The Human Be-In

THE

HUMAN BE-IN

Helen Swick Perry

Basic Books, Inc., Publishers

NEW YORK LONDON

Library of Congress Catalog Card Number: 73-116853
SBN 465-03111-0
Manufactured in the United States of America
DESIGNED BY VINCENT TORRE

For Stewart, who takes the road
less traveled by . . .

Acknowledgments

The process of writing a book on the young in these days of swift and continuous action requires direct and indirect support of a special kind. In order to even venture onto such a controversial subject, one must cling to the idea of the sympathetic reader; even at that the fantasied negative reader takes over from time to time, and the task then becomes formidable. Yet in the end, I have always found at the critical moment a group of friends who have spurred me on, as I moved from one city to another and then to a third; without their symbolic and actual support, the book would have been abandoned. The steadying influence throughout has been my husband, Stewart E. Perry, who has insisted that I finish this book when I yearned at times to turn to another project in progress, more firmly rooted in the past and therefore an escape from the tremendous problems of the current era. Another steadying influence has been that of Margaret E. Adams, who has followed the progress of the book through two cities and several versions.

Some small part of the bread for this enterprise was supplied by the National Institute of Mental Health (under grant USPHS MH-8375), which for eight and one-half months allowed me to wander for part of my working day through the streets of the Haight-Ashbury neighborhood. The rest of my wandering—at nights, on weekends, and after the grant was over—and the actual writing of the book were supported entirely by my husband.

In San Francisco and Berkeley, a crew of the young, most of whom must remain nameless, took on the general task of reforming and educating me. In addition, the following people gave me crucial and special help: James T. Carey, Aune Helenius, Roger Howe, Erwin L. Linn, Sandra R. Luft, Harriet

Roberts, Vicki Wentworth, and Gay Yambert. In a less immediate way, Ralf Gleason and Cecil Williams elevated some of my ideas into other than autistic observations, so that by listening to them talk about the young people, or by reading Gleason's columns in the San Francisco *Chronicle*, I dared early to run against the main stream of superficial distrust of the young people.

In Washington, D.C., where the book was mainly written, Louise Greenfield, Katherine S. Henry, Mattie R. Johnson, Susan Tertell Kiehne, Marjorie and Bill Schlecht, and Margaret E. Tepper gave tender and often skilled support to the main task. And finally, in Cambridge, Wynni De Witt, Margit Pearson, and Katharine P. Pollock did special finishing-up tasks with generosity of spirit.

At a more distant level, I am centrally dependent on the thinking of Harry Stack Sullivan. From another direction, I have been for many years influenced by the writings of the Concord group in New England and by those who have compiled and written on that movement. In particular, I would like to mention the work of Van Wyck Brooks, Clara Endicott Sears, and Odell Shepard.

More explicitly, I wish to gratefully acknowledge permissions for the following special or extensive use of the work of particular authors:

"Peter Proudfoot" from *Collected Poems (1905–1925)* by Wilfred Gibson. Reprinted by permission of Macmillan and Company Limited, England, and Mr. Michael Gibson.

"Plea" from *Golden Sardine* by Bob Kaufman. Copyright © 1967 by Bob Kaufman. Reprinted by permission of City Lights Books, San Francisco.

Passage from "Notes for a Hypothetical Novel" from *Nobody Knows My Name*, by James Baldwin, published by The Dial Press. Reprinted by permission of The Dial Press, New York and John Farquharson Ltd., London.

Passages from *The Flowering of New England* by Van Wyck Brooks. Copyright 1936, 1952 by Van Wyck Brooks. Renewal © 1964 by Gladys Brooks. Reprinted by permission of E. P. Dutton & Co., Inc., New York.

Contents

Endpaper photo by Richard Crone:
"Be-In" in Golden Gate Park, February 1967

The Human Be-In

To refrain from harming any living
creature, I undertake . . .

FIRST PRECEPT FROM
THE TEACHINGS OF GAUTAMA BUDDHA,
AS TRANSLATED FROM THE PALI BY
WILLIAM G. SCHLECHT

Prologue

December, 1967
Washington, D.C.

For almost a year, from October, 1966 until September, 1967, most of my waking hours were focused on the flower children in the Haight-Ashbury neighborhood of San Francisco. Periodically I would tear myself away from this absorption and perform other tasks that were formally required of me. But the other tasks came to be only a backdrop for an ongoing sorting of my own values and of how they were changing under the influence of the flower children, or the "young seekers" as Allen Ginsberg has called them. In the end, I could only come to one conclusion: I, too, was a "hippie." I did not like the word any more than many of the young people in the Haight-Ashbury; but when I was asked to stand up and be counted, then I had to say that I was a hippie and had always been one, although somewhere I had lost my way so that I wore the protective coloration of a middle-aged, respectable, middle-class American. In that eleven-month period, I had undergone a transformation that affected almost every area of my life, so that it was becoming more and more difficult for me to feel comfortable in the square world.

In September, 1967, I moved from San Francisco to Washington, D.C., and shortly afterwards I found out that the Haight-Ashbury thing was over, that there had been a funeral procession one day for the hippie in the Haight-Ashbury, that this had been followed by a day of mourning, and that on the third day there had been a resurrection; that the hippie would now be the "free man" and that he would spread out from the Haight-Ashbury to the rest of the city and the surrounding countryside. From what I had seen of Haight Street during the summer, this action seemed responsible and inevitable; but it did not lessen my sense of mourning. It was like knowing that a dear friend has cancer in a terminal stage; one knows that death is inevitable, but there is no adequate preparation for the moment of its coming. I truly think that I was in a state of shocked depression for a short period of time; for I felt that I had witnessed the end of a noble experiment—an attempt at a new kind of Utopia. All of the negative components so that experiment had been emphasized in the press and on national television; but this negative focus could not forever do away with the nobility of the task that was undertaken.

In the nineteenth century there was a moment in time and space when our country had become a kind of Haight-Ashbury for at least the Western world, and that was when the Statue of Liberty was erected in New York Harbor and the words of Emma Lazarus inscribed upon it:

Give me your tired, your poor,
Your huddled masses yearning to breathe free,
The wretched refuse of your teeming shore,
Send these, the homeless, tempest-tossed, to me:
I lift my lamp beside the golden door.

Some time after that, the apple-sorting process started, and the nation began to use immigration quotas in order to satisfy its need for rejects, culls, in the drive for its self-esteem. From then on, that dream was over, until finally even such public-spirited institutions as hospitals and schools in the Republic had their own apple-sorting machines and their quotas. Some years ago now, I discovered that one of the homes for unwed mothers run by the Salvation Army had a policy of automatically rejecting young women who had already been rejected by the Florence Crittenton Home; otherwise, the social worker told me cheerily, our population would simply be composed of rejects from the Florence Crittenton.

But for one brief year, in the Haight-Ashbury, the upset young people from a nation, and indeed from overseas, were accepted; there were no rejects. Until finally the task became too great; only an enlightened city government in the spring of 1967 could have averted disaster, could have helped the valiant band of St. Francises in the Haight-Ashbury—who called themselves Diggers—plan for the Summer of Love. In that spring there were various informal emergency meetings throughout the city of San Francisco, in an attempt to avert disaster and to plan for the influx of young people; but the city fathers took the attitude that the young people must be discouraged and that the best way of discouraging them was to make no provision at all, to let nature take its course. In their own cynical way, the city fathers planned well. Mark Twain once said that the coldest winter he ever spent was one summer in San Francisco; and many a young person who went to San Francisco with no visible means of support in the summer of 1967 will remember all his life the cold fog drifting up Haight Street and the smell of garbage and filth; he will remember, too, the despair and the loneliness of other young seekers like himself. But if he was one of the lucky ones, he will remember also the tenderness of strangers, the concern of the more established seekers in the area, the shared food and living quarters, the valiant attempt on the part of those who had been there longer to stop disaster from happening. And this remembered personal concern will be of an intensity that will be cherished for a lifetime; for it emerged from a simple rule of human conduct that had been forgotten in most of America by 1967, and it was not an idle slogan in the Haight-Ashbury: *Love thy neighbor.*

Since the Haight-Ashbury had no eligibility requirement—no barriers of age or color of skin, no written creed, no rigid rules for dress or language—it also had no rules for the degree of emotional stability. By the winter of 1966–1967, the Republic had reached a new peak in the proportion of young people, many of whom were in considerable distress; thousands of these young people in distress found their way to the Haight-Ashbury. No one was turned aside; and even the most disruptive were led gently toward the Utopian ideas of the flower children. There were of course many young people who had disastrous experiences there. In the beginning, I myself was consumed by the distress that I witnessed in the faces and the actions of many of them; but at the same time, I early glimpsed the hope and kindliness that flourished there and never entirely disappeared.

Before and during the same general period, I had occasion to go on the back wards of one of the California state hospitals every six weeks. In this work I came to know something about the lives of forty-eight women who had come in to the mental hospital as young women and had been hospitalized, twenty, thirty, or, in one case, forty-five years. I read the stories of these women in their case records, and I met and talked with them. Their stories were not significantly different from the stories of young people in the Haight-Ashbury. They, too, had been seekers when they were young, and they had faced some of the same youthful crises. I felt that a good many of them would have had different lives had there been a Haight-Ashbury for their crises in the California of their early years.

In American society, we seem to have a built-in crisis in the adolescent years for everyone; in an atomic age, this crisis has escalated, and the words "kill" and "overkill" threaten all of springtime. As John Lennon and Paul McCartney have said: "I read the news today oh boy . . ." For a brief moment, the Haight-Ashbury offered some relief from doom; for many young people, I believe that it was an alternative to suicide, or being a patient in a mental hospital, or becoming a criminal; and these three alternatives threaten too many of our young people today as the only ways out in the present situation of world crisis and vast continuing injustice.

Some thirty years ago, the American psychiatrist Harry Stack Sullivan suggested that preadolescence is the nearest that most people in America come to untroubled human life—"that from then on the stresses of life distort them to inferior caricatures of what they might have been." Somehow the young seekers in the Haight-Ashbury changed this timetable. They extended the period of promise and hope beyond preadolescence into the adolescent world, in some cases into the world of the adult, so that there was a golden period. It was an awesome thing, the vision was frightening; and there had to be awesome risks. In a world dependent on chemicals for life and death, for hope and despair, the young seekers in the Haight-Ashbury felt that they, too, had to have their own chemicals. There were always wise heads among the seekers who saw the dangers of this need and tried to keep it within bounds, tried to define it as a *rite de passage* to the new Utopia, but only as an interim step. But the establishment and the mass media focused on the drugs and their dangers and in focusing saw nothing else, so that in the end this flaw, which might have been overcome by the young seekers in time, became the fatal flaw through which the cancer of the larger society could attack the new young society.

It would be a mistake to look upon the Haight-Ashbury community as another Bohemia, except insofar as any Bohemia has within it some of the seeds of Utopia; for the seekers in the Haight-Ashbury were not simply trying to escape from the sick values of the central society—they wanted to build a new world. In a very real sense, they belonged to the tradition of Bronson Alcott's Fruitlands, for like Alcott they venerated the innocence of children, they abhorred brute force, they withdrew from materialistic values, they wanted to do something about the lot of oppressed peoples, they wanted to change the education of the young, they wanted a leveling of society and an end to status, and above all they cherished Nature and the peaceful life. In most ways, Fruitlands was the direct forerunner of the Haight-Ashbury, as if Alcott's lost records of that Arcady had somehow found their way into the hands of the hippies. Fruitlands, too, lasted less than a year—from June 14, 1843 to January 14, 1844. In the beginning of that experiment, Emerson, Alcott's neighbor in Concord, had journeyed to Fruitlands, and Odell Shepard, Alcott's biographer, reports on this trip and on Emerson's reaction:

Emerson came early in July—Emerson, whom Alcott would rather have pleased than all the world beside.

"The sun and the evening sky do not look calmer," he wrote, "than Alcott and his family at Fruitlands. They seem to have arrived at the fact—to have got rid of the show, and to be serene. Their manners and behaviour in the house and the field were those of superior men—of men at rest. What had they to conceal? What had they to exhibit? And it seemed so high an attainment that I thought—as often before, so now more, because they had a fit home, or the picture was fitly framed—that these men ought to be maintained in their place by the country for its culture. Young men and young maidens, old men and women, should visit them and be inspired. I think there is as much merit in beautiful manners as in hard work."

So much he said by way of wholehearted approbation; but then came the cautious Yankee afterthought: "I will not prejudge them successful. They look well in July; we will see them in December."[1]

It was a New England winter that finally ended Fruitlands just as it was a cold San Francisco summer that in part ended the Haight-Ashbury experiment. At the end of Fruitlands, Bronson Alcott wanted to die, and it was only his debts and his sense of obligation to his family that maintained life in him; he could not afford the luxury of dying. But Fruitlands had a resurrection, a continuity in the American scene. For one brief fall, winter, and spring, it clearly blossomed in San Francisco. It is in the hope of its blossoming again that I want to tell this story of my own encounter with this Utopia and of how it renewed my youth and my hopes. I began my sojourn with fears, and I witnessed many tragedies there. But the main outlines of this experiment were noble, and I mourn the golden moments and the tender hopes.

[1] Odell Shepard, *Pedlar's Progress* (Boston: Little, Brown and Company, 1937), p. 366.

CHAPTER 1

Strangers and Friends[1]

If I had suddenly found myself at Fruitlands, in the winter of 1843–1844, discoursing with Bronson Alcott and eating a dinner of apples and unleavened bread, I fancy that I would have found myself more at home with the dress, the cold, the outside bathroom facilities, and the nineteenth-century transcendentalist conversation than I did when I first went on to Haight Street in October, 1966, and looked at the young society there. Initially I could not fathom my own sense of fear, of exposure, of strangeness, for I had followed the young for a period of years, intensively and sympathetically; nor did I dream that these young people were engaged in building a new version of Alcott's Fruitlands. Their numbers were still small—less than a thousand in an urban neighborhood of about 30,000 people. Yet their visibility was great, since they wore what seemed then to be outrageous costumes, had a street society in a city with a relatively good climate, and engaged in unpredictable behavior; neither the long-established residents of the neighborhood nor I could disregard them for long, particularly as the streets became more crowded with them day by day.

Their presence in the neighborhood seemed a complication to me in making a brief study of community mental health needs there and in some of the smaller neighborhoods, like

1 This chapter title emerged from my own experience, it seemed to me; yet retrospectively I recognize that I read Hortense Powdermaker's *Stranger and Friend: The Way of an Anthropologist* (New York: Norton, 1967) shortly after I began my study of the Haight-Ashbury neighborhood and that her expression and feeling merged with my own experience.

Finn Town, that edged the circumference of the Haight-Ashbury. My colleagues at the Langley-Porter Neuropsychiatric Institute suggested to me that these new young residents, while interesting and bizarre, were not consequential for my study. Bohemias in San Francisco did not last long, they noted, and they cited the example of North Beach of the 1950's, which I myself had visited briefly in its heyday.

Yet from the outset the costumed people in the Haight-Ashbury did not seem to form simply a new Bohemia. Almost immediately I referred to them in my field notes as "costumed people," partly because I had not yet heard the term "hippie," but also because I recognized that they could not be easily classified, that they did indeed hear a different drummer, that the meaning of their drama was hidden from me. Nor did my immediate colleagues use the term "hippie" at that time, referring instead to "the young tourists" or "the acid-heads." A young social worker who worked at the Institute and lived in the Haight-Ashbury neighborhood immediately adjacent to the Medical Center[2] initiated me into the use of the term "hippie," and I remember asking her to spell it for me when I finally realized that she was not using the older term "hipster." At about the same time as I began work, a long story appeared in the San Francisco *Chronicle* on a commune of "acid-heads," who lived in a large old house in a poor neighborhood, not too far from the Haight-Ashbury; the word "hippie" was not used in the story at all, although in another month—so swiftly did the term catch on—the local newspapers were generally using the term imprecisely for various costumed young people anywhere in the Bay area.

In part, the idea that many of these young people might be acid-heads made me feel unwilling to explore too deeply into their life styles. Some years before I had worked in a research

[2] The Medical Center was a complex of loosely affiliated institutions and buildings in which the University of California in San Francisco trained students in the various health disciplines, notably doctors and nurses, and maintained various hospitals and clinics for training in clinical practice and research. Langley-Porter was affiliated with this whole complex, specializing in training for clinical practice and research in mental disorders; it also had a training program in community mental health, of which I was a part.

hospital where experiments with LSD had been carried out, and I knew the dangers of casual use of the drug; I did not at all approve of the way in which LSD had become a part of the young people's way of life in the Haight-Ashbury. Moreover, in agreeing to do a brief study of an urban community and its mental health needs, I had felt that I was moving away from the more distressing work of observing on mental hospital wards, which I had been engaged in previously.

For a long time I had believed that preventive psychiatry, focusing on people living in communities, represented a more hopeful approach for psychiatry. The neighborhood that I was to study had had a long history of tolerance and respect for diversity of life styles, so that I had felt that I would be able to observe an urban community that was working well. The hippies changed that picture. The neighborhood reacted as I did in the beginning: these kids are mostly sick, they said; they are opting out of the need for political reform; most of them need baths and good food; they are spoiled; and so on and on. Yet the attention of the entire neighborhood was focused on these young people. Shortly my attention was similarly focused. Within a matter of weeks, no subject was of such overwhelming interest to the whole of the city as the hippies. By early spring, the news of the young colony had begun to be the subject of national and international attention.

As the circle of attention widened, some of the criticism increased. But within the smaller circle, some acculturation was taking place. Both the neighborhood and I were discovering that the new young community was not simply participating in a psychotic-like dance to St. Vitus. Somewhat reluctantly we began to feel as if we were indeed friendly to some of their ideas and that their life styles were admirable in many respects. While this acculturation was swift for me, it was also painful and at times abruptly funny.

Although I had been familiar with the general neighborhood for some time, my earliest encounter with any kind of organized activity there took place on Sunday afternoon, October 30, 1966, in the Panhandle—a slim extension of Golden Gate Park; this had been advertised as a Festival of Peoples, and I had presumed that, of course, this would include the young costumed people that I had seen on Haight Street on previous days, as well as other people who lived in the neighborhood. In part the Festival was to serve as a political rally, for this was just before the 1966 election, and the city newspaper announced that one of the speeches was to be given by a state legislator, Willie Brown, a Negro[3] who lived in the neighborhood with his family. When I arrived with a companion about two o'clock, I found a rather depleted line of booths down the center of the parkway, each booth announcing its identity; various church and community groups had displays in these booths, most of which served some kind of food, including "soul" food, hot dogs, popcorn, and so on. One of the booths was manned by the Christian Science Church, and after we had strolled by it, a man came running after me to present me with a free copy of the *Monitor.* On Monday morning, I wrote my field notes on this afternoon, expressing my sense of discouragement about the young people in the Park that day:

We went a little before two P.M. and stayed a couple of hours. I found it very depressing, much more so than walking on Haight Street. There was little interaction between young people, some between children. . . . It seemed to me that there were a good many unattached young males; my impression was that the young females tended to be with someone. Most of the young men looked schizophrenic to me. . . .

A young white woman, with long blond hair, played with a group of three young Negro girls, quite dark in complexion. She sat near us on the grass, had been earlier talking to another white girl who did not play with the children but read Freud's *Civilization and Its Discontents.* The first woman was obviously acting in a play, partly for our benefit. She had a rather large and heavy ball which she tossed back and forth to an eleven- or twelve-year-old Negro girl. There were two younger Negro girls who tried to participate in the game, but the white woman was not adept about including them. Occasionally one of the younger Negro girls would stroke the young woman's blond hair; she was like the fairy princess, and she would allow them to touch her. She did not stroke the children's hair in response or indicate affection to them at

[3] I use the terms Negro and black interchangeably in this book, which is simply a reflection of my field notes and of the general usage at that time by the people whom I was studying.

all. It seemed like an act in which she was Lady Bountiful. Finally the smallest girl went over and hit the fairy princess, who then gathered up her gear and moved away with the children in tow. They were obviously her charges, for she took out money for them to buy popcorn, and so on. It was interesting to contemplate how she got herself into this position with them, for she was obviously of another social class, perhaps a student, and not altogether comfortable with what she was doing. The children were poorly dressed and their underclothing in particular was torn and unkempt. . . .

I saw no particular evidence of a festival. Everyone seemed fairly glum, except for some horseplay between the young Negroes grouped around Willie Brown. I wondered if there had been some disappointment in the crowd and whether people had drifted away before I came. I felt the almost complete anomie of the group. I saw no evidence of dancing, folk singing, etc. In fact, Willie Brown was unable to get anyone to sing with his wife (and guitar), even the most familiar songs like "Michael, row your boat."

My mood today (Monday) is of great extreme depression, the worst that I have experienced on this job. I feel as if I can't stand it, the signs of so much real misery and sickness among the young.

This excerpt from my field notes highlights my own sense of disaffection for the young people there that day, my sense of panic about the degree of mental sickness in evidence, and my failure to understand the nature of the scene before me or to properly evaluate the cues. This Festival was an annual event for the Haight-Ashbury Neighborhood Council (HANC as it was usually called), an established and enlightened organization in the area, but I had assumed from the name "Festival of Peoples" that it was a hippie-organized event, or what I later came to know as a "happening."

I had known for some time that the Haight-Ashbury neighborhood represented an advanced example of what an urban neighborhood could be, and that HANC was a vital force in the neighborhood. In the spring and summer of 1966, for instance, HANC had provided much of the community leadership for a stunning victory over the city, state, and federal highway planners by opposing the placing of a freeway along the Panhandle, leading to the Golden Gate Bridge. HANC had aroused the citizens in the area to the danger to their neighborhood from any such major artery through the center of the area, cutting the neighborhood off from the greenery of the Panhandle. There had been a successful liaison in the neighborhood between the older citizens of whatever ethnic background or class, the students, the artists, and the few hippies who were already living in and around the Panhandle. Most of the old houses along the Panhandle had hand-painted anti-freeway signs in the windows, and there were massive meetings and protest from the whole neighborhood. In the end, the neighborhood had won its fight; a senior federal highway engineer told me authoritatively that this freeway fight was one of the few successful stands made by any group of residents in any large city in America against the combined recommendations and planning of all three jurisdictions—local, state, and federal.

To some extent, this freeway fight may have encouraged more young seekers to move into the neighborhood; at any rate, during the summer and fall of 1966, the number of visible costumed young people in the neighborhood had doubled, according to most old residents. Although HANC had a history of being willing to welcome all people to the neighborhood, members began to have second thoughts about the newest residents. The neighborhood and HANC were caught in much the same stance that I was: they saw the new young people as disturbed and in need of help, they worried about their use of drugs and their possible "bad influence" on their own children who had been steadfastly kept in public schools in the neighborhood, in an attempt to stop the shift of families to the suburbs of Marin County across the Bay.

The new young residents began to feel, in turn, that HANC was unwelcoming of them, and they felt resentful of this in particular because various hippie leaders had been effectively supportive of HANC's stand on the freeway. So the new residents had deliberately stayed away from HANC's Festival of Peoples. I later found out that there had been signs in some of the hippie shops on Haight Street suggesting that the Festival, like exclusive clubs and welfare rolls, had its own eligibility requirements and that it would be a good thing for the flower children to keep away from the Panhandle that Sunday, although it was usually a favorite gathering place.

Some of the old residents who participated in the Festival had been unhappy about this rift between the young people and HANC, so that the occasion had been rather dismal by comparison with other years.

In general, the young men that I had seen at the Festival, many of whom were alone and appeared disoriented, were like me undoubtedly strangers who had read about the Festival in the newspaper and were looking for the young community to observe and make contact with. A street worker at one of the city agencies later told me that a number of young newcomers to the Tenderloin section of San Francisco, who traditionally earned their living by homosexual prostitution, had drifted up into the nearby Haight-Ashbury neighborhood during that particular period because one of the periodic police clean-ups was going on in the Tenderloin district. Their isolation and posturing reminded me of young male patients in the mental hospital who had become schizophrenic as a way of avoiding their fears of being deviant. Later I knew some young people from the Tenderloin district who came to live in the Haight-Ashbury; many of them found the experience of living there therapeutic and reassuring. But on that Sunday in the Panhandle, I was appalled by the presence of these isolates who seemed in a state of anomie and upset; and they, in turn, must have been disappointed to find people like themselves wandering about, alone and unsure, and an occasional square like me walking around in a state of shocked dismay.

Or again, my perception of the young white girl with the Negro children was clearly unsympathetic and overly critical. I was not yet aware that students from San Francisco State College, many of whom lived in the neighborhood, had begun an intensive program of seeking out lower-class Negro children newly come into the neighborhood from the redevelopment razing of slum dwellings east and north of the Haight-Ashbury, in an attempt to provide some enriching experience for these deprived children. These early attempts of middle-class white students were often socially gauche; but they were eager to learn, and they became increasingly effective as time went on.

I mention these instances of my obvious distortions in order to account for much of the later, more widespread distortion that has emerged in the mass media and in scientific journals about what was going on in the Haight-Ashbury, based primarily on observations made in the summer of 1967. During the previous fall and winter, there were few observers in the neighborhood, except for occasional local newspaper reporters; and though I came to know many researchers who later went into the neighborhood, I think that I was one of the earliest observers to spend long and continuous periods of time there.

Even though I had an opportunity to observe the neighborhood in a more authentic and benign period of growth and development, I still found myself prey to my own lack of information and my middle-class fears; by the summer of 1967, the opportunity for distortion was considerably greater for observers newly arrived. There were literally scores of magazine writers, graduate students, professors from various colleges and universities, garbed, as they thought, in Haight-Ashbury mufti, running around Haight Street interviewing each other and the bewildered young newcomers to the district; and the tour buses had begun to include the Haight-Ashbury as an important sideshow in their journey through the city. Many of the more established parts of the winter and spring hippie community, sensing the change on Haight Street, had bundled up their novitiates in the late spring and carried them off to sylvan communes at Big Sur, or into the more remote parts of Marin County, or up north to the coastal areas around Mendocino. What went on on Haight Street in the summer of 1967 was infinitely more misleading than my encounter at the Festival of Peoples.

Shortly after the Festival, I attended a meeting of HANC during which one of the people responsible for planning the Festival reported in a reassuring way that not too many of the young "tourists" had attended and that the event had been quite successful. In a listing of some of the organizations represented, she mentioned the fact that a specified number of Christian Science *Monitors* had been distributed free in the Panhandle; and, to my surprise, she added that she could vouch for the fact that these copies of the *Monitor* had been given only to the "right sort of people, if you know what I mean." Since I had been given a copy, I found myself upset and angry at being classed as the "right sort of people." This was a Festival for all people according to the announcement, and I began to participate in the young people's sense of outrage at deciding a person's ability to be a person because of his dress. Thereafter I resolved to dress more in sympathy with the young people, and I adopted to some extent a modified attire both in the neighborhood itself and even at the office. It was the beginning wedge of my accommodation to the values of the young.

My acculturation went much more swiftly as I came to know something about the activities of the Diggers, for they were the acculturating elders of all the tribes of the young in the Haight-Ashbury. Later I shall describe in more detail their formation and meaning, but a description of my first encounter with a Digger—Albert—will perhaps convey some of the process by which I was swiftly forced into an appraisal of all my values. I first saw Albert and some of his friends in the kitchen of his small and very clean apartment where he was fixing a rice pilaf for their supper. A friend of Albert's had volunteered to take me there and had introduced us. I began by telling Albert that I was looking over a large section of the city, which included the Haight-Ashbury neighborhood, with an eye toward seeing what its mental health needs and resources were; that my work was part of a long-term examination and that it would be several years before there would be any clinical service at all available to the general public in the neighborhood, that in fact it might turn out that Langley-Porter would not undertake such a responsibility or else undertake it in another part of the city.

Albert and his friends reacted to this with utmost dismay and surprise. They assured me solemnly that this would do no good, that the world was moving too fast. When after several minutes of this conversation, I stated that I had to leave because I had a dinner engagement and that I would make an appointment to see them later, they pointed out that it was very difficult for them to make appointments, because they never knew when something important would come up, and that Albert in particular was hard to find because he was so busy. In addition, they wondered if I was hungry, was that the reason I had to rush off to another dinner; and they indicated that they would be glad to cut me in on the rice pilaf. Anyway, I stayed for quite a long time and was late to dinner at my friend's house; since there was no phone in Albert's apartment, I was not able to call my friend and tell her I would be late.

Near the end of my visit with Albert and his friends, Albert warmed to me a little as if he felt that perhaps I *could* learn what the values of this new society were and at the end we exchanged phone numbers. He gave me a number where I could leave a message for him, and I gave him my number at my office, located in an old house, once a private residence, near the main buildings of the Medical Center and a few blocks up the hill from Albert's apartment.

Much to my surprise, a few days later I received a call at Langley-Porter from "Albert, the Digger," in which he informed me that it had just occurred to him how Langley-Porter could begin to do something right away. "Do you sometimes have a wing of the hospital vacant? Or a few beds anyway? We often have a few kids—runaways, you know—who need a good place to stay for a few nights and to get something off their chest and then they'll go back home."

I almost panicked as Albert talked. I thought of trying to explain Albert's point of view to my colleagues. I often saw hippies walking around on Parnassus Street near where I worked, and it was possible indeed that Albert would walk by some day, see the sign in front of our building, "Community Mental Health Training Program," and walk in and ask a few questions:

"What part of the day is the building used?"

"Only from eight-thirty to five usually."

"And how many bathrooms?"

"Well, in fact, there is one full bathroom, one half-bathroom, and an additional toilet."

"Good. And are there closets large enough to accommodate sleeping bags during the day, so that overnight guests could store their sleeping equipment during the day when the offices are being used?"

I fantasied myself hedging and pointing out that, well, sometimes we did have evening meetings. "How often?" I could hear him ask.

Yet in another part of my mind, I began to consider abruptly the real possibility of using the very house in which we worked as an overnight hostel. My colleagues were engaged in teaching medical residents in psychiatry about community mental health. What better way was there for us to learn about the problems of establishing a viable community of young and old than by attempting to accommodate to each other within these four walls? And I began to think, rather practically, that there would have to be some shower rooms installed in the basement, that there would have to be firm rules about airing sleeping bags on sunny days, about the use of drugs on the premises, and so on.

But all I could say to Albert was that, no, I didn't have anything to do with the hospital proper; and that I didn't know of any arrangement that could be worked out. I felt very unhappy about making this statement to Albert, and he was disappointed in me, although he did not give up. On later occasions, he suggested other alternatives to me. Somewhere along the way, I began to feel more at home with Albert's viewpoint than with the outlook of the Institute on a good many issues.

Thus within the space of a very few weeks, the nature of my feeling about these young people changed drastically. Mistakes they made, but they recognized them; they were critical of themselves; and they were flexible. To my amazement, they read many of the books that I had read as an undergraduate over thirty years before—D. H. Lawrence, Freud, James Joyce, Aldous Huxley, for example; and well-worn copies of books by these authors were pored over in the Psychedelic Shop, which periodically seemed to operate mainly as a library. Moreover, they were concerned about the problems of child-rearing practices in middle-class American society and were exploring alternative solutions, such as the kibbutz in Israel; such books as Melford E. Spiro's *Children of the Kibbutz* were regularly borrowed back and forth by members of the young community whether they were parents or not. Under their influence, I read some of the books that they liked but that I had never gotten around to reading, although most of them were at least familiar titles to me; the Tolkien books are notable examples. I discovered the importance of these books for the young people. Although Tolkien has denied that he was writing an allegory about Western civilization and the fear of nuclear destruction, the hippies read his books as an allegory for their time and position. The consistently good people in the Tolkien books are Hobbits and they have the lowliest status of all the groups of characters in the books. The hippies thought of themselves as being or becoming Hobbits; from time to time as the winter wore on, a sign would appear in the window of one of their gathering places to this effect: *Do not add to the street confusion this weekend. There may be busts. Be good little Hobbits and stay home.* I came to understand that the hierarchy of status in the establishment was one of the serious concerns of this coalescent group of young people. As a member of the second sex and as a marginal person in my own professional world—whatever that is—I found this concern congenial to me. What I am suggesting here is that with the passage of a relatively short time and some openness to this young community, the stranger began to feel at home. This was not a phenomenon particular to me; I will cite two quite disparate examples of what I mean.

Sometime in that winter, my husband, who had accompanied me on some of my evening observations in the Haight-Ashbury neighborhood, became interested in a new experimental street school in the making—Happening House, as it was optimistically called—which had been rather casually envisioned by some of the hippies and by Leonard Wolf, a professor at San Francisco State College who lived in the Haight-Ashbury neighborhood. The planning sessions for this college were held weekly in various spots in the Haight-Ashbury. One evening, my husband reported to me with some amusement that he had spent over an hour that afternoon weeding in the garden surrounding the parish house of All Saints' Episcopal Church in the heart of the neighborhood. It seemed that there had been a meeting called of people interested in Happening House, that day at the parish house, for one-thirty; but HT (hippie time) had some of the characteristics of CPT (colored people's time) and JT (Jewish time) as it is jokingly called by members of those groups; if a hippie found something more important to do, a conflicting appointment was not of the essence. My husband arrived promptly, but the meeting did not begin until almost three o'clock. He explained to me that ordinarily he would have been very annoyed if a student had been late in keeping an office appointment with him in his office at the Medical Center; but in the Haight-Ashbury, this kind of preoccupation with time did not bother him; he cheerfully began to weed the parish garden, which needed it, and he was joined in his task by the next arrival, who straggled along a half hour later. There was a contagion and joy in what was going on in the neighborhood, once one had tidily put away his rules and regulations for living and left them in the more established part of his existence.

A more significant example is found in the experience of a medical student who spent ten weeks studying the hippies as part of his training program. At the end of his project he gave a presentation of his work to faculty and students. Several faculty members suggested that he had erred on the side of presenting only the positive aspects of the young society, and the medical student finally countered this charge:

I sort of asked myself a couple of nights ago if I could think of anything negative about the hippie culture; my acculturation has been complete enough that I can't. And I feel very defensive when I'm cornered in a situation in which I'm discussing the hippies, and someone begins to attack them. This has happened several times with my classmates. I become defensive in a situation like this because in a real sense, over the course of ten weeks, *they've become my people and my culture in a very real way*. I didn't go into the Haight-Ashbury with the idea of being acculturated or assimilated into the hippie society in a real way; but I was. And this in itself sort of speaks for the positive values in the society. I find myself at a loss to attack hippie society in any way—aside from a public health aspect, which is a little bit appalling to me, but I'm not about to move into a commune or anything of this nature. But in terms of the manifest values and the way that they operate, I find myself [in almost complete sympathy].[4]

[4] From a transcription of the tape-recorded seminar. Italics mine.

This becomes more remarkable when one looks at the general background of this medical student; he had been raised in an upper middle-class background and he was in sympathy with the general goals of his parents. He had been a very successful medical student, drove an expensive car, was married, belonged to the Playboy Club and had enjoyed the entertainment and exclusiveness of belonging, and planned a lucrative and usual medical practice after he completed his military requirements. Subsequently he told me that his career plans had drastically changed as a result of his experience in the Haight-Ashbury.

The path by which I achieved some feeling of myself being able to say, "They've become my people and my culture," was less spontaneous and immediate perhaps than that of the medical student, but I think that it was basically the same path. More remarkable, various formal institutions in the area—notably the churches and HANC itself—gradually were won over to the meaning of the hippie culture; yet basically it was the formal institutions throughout the society that were most upset by the appearance and the habits of this young colony. If I were to make a rule about the hippies and their acceptability to individuals and to institutions, I would say that, in general, those furthest removed remained the most intolerant. As the months wore on, the immediate neighborhood became increasingly protective and sympathetic toward the responsible leadership in the new community; at the same time, the city fathers and the city-wide institutions became more and more punitive, more frightened. There was at least one important exception to my generalization: the police at the nearby Park Station in the neighborhood became progressively more punitive and finally frankly harassed the young people.

In the spring of 1967, the city officials began a series of actions designed to officially discourage young people throughout the United States from coming to San Francisco in the summer of 1967. In March, the Mayor proposed a policy of official condemnation of the free movement of "indigent young people" into the city. In a letter to the Board of Supervisors of San Francisco, Mayor John F. Shelley stated, in part, as reported in the March 24, 1967, issue of the *Chronicle* on the front page:

I wish to emphasize at this time I am strongly opposed to any encouragement of a summer influx of indigent young people who are apparently being led to believe by a certain element of society their vagrant presence will be tolerated in this city. . . .

I believe the Board of Supervisors should go on record as declaring as its policies that such migration is unwelcome; that existing ordinances be strictly enforced and that such migratory persons cannot be permitted to sleep in public parks or otherwise violate laws involving public health and the general peace and well-being of this community.

Information should be widely promulgated that the City of San Francisco cannot provide food or shelter for such persons and that their presence here without adequate prior planning on their part for their necessities can only result in a chaotic condition detrimental to themselves and to the residents of San Francisco.

Mayor Shelley's action was timed to coincide with a full range of harassment of the young people in the Haight-Ashbury, including a public health inspection of 1,400 buildings in a fifty-block area of the neighborhood. This inspection, incidentally, did not turn up any unusual indictment of the young people's living habits. "The situation is not as bad as we had thought," the city health director stated ruefully, according to the March 29 story in the *Chronicle*. It was at this juncture that HANC issued a statement of its own, asserting its support of the hippies and defining the character of the neighborhood as being for all people, including the hippies. The following is excerpted from the full report as issued in the April, 1967, issue of the official publication of HANC:

Haight-Ashbury is a state of mind as well as a geographic area. Almost accidentally, the area itself has become a focus of international attention because the neighborhood is to a degree unique in its cosmopolitan character, its congenial climate, its tolerance of diverse peoples and life styles. . . .

We think it irresponsible of local officials to raise the spectre of bubonic plague or other pestilence on the strength of rumor alone, for it is by no means established that the health standards of the Haight-Ashbury are at variance with those of any other crowded urban area, here or elsewhere. . . .

By far, the residents of the Haight-Ashbury, both hippies and non-hippies, are reasonably law-abiding and responsible citizens.

To attempt to restrict the movement of citizens on the mere suspicion that they might not be law-abiding is unconstitutional.

War against a class of citizens, regardless of how they dress or choose to live, within the latitude of the law, is intolerable in a free society. We remember the regrettable history of officially condoned crusades against the Chinese population of San Francisco whose life style did not meet with the approval of the established community and whose lives and property were objects of terrorism and persecution.

Harassment of our community, however well intentioned, is likewise intolerable. Local police have been instrumental in creating problems where none existed. They have contributed as much as any group toward making the area attractive to the curious. . . .

What we who live here see happening is that the area is being singled out for selective law enforcement, not because the area is in particular need of such attention, but because public officials or others object simply to a new life style which is implicitly critical of the hypocrisies of the dominant culture.

Many of the criticisms directed at the hippies might be more appropriately directed toward the landlords who are derelict in their responsibilities to see to it that their rental units comply with the housing and health codes of the city.

Other criticisms should properly be directed to those agencies of public maintenance who have neglected to provide litter and street cleaning facilities proportionate to the number of permanent residents and visitors to the area.

In magnifying the problems attendant upon diverse urban populations, permanent or transient, public officials have yielded to fear and have helped create panic where none existed. Hippy culture is a native development, a product in part of the alienation that the young feel when the society has not made sufficient efforts to accommodate them. Persecution, harassment, and police crackdown can only further divide a community that has made a great effort to integrate its diverse populations and accommodate to what its citizens regard as the good life.

We welcome the cooperative efforts of city bureaus, the Chamber of Commerce and others who respect the Haight-Ashbury community as it is or appreciate its unique character. But we repeat that because Haight-Ashbury is a state of mind, it is a natural focus of international attention, and we will resist any efforts by city officials or others to persecute or brutalize citizens in the mere act of being themselves.

It ill accords with the best of San Francisco traditions to seek to outlaw one life style in favor of that life style apparently more congenial to public officials whose only duty, after all, is to serve the public—and not dominate it.

With this statement, the most responsible members of the older community in the Haight-Ashbury signaled their emancipation from the standards of most middle-class people throughout the United States and welcomed the hippies into a symbolic Festival of Peoples. These old-time residents in the Haight-Ashbury had lived most closely to the young community and they had had their crosses to bear through the preceding months. Yet in the end they had been acculturated to the morality of the young, had seen the heart that beat beneath the complicated paraphernalia of dress and cults. In the sense that I have used it for my own experience, they, too, had become hippies in the process of living near them and listening to what they had to say. The tragedy is that in this fight, unlike the freeway encounter, HANC was unsuccessful. By then the forces of an entire nation were being mobilized against the hippies and the Haight-Ashbury.

CHAPTER 2

The Haight-Ashbury Before the Tour Buses Came Through

Some years ago, I visited Fruitlands, near Harvard, Massachusetts, the house and the spot where Bronson Alcott tried to establish a new and better life for mankind. Over a century has intervened, but the area still seems remote, unspoiled, almost unchanging—an unbelievably beautiful slope of land on a hillside overlooking the Nashua River and the surrounding hills. Although the Haight-Ashbury neighborhood had some blocks that were sordid and increasingly so as time went on, it contained or was contiguous to storybook forests, quiet hilltops, sweeping views that rivaled the solitude and splendor of Fruitlands. Most Utopian attempts in America—Walden Pond, Brook Farm, the Oneida community—have had their fingers on the pulse of Nature's beauty; to miss this part of the Haight-Ashbury experiment would be to overlook a great deal of what happened. Thus a few minutes of brisk walking in almost any direction from the center of the neighborhood—the crossing of Haight and Ashbury streets—brings one to some of the most enchantingly remote and beautiful spots in San Francisco. The young seekers in this neighborhood knew these spots well;

whenever I went on Lone Mountain, or on Buena Vista Hill, or on lofty Edgewood Avenue in the early spring—when the pink plum blossoms fell against the dark forests of Mount Sutro—I always found the young costumed ones there before me, reading, talking, contemplating, listening, watching the sea and the sky from these hilltops.

Yet by 1966, the advantaged young in America also had the firm conviction that they had to gain some new perspective on the world as it was, with its violence and its miseries. This perspective was not to be found in most of the university classrooms in America or in the suburban areas in which many of them had grown up. Thus the search for a new Utopia had to be centered in the city, because the city was the new frontier, the unexplored, the lost, desolate part of America, the place where the poor lived out their lives of quiet and increasingly unquiet desperation. This is where the reforms were needed; and the advantaged young of each generation still dream, however briefly, of the unfinished American promise, of the right of any child to realize some of that promise.

In the new Fruitlands, the ghettos were as near at hand as the hilltops. Ten blocks east from the intersection of Haight and Ashbury streets, walking along Haight Street, was the Haight-Fillmore district, one of the worst slums in San Francisco, now inhabited largely by poor Negroes. By 1966, the advantaged young had reason to be fearful lest they in fact had nothing to offer the poor; but they also had the obvious need to keep in touch with the ghetto; in time this would become a mutual need and Haight Street would be a ribbon of life, moving in both directions. In the late fall of 1966, signs in shop windows along Haight Street carried reminders of this commitment to the poor, particularly the Negro. One sign read: "Let's not forget about the Spades." This was a continuing theme. There was no formula as to what was to be done; but the necessity for awareness was omnipresent. As Paul Simon wrote in the song, "The Sounds of Silence": "The words of the prophets are written on the subway walls and tenement halls. . . ."

Thus in two important ways, the neighborhood offered easy access to two necessary ingredients for a new experiment in

Utopia—the beauty of Nature and a beginning contact with the life of the poor. The second ingredient was historically new in American Utopias. While Bronson Alcott had an abiding concern for the oppressed Negro living in slavery in the South—and for this reason the wearing of cotton, produced by slave labor, was not countenanced at Fruitlands—he did not have to maintain contact with the poor; he had been poor himself, had known privation in his early life, and had not been touched with the kind of isolating affluence that the young advantaged have felt in the twentieth century.

Thus the early young community in the Haight-Ashbury was not simply another Bohemia, although many artists came there, developed there, or were already there when the young seekers moved in. Traditionally the whole Bay area, as well as the nearby coastal towns, had been a haven for the artist for a long time. Like other Bohemias, North Beach, an Italian-American neighborhood, had for a time in the 1950's supplied a nurturing environment for young artists. Certainly both North Beach and the Haight-Ashbury had their own set of tolerances and understandings for the eccentric and the artist; historically this had been true of many parts of San Francisco. But the one world of the Haight-Ashbury was a broader canvas for the seekers of 1966; it had been in existence for some time before the advent of the seekers.

The very fact that the Neighborhood Council could have rallied within the space of a few months and taken a clear and strong position for the hippies is evidence of a vital tradition that had preceded the year of crisis. In my first ventures into the neighborhood, old-time residents bragged to me of the fact that one block on Belvedere Street had been cited by a national magazine some years before as the best integrated block, by ethnicity, race, and class, in urban America. Although I have made a rather intensive search for this particular story, I have been unable to uncover it; yet the importance lies not in the source for this fact, but in the pride with which the neighborhood identified itself with this reputation, so that it had the quality of legend for the long-time residents.

It has seemed to me that the history and tradition of the area did not alone account for this pattern—that in fact the physical geography of the area, natural and man-made, had kept more or less intact a quality of one world that was once characteristic of several neighborhoods in San Francisco but somehow survived longer in the Haight-Ashbury. When I first began to go into the neighborhood almost daily, I would customarily come from my office high on the hill over the area; and often I would ride down on a bus which circled through the upper reaches of the area, known originally as Ashbury Heights, settling down finally on Haight Street from which it would go eastward into the center of the city. I came to think of Haight Street as the delta of a river. The bus collected some portions of all the different strata and altitudes through which it flowed, carrying them downstream in a tumbling and merry confluence of all kinds of people, who pleasantly jostled each other without abandoning their own identities.

This quality was also characteristic of the local Catholic parish of St. Agnes, whose parishioners looked like a "human be-in" as they gathered on the steps of the church after Sunday mass. By good fortune, I have had access to a series of photographs of parishioners leaving St. Agnes on a Sunday morning in 1958, long before the advent of the flower children, of course;[1] almost a decade later, the diversity of the parishioners had not changed substantially, although the proportions had. Some of the Filipino women who lived in the neighborhood still went to mass with embroidered shawls over their heads; the young Italian-American girls had slender wired earrings in their pierced ears; black men in working clothes mingled with well-dressed middle-class and upper middle-class white and black families who lived in the area; here and there was a bus driver from the municipal transportation system, still wearing his uniform after an all-night shift; and so on.

The very fact that St. Agnes served the hills as well as the

[1] These photographs, taken by Mr. Code Beverly, are included in an unpublished M.A. thesis written by Sister Mary Bernadette Giles, P.B.V.M., a teacher at St. Agnes Convent in the Haight-Ashbury neighborhood: "A Changing Urban Parish—A Study of Mobility in St. Agnes Parish, San Francisco, California," Gonzaga University, Spokane, Washington, June, 1959.

valley had determined part of the variation in class structure, since real estate shows a marked inclination to rise in price as it climbs, even in cemeteries; but the variation in ethnicity and race could not be so easily traced. Even in cosmopolitan San Francisco, the diversity of this pattern was notable. In North Beach, for instance, where the beatniks had found shelter earlier, the twin spires of St. Peter and St. Paul summon mainly the Italian-American community to Sunday mass. All over San Francisco—in fact, all over America—this kind of apple-sorting for church congregations goes on almost automatically following the pattern of housing in the cities and the suburbs, and often ordering their congregations by variables of class and ethnicity in a surprisingly systematic fashion. At St. Agnes, and on the buses that served the neighborhood, diversity, and even eccentricity, were happy realities.

With the exception of the eastern gateway to the central part of the city, the neighborhood had clear boundaries, natural and man-made, that undoubtedly helped to preserve its village quality and its quality of one world. These boundaries had definite ecological advantages for the experiment undertaken by the flower children, as they had served to unify diverse peoples at an earlier period. It was an area rich in natural beauty, as I have already suggested; but even the beauty was diverse for an urban neighborhood.

Haight Street, running almost east and west, is amazingly flat for most of its length, lying along the floor of a valley. The valley itself stretches from the Bay in the east to the Pacific Ocean in the west, but Haight Street itself extended for about twenty blocks, terminated eastward by the diagonal Market Street which northward and eastward led to the Bay Bridge. Westward, only four blocks from the intersection of Haight and Ashbury streets, was the man-forced greenery of Golden Gate Park, wrested from the sand dunes some seventy years before and stretching for about fifty blocks to the ocean. For a long time, the young people talked of placing a statue of St. Francis on the edge of Golden Gate Park, with his arms outstretched facing eastward down Haight Street. This statue, they fantasized, would be carved from a great redwood, and it would symbolize the neighborliness of the Utopia they planned; it would be fitting for St. Francis to greet the young and distressed from everywhere. There were many schemes for financing this undertaking, locating artists equipped to do the carving, and so on; and they were good dreams, although they never reached any fruition as far as I know.

Entering the Park from Haight Street, one walked along the edge of a small man-made pond and then under a short pedestrian tunnel—over which a Park roadway ran—to a green slope which became known as Hippie Hill. The access was short and easy, and within a few minutes one could be away from the sharp sound of street traffic, still hearing the low hum of more distant traffic in the Park, but mainly protected from sight of it. This was the back dooryard for the young people; here on a sunny day could be found children and dogs and adults of all ages. Over time, the winos from Market Street learned their way to Hippie Hill. Many of the winos found the young people gentle and understanding of them; they learned to live with each other on Hippie Hill and sometimes shared food and wine. For a long time, Hippie Hill was largely off limits for busts from the nearby police station; they were out of sight of the more populous streets of the neighborhood where the squares were more apt to complain about their musical instruments and their loafing around on the streets in the afternoon and evening. The sharp smell of pot was common in this area of the Park, but again it seemed about as dangerous as kids smoking corn silks behind the barn, and no one particularly objected.

Looking north, down any of the cross streets along Haight Street, was the slender piece of green park known as the Panhandle; it was a thin extension of Golden Gate Park itself, forming a pleasant island of green for eight long blocks and running parallel to Haight Street. Along the near side of the Panhandle, traffic flowed from the Sunset District south and west of the Haight-Ashbury to the downtown area; the other side carried one-way traffic going in the opposite direction. Beyond the Panhandle was a rather sharp slope leading up to the white spires of St. Ignatius on Lone Mountain. The Panhandle represented the staging area for the flower children's gospel work with the larger community. Here within sight and sound of a large proportion of the flower children living on both sides of the Panhandle were staged the functions of the new community—free concerts given by the Grateful Dead and other local bands; the serving of free soup by the Diggers in the late winter afternoons; the "chalk-in" on a March Sunday when the city fathers relented briefly and allowed young and old to draw with colored chalk on the long pavements down the center of the Panhandle; and so on. This was the platform from which the community could proselytize the larger community, advocating a free and peaceful world in which no man was turned away. This barrier did not mark the end of the neighborhood; people living on the north side had been drawn more and more into the community of the Haight-Ashbury by way of the freeway fight. But the Panhandle did act as a punctuating greenery for the southerly part of the most central area. By happenstance, too, the traffic along both sides of the Panhandle, one-way and swift-moving, had lowered nearby property values, so that the large Victorian houses, once pleasantly peaceful as they faced the Park, had declined in value as the noise and fumes of automobiles increased, and rented for prices that were attractive to the young people in the area.

But it was the high area to the south of Haight Street that gave the neighborhood the character of a small town in the West. That way lay the foothills of Twin Peaks, with the Peaks themselves looming behind. When I walked along Haight Street in the fall of 1966, that view to the south always gave me a start. The warm winter rains had not come yet, so the Peaks themselves looked bare and brown and immense. I felt as if I were in a frontier town; and when I saw a cowboy or an Indian come walking down one of the hilly streets toward Haight Street, as I often did, I would feel almost disoriented. The scene up the south slope encapsulated the loneliness and the grandeur of the West as the Easterner experiences it on his first trip by land across the continent. The surprise was that this quality existed in the heart of a city. Actually the foothills were rather thickly settled, but the houses were partly hidden by a dense growth of evergreen bushes and trees; moreover, the empty stretches of Twin Peaks beyond were not in fact high enough to be truly grand. But distance and space change dimensions in the city, so that I always felt lonely as I looked toward the south from Haight Street, as if I were in a railroad town near the Continental Divide. In this direction was Mount Sutro and, further east, Buena Vista Hill. On these high points of land from which one could glimpse the Bay and the Ocean, the various tribes of young people held their ceremonials—sunrise services, meditations, a spring solstice festival, and finally their ceremonial burial of the hippie when, like Fruitlands, the experiment in the Haight-Ashbury was over, at least for the older tribes.

Before the young seekers came, Haight Street itself, the main business street in the neighborhood, had been a shabby and deteriorating shopping area. But in the early months of 1966 several new and colorful stores appeared on Haight Street—In Gear, the Psychedelic Shop across from it, and the I-Thou coffee shop further down. Any village needs a main street for its temples of wisdom and its marketplaces; and without the availability of store fronts at cheap rentals on Haight Street, it is doubtful that the new community could have developed. The older merchants on the street, who had somehow managed to survive through the lean years, looked upon the new merchants with a jaundiced eye. It was true that the old merchants began to prosper because of the new stores and the new customers. But the brisk sound of hammering and the smell of new paint on Haight Street must have been a sad reminder of their own youthful days when the street had contained many fine and flourishing small businesses. At any rate, it was obvious that of all the neighborhood groups who were leary of the new residents, it was the old merchants who fought hardest to clip their wings, particularly the wings of the new merchants. The old servitors of Mammon did not take kindly to the new servitors, who had strange ideas of the meaning of dollar bills and who seemed nevertheless to make as many trips to the local banks as the most prosperous of the old merchants. There were rumors that the Psychedelic Shop had applied for nonprofit status; such a heresy had never been heard of on Haight Street before, although the old merchants had long extended special credit and prices to old neighbors living on slender incomes.

In particular, a growing storm centered around a large abandoned five-and-dime store on the north side of Haight Street, almost directly across from the Psychedelic Shop. Partly because it was one of the largest store fronts on Haight Street, the old merchants took an unprecedented interest in its purchase by Mr. Morris Moscowitz in the fall of 1966. Mr. Moscowitz had for some time run a very popular bookstore on Telegraph Avenue in Berkeley, known widely as Moe's Book Store. As the new owner planned it, the store on Haight Street would be a secondhand bookstore stocked with about 50,000 books. The old merchants generally agreed that they did not want a Telegraph Avenue developing on Haight Street, and they felt that a bookstore would attract the wrong kind of people. One of the old merchants stated that one of the peace marches in Berkeley had formed "in front of Moe's store," so that it was obvious to him that this was a bad precedent for what might happen on Haight Street.

The fear that Haight Street would become a Telegraph Avenue was realistic in some ways, for there was a continuing and historical dialogue going on between the students in the Bay area, touched off by the early symptoms of student unrest in Berkeley. But the cutting-off of the bookstore did not delay this dialogue. Students from Telegraph Avenue increasingly came over to Haight Street during the winter of 1966–1967, and, ironically, they often gathered in the large display room of the old five-and-dime store. The old merchants' association had fought the opening of Moe's Book Store on Haight Street so successfully through the winter and spring of 1966–1967 that the issuance of a permit for the opening of a bookstore was delayed by various legal procedures. But temporary occupancy was allowed, and a store known as the Print Mint had opened its doors. Throngs of peace lovers, students from Berkeley, costumed ones from all over Christendom, and finally jostling and eager tourists pushed their way through its doors, buying the famous Fillmore posters, peace posters of all kinds, salacious and/or political buttons, large blown-up photos of every daring artist anyone had ever heard of; in time, even one of the old merchants would enter the Print Mint rather sheepishly to make his own purchases for "interested relatives" in another part of the country, he said.

As time went on, more and more people who basically belonged to the square world began to express sympathy with the young people; and I began to understand that there were many *hidden seekers,* or hidden hippies, throughout the Haight-Ashbury, indeed throughout society. As the contagion began to spread, the situation reversed itself, so that it was the square people who hid their identity, coming home from work and donning a costume for an evening of meditation, playing chess, listening to country music, or going to the Fillmore for rock-and-roll events. Many of these hidden seekers had lived in and around the neighborhood for a long time; the experiment of the young people simply allowed them to come out in the open. Particularly after the "Gathering of the Tribes"—the "Human Be-In"—in Golden Gate Park on January 14, 1967, these hidden seekers donned the costume and came out in the open.

This concept of hidden seekers was first borne in upon me by my own encounters with people in the neighborhood whom I knew elsewhere in the social system in other roles and literally in other clothes. Yet they subscribed to the philosophy of the seekers in many particulars and considered themselves novitiates in the search for a better way of life. In many instances, people in the professions expressed clear and growing disaffection for their way of life as professionals, and in one instance I happened to hear a public announcement of this disaffection.

In late November of 1966, the Ad Hoc Committee for Betterment of the Haight-Ashbury Neighborhood held a kind of town-hall meeting to which everybody was invited. This turned out to be a fairly bitter meeting in which there were clear political factions developing; in particular there was a bitter fight going on between the new merchants and the old ones. A second major fight, more hidden from sight but even stronger, was the feeling that the institutions within the area, particularly the universities, were going to try to control the neighborhood. Various questions were posed by the audience as to whether a person working in the neighborhood—at the Medical Center, for instance—but not living in the neighborhood could qualify for participation in any formal decision-making for the neighborhood. I had some qualms as to whether I should be at the meeting, since I was clearly ineligible under that definition. But as the meeting progressed, this definition was abandoned; no one, old or new residents, wanted much to do with eligibility when the chips were down.

At one juncture, statements were invited from the floor, and a young woman unmistakably dressed in the costume of the flower children went up to the microphone. She advocated a clear working together of all groups within the neighborhood, so that outside professionals would not have any rationale for telling the neighborhood what to do; in particular, she noted that nobody in the neighborhood wanted a bunch of social workers coming in and telling the local people what to do—a remark that was greeted with applause from the audience. This young woman looked familiar to me, and I had the distinct impression that I had seen her a number of times in another role, but I could not place her. After the meeting was over, she was surrounded by a group of people and I wandered over to get a better look at her. She spoke to me, and I realized abruptly that she was a young social worker at the Medical Center who lived in the Haight-Ashbury neighborhood. Within her personal world, she had clearly opted for a way of life that transcended narrow professionalism.

Another illustration was supplied me by a personal friend who happened to be a lawyer. He told me that he had taken his young son to a children's playground on the Panhandle on a Sunday afternoon and had been surprised to see his middle-aged law partner with his wife and children participating in the chalk-in on the Panhandle; they were all dressed for the occasion, and it was clear to him that they felt much at home in their costumes. He knew that they lived in the Haight-Ashbury neighborhood, but it had never occurred to him that they had become acculturated to the new movement there.

In my evening excursions into the neighborhood, I often met young women who worked as secretaries during the day at the

Medical Center. They were dressed as flower children, indistinguishable from the more full-time members of the new community, and they were obviously considerably more animated than they were during the day. In the pecking order of the general society, secretaries were usually defined as servants by non-reciprocal first-naming; and this served to keep them in their place in the status system. In the Haight-Ashbury, they were also known by their first names; but in the absolutely reciprocal, non-status system of the new community, a first name came to represent identity and respect.

One last example of this doubling in brass was found in San Francisco State College students who lived in and about the neighborhood and who were devoted followers of the new Utopia. I knew several State College students who had lived in the neighborhood before the appearance of the costumed ones. Retrospectively, I realize that they predated the appearance of the movement; earlier I had thought of them as characteristic of the somewhat eccentric population of State College; I had not realized that they were flower-children-in-the-making, that they had already begun to celebrate life. They had been concerned about war, about civil rights, and they still were; but they talked at times, rather self-consciously to be sure, of the joy of living, of the beauty of children, and the like, almost as if they were transcendentalists on a hillside at Fruitlands.

Although State College was located a few miles from the neighborhood, Haight Street and its environs had been an informal campus for some of its students for many years. At one time, State College had been located just east of the Haight-Ashbury neighborhood, but it had grown beyond its allotted space and been moved out to the edge of the Sunset District. Most of the students could not be accommodated in the few dormitories on the campus, and the houses in Sunset were largely small one-family dwellings; thus, many of the students commuted on the city's transportation system. After classes were over for the day, these students took the trolley that went almost immediately through the tunnel under Twin Peaks, emerging at the southeast corner of Buena Vista Park, which formed a part of the Haight-Ashbury neighborhood. From that east portal of the tunnel, the students fanned out in all directions, living in Noe Valley, the traditional home of Scandinavians and the Finns, or in the Mission District, largely inhabited during this period by Spanish-speaking people, or preferably in the big old houses and flats of the Haight-Ashbury neighborhood, where many students lived communally before the advent of the costumed people. Afterwards, students from State College who lived in the neighborhood became indistinguishable from the flower children; or, to put it another way, the students had their costumes hanging in the closet, so that when the play started they had only to don them.

One evening in January, I went to hear some country music at the I-Thou coffee house, which incidentally was run by a man who had written his M.A. thesis on Martin Buber at State College. As the audience gathered that evening, both men and women came in carrying long-stemmed, peppermint-colored carnations. Although I do not know the event that occasioned this particular flower-carrying, I presume that it was used to announce the opening of a new shop in the neighborhood, for instance, or perhaps the birth of a child, flowers being more appropriate than cigars to the seekers. During the course of the entertainment, the leader of the band made several jokes between numbers about registration at State College, which was then taking place. To my amazement, most of the customers laughed—it was an in-joke. Granted that the I-Thou coffee house may have been particularly frequented by State College students that night, or any night, no outsider would have known, without the jokes, that the audience was composed mainly of students from State College.

Thus the neighborhood was in many ways ripe for the events that took place in such intensity during the period of which I write. It included a population geared in many ways to the young and to new ideas, in particular to the idea of one world. Its flexibility can be demonstrated by the very fact that throughout the winter and spring, in spite of the influx of young people whose numbers increased at an almost unprecedented rate in the life of any city, the neighborhood became increasingly accepting. By June, various estimates were made that about 15,000 young flower children were living in the neighborhood;

and most of this growth had taken place within the space of a few months.

In many ways, they were a motley crew by the early spring of that year—students and non-students, Ph.D.'s and high school drop-outs, rich and poor, meat-eaters and vegetarians, for drugs and against drugs, and clearly from every ethnic and racial group in America. In part the cement that held them together was the actual neighborhood, the real village life. But there was a groping for new values on the basis of the obvious failure of old values, and this was a part of what was going on generally among the young particularly in the Republic in the 1960's, as it was going on also in many other parts of the world. In spite of the diversity, the central dialogues could be clearly understood as soon as one began to listen to the words of the songs that the young sang and to trace out the various attempts at reform that had been undertaken by the young in the 1960's.

CHAPTER 3

Transcendental Reform

You say you'll change the constitution
Well you know
we all want to change your head
You tell me it's the institution
Well you know
You better free your mind instead

—from "Revolution 1" by John Lennon and Paul McCartney

After many years passed in admiration of a better order in human society, with a constant expectation that some beginning would shortly be made, and a continued reliance that some party would make it, the idea has gradually gained possession of my mind, that it is not right thus to linger for the leadings of other men, but that each should at once proceed to live out the proposed life to the utmost possible extent. Assured that the most potent hindrances to goodness abide in the Soul itself; next in the body; thirdly in the house and family; and in the fourth degree only in our neighbors, or in society at large; I have daily found less and less reason to complain of public institutions, or of the dilatoriness of reformers of genetic minds.

—from letter on "The Consociate Family Life" at Fruitlands, signed by Charles Lane and A. Bronson Alcott, August 1843.[1]

[1] Cited in *Bronson Alcott's Fruitlands,* compiled by Clara Endicott Sears (Boston and New York: Houghton Mifflin, 1915), p. 41.

There are and were many myths about the young people who began to gather in the Haight-Ashbury in 1966. One of the most prevalent myths is that they were non-political, that they, by contrast with the civil rights workers in the early sixties, were uninterested in doing anything to reform the society, that they were interested only in drugs and sex and obscenities. This seems to me very much like saying that Jonathan Swift's *Gulliver's Travels* is not political because it is a book describing utterly imaginary voyages. There were indeed many trips undertaken by the young people in the Haight-Ashbury, some of them dangerous, and their experimentation was as diverse as America itself. But they had a clear compass for their main journey, and their side excursions even by way of drugs did not obscure their central political objective—to find a way for mankind, all of it, to survive by directly reforming the ethical values of the society at a personal, family, and neighborhood level.

Bronson Alcott's central conviction that reform begins within the person was not essentially different from the conviction of the seekers in the Haight-Ashbury. "Revolution 1," as subsequently sung by the Beatles, stated the position again. The argument about whether reform of the society should begin in the person or in the major institutions is an old and continuing one, of course, but it had a new thrust and a new urgency for the advantaged young in America of the 1960's. Throughout the first half of the decade, there had been a rapid succession of enthusiastic attempts, particularly on the part of college students, to participate in the amelioration of social injustice by the peaceful reform of existing institutions. Many of these attempts had met with failure, but these young people were not easily discouraged; they regrouped and began again. Many of their songs chronicle their hopes and their enthusiasms; eventually some of their songs would begin to chronicle their conviction that the institutions per se could not be reformed, that a new beginning was necessary.

If one is to begin to understand the nature of the task undertaken by the young seekers in the Haight-Ashbury, then it is imperative that one look briefly at the history of student movements in the Bay area in the early 1960's, focusing particularly on the Free Speech Movement at Berkeley in the fall of 1964, and its aftermath.[2] The importance of this history for the seekers was first brought home to me by an interchange with a middle-aged friend of mine in the Bay area who was the mother of three children involved in the Free Speech Movement. We were talking about the flower children in the Haight-Ashbury shortly after I began my study there, and she said with anguish in her voice, "How *can* the adults be so critical of the young these days? *Don't they ever listen to the words of their songs?*" She and her husband had understood the social and political concern of their own children and had stuck with them throughout the long legal complications following the Free Speech Movement—and this eventually would include a term in jail for one of them. As she spoke, I began to look afresh at the flower children in the Haight-Ashbury, understanding that, of course, they were but one part of a single process that the young had been involved in in the 1960's, particularly since President Kennedy's inauguration, and that had reached an early crisis in the Bay area with the Free Speech Movement.

I begin with President Kennedy's inauguration because his term of office, as it began and as it ended, was a built-in milestone for all the young people and the dispossessed people that I talked with in the intervening years. The young people in the Haight-Ashbury were no exception to this rule. Thus on November 22, 1966, the leaders of the new community held a press conference, covered by the metropolitan dailies, to counter a charge of obscenity raised against Lenore Kandel's *The Love Book* on sale in the Psychedelic Shop. They began the conference by noting that it was the third anniversary of President Kennedy's death and then stated: "We wanted to make you know we are conscious of our country's history." Such deliberate references to President Kennedy's leadership and death were a part of the formal and informal communication of the young community on both sides of the Bay. As I began to get acquainted with the members of the black community who

[2] The Bay area was, of course, only an early and visible part of what was taking place on campuses throughout the country in the same general period.

were involved in the Haight-Ashbury experiment, I found that they, too, dated history from these two events, although Malcolm X's death, on February 21, 1965, fifteen months after President Kennedy's, was equally significant to most of them. As time went on, other heroes of the young would disappear, often by the assassin's bullet. For both groups of young people, advantaged and deprived, there was a growing conviction that actual survival was at stake for people in leadership positions who told it "like it is." Yet the necessity for speaking out became increasingly obvious to the thoughtful as the decade progressed.

For the young, President Kennedy was the earliest classic example of someone at the highest level telling it "like it is." In his inaugural address in 1961, he used words that clearly defined his common cause with the young and the dispossessed: "Let the word go forth . . . that the torch has been passed to a new generation of Americans . . . unwilling to witness or permit the slow undoing of those human rights to which this nation has always been committed." The students' view of the Free Speech Movement, as it was published in 1965, shortly after their apparent victory, carried this excerpt from the inauguration address on the first page.[3] Shortly after the inauguration, President Kennedy strongly fortified his position with the young and with the dispossessed by his statement on the Bay of Pigs: *He told it like it was, and he took responsibility. The President of the United States said that he had made a mistake.* With that act, he had the young and the dispossessed in his hand. The early success of the Peace Corps, initiated early in his administration, is further evidence of his importance to the young. Like the young in all times and all lands, the young of the 1960's yearned to be Robin Hoods, Lone Rangers, King Arthurs, John F. Kennedys; and the television fortified their consensus on the ancient wrongs that must finally be righted.

President Kennedy's death in 1963 shocked all of us; but it was totally unbelievable to the young. It occurred in an area of the Republic that had opposed his civil rights stance and in which the immoral disposition of the offshore oil lands repre-

[3] *The Trouble in Berkeley,* with text by Steven Warshaw (Berkeley and San Francisco: Diablo Press, 1965).

sented the last and most powerful stance of the bad men, as the young defined it. In the words of a television generation: The Lone Ranger had been murdered, and the bad guys were trying to cover up. Most of us in America subscribed to this belief, in part. By the latest polls, most Americans of all ages still believe that the Warren Report was less than candid and that we have not been told vital information on that death.

For those of us who had grown up in an earlier generation, President Kennedy's death merely confirmed our cynicism about the world; there had been a brief period of hope, and then, as always, it was dispelled. For the young, the reaction was different. In the summer following President Kennedy's death, an unprecedented number of advantaged young people went into Mississippi to work with the black members of SNCC on the political rights of the impoverished black people in the South. This task was seen by many of them as being what President Kennedy would have wanted them to do, and this was stated matter-of-factly by students of my acquaintance who participated in this movement. Three civil rights workers were murdered in Mississippi that summer. But their young friends and comrades in Mississippi, however saddened, continued with their appointed task, proceeding more cautiously and setting up more stringent rules for periodically checking in with their communications center, as they fanned out through the state and tried to help in the legitimate selection of a list of delegates for the Democratic Convention in Atlantic City, scheduled for September of that year. I talked to some of the young people who went to Atlantic City and watched, as they said, their summer's work go down the drain, for the National Committee completely rejected the slate presented by the Mississippi Freedom Democratic Party.

After the Atlantic City rebuff, the young white students were noticeably discouraged and downhearted. But again they regrouped, re-evaluated their mistakes, moved in new directions; *they did not become cynical.* Their new focus of attention evolved in part from the challenge of the black students in SNCC who had been more pessimistic than the white students about the outcome in Atlantic City. After Atlantic City, these black students told the white students: Go back to your own white communities and institutions and reform them; that's where the trouble is and that's where the reform has to begin. Some of the graduate students in sociology who had been in Mississippi and Atlantic City drove directly on to Montreal where the sociology meetings were then in progress and presented their dilemma to their senior professors; for the most part, I agreed with the students that the professors were ungiving, conforming, playing it safe. At that time many professors did not feel that academia and political action belonged in the same bag; and they felt that the students who had gone through the summer's ordeal were understandably tired emotionally and overreacting.

Students returning to Berkeley from their summer in Mississippi faced, if anything, an even more formidable task than students in other parts of the country. For the University of California at Berkeley was huge and impersonal, and undergraduate classes in particular were overcrowded; the lecturer was often known to the undergraduate only as a voice over the microphone. I knew, for instance, a professor who regularly hid out from undergraduate students during his regular office hours, in order to make time for his graduate students. Thus the task of reforming the University administration at Berkeley seemed formidable by comparison with the smaller and more relaxed student-faculty relationship at San Francisco State College, for instance. Yet the young people at Berkeley immediately plunged into a round of new activities, raising money for SNCC, for CORE, talking to their teaching assistants about what might be done to inaugurate new classes centering on urban slum problems, and so on.

One group of politically active students, shortly before the fall term began, decided that the Republican Convention, meeting in San Francisco that year, should be liberalized and that a candidate other than Mr. Barry Goldwater should be offered to the American public in 1964 (some of them were supporters of Governor Scranton, for instance). These students organized a picket line at the Cow Palace in San Francisco, where the Convention was meeting, and they began to recruit pickets, as was traditional, on the edge of the Berkeley campus. Their recruitment stirred the repressive forces in the broader community, most of whom were for Mr. Goldwater, so that shortly new rules for the setting up of tables for advocacy were enforced by the University administration upon the students. The new rules hit hardest on those students who were working for CORE, SNCC, and other civil rights programs. In this way the Free Speech Movement came into being, and a young student, Mario Savio, who had been in Mississippi that summer, became the voice for a number of students who gathered in front of Sproul Hall at noon each day to listen to an account of the latest repression on the part of the University administration. The record of that period, from the opening of school in late September to the occupation of Sproul Hall by the students on December 2, 1964, is part of the social history of our time, and I shall not attempt to detail it here.[4] Suffice it to say that the continued struggle between the University administration and the Movement—after the initial encounter—centered on the administration's wish to single out some students for punishment and the students' continued demand that if one or two were to be punished, then a large number of them should also be punished.

After the noon rally on December 2, 1964, Joan Baez and Mario Savio led a thousand students into Sproul Hall for a non-violent sit-in, singing Bob Dylan's "Blowin' in the Wind":

How many roads must a man walk down
Before you call him a man?
How many seas must a white dove sail
Before she sleeps in the sand?
Yes, and how many times must the cannon balls fly
Before they're forever banned?
The answer, my friend, is blowin' in the wind.
The answer is blowin' in the wind.

"When you go in, go with love in your hearts," Joan Baez told the students, using the basic words of Martin Luther King and the civil rights movement. Eight hundred of the students were arrested in the middle of that night; the police did not enter Sproul Hall with love in their hearts, and many students were

[4] The most accurate report that I have seen of this period is found in the pictures and text for *The Trouble in Berkeley*.

injured. Some weeks later, almost everyone at Berkeley, including most of the faculty, agreed that the students had made a brave and courageous stand, that they had implemented needed reform. Thus amnesty for *all* those who participated was granted, belatedly, within the confines of the University. Yet this amnesty was not granted in the larger society; nor did faculty and administration feel that they had an obligation to fight for a legal amnesty in the larger community, even though there was general agreement that the whole campus had benefited. The conversion of the faculty to the ethical principles of the Free Speech Movement did not seem particularly meaningful to those students who chose to take jail sentences rather than give up their right of advocacy—a probation condition for a suspended sentence.

For two years after the hopefully successful outcome of the Sproul Hall sit-in, the student activists at Berkeley would periodically make the same stand; the particular event would be different, and the issues would center more and more around the immorality of using napalm on civilian populations, the students' unwillingness to have recruiters from the Armed Services on campus, and so on. But the basic issue with the administration continued to be one of community: *You cannot punish one for what many of us believe. We are a community, and we will not let you single out one of us to be thrown to the wolves of public relations. We will not compromise on principles. We will not be expedient with one of our group for the political advantage of most of us.* To a society steeped in demi-morality at all levels, such basic ethical stands seemed the essence of bravado and youthful impudence.

By the fall of 1966, the student movement of the 1960's was changing throughout the Bay area, as it was changing throughout the country. Two facts of life had forced this change. First, it was clear to most activist students on both sides of the Bay that there had been a gradual and dangerous erosion of the principles enunciated and supposedly implemented at Berkeley by the Free Speech Movement. Students at San Francisco State College had never had to fight so intensively as they had at

Berkeley for the right of free speech; but State College students and faculty saw the erosion of those principles at Berkeley as a threat to what might happen to them under an increasingly repressive state government. And second, there had evolved in the two years since the Free Speech Movement a new and more frightening danger to the whole society, to the whole world—the escalation of the war in Vietnam. This second danger was defined by many students as simply an extension of the racist philosophy in the United States to the continent of Asia. In the scheme of things as they were in the Republic, the young male black high school drop-outs in the slums on both sides of the Bay were being drafted—even welcomed the draft in many instances as a way out of futility—while the male students at State College or on the Berkeley campus had deferments. Deprived men of color were being sent to kill and be killed in a foreign land; their enemies in Asia were also deprived men, women, and children of color. Many college students were faced with the dilemma of conscience: It was not democratic for the draft to protect the privileged and fall on the deprived; at the same time, many of these advantaged young people felt the war to be morally repulsive.

More and more college students in the Bay area, as elsewhere in the country, were beginning to see dropping out of school as a beginning step toward some resolution of the moral dilemma; I speak now particularly of male students subject to the draft, of course. The victories of these young advantaged students in the various reforms that they had undertaken had been Pyrrhic, as far as many of them could tell; and the possibility of being able to stop the escalation of the war in Vietnam by a reform movement, patterned on the Free Speech Movement, for instance, seemed terrifyingly futile. But, as I often heard the young say, they were all programmed by family and teachers for college education and success through academic achievement. To drop out of school was a step of some magnitude, particularly to the students at Berkeley, who in the state system of colleges and universities had been accorded, by the apple-sorting process, considerably more status than the student at San Francisco State College.

Into this dilemma of conscience and programmed aspiration,

the call of Timothy Leary to "turn on, tune in, and drop out" had a peculiar relevancy. It became the battle cry for a new alternative: If the establishment refused to be reformed, give up on it. One could at least tune in on one's own values, find out what they were, find perhaps a chemical breathing space by experimenting with the psychedelic drugs. Above all, by dropping out of school, one could force oneself to make a moral decision—would it be Canada, prison, or the fake-out? —for most draft boards moved quickly once a student had dropped out of school.

On both sides of the Bay, the advantaged young began to seriously consider the possibility of a psychedelic revolution. In much the same way, Bronson Alcott disengaged himself from the political activism of his own time. Before Fruitlands, he had made various attempts to actively reform the government, being a founding member of William Lloyd Garrison's original Anti-Slavery Society, and refusing to pay his poll tax as a protest against the immorality of the government. After Fruitlands, although he had moved far away from political reform by then, he, like Emerson and Thoreau, was finally radicalized by the government's continued immorality on the slavery issue into actively giving moral and financial support for John Brown's stand at Harper's Ferry in 1859. There were thousands of Alcotts, Garrisons, and John Browns in-the-making on both sides of the Bay by 1966, fluctuating back and forth, debating the old issues with new intensity and urgency, centering their concern once again on the basic American problems—the enslavement of the oppressed and the periodic sacrifice of the Republic's young men to the drive for an ever larger economic empire.

There was never a monolithic definition of how the psychedelic reform would be accomplished, although certainly the drugs were defined as a viable pathway, a reasonable *rite de passage*. In the beginning of the Haight-Ashbury experiment, many student activists at Berkeley tended to feel bitter about the seekers in the Haight-Ashbury, seeing them as cop-outs who were escaping by drugs and abandoning political reform. The student activists at Berkeley had undergone an intensely bitter experience in their fight for reform; and it is understandable that they initially defined the seekers in the Haight-Ashbury in more absolutist terms than the students at State College where freedom of speech had never been so directly in danger. From my own limited observation of drug use on Telegraph Avenue in Berkeley, as compared to its use on Haight Street, I would suggest that the political disappointments in Berkeley did produce in some young people there a kind of commitment to drugs as a way of life which was not as prevalent in the Haight-Ashbury in the period of which I write. In the Haight-Ashbury, drugs were never the exclusive way of accomplishing the reform of the person and his daily life, and the early seekers did not see them as an end in themselves—although eventually that would change, too. Meditation centers, patterned after various Asian religions, were an important part of the tools for psychedelic revolution in the Haight-Ashbury. Macrobiotic diets (mainly rice and tea and no meat) were popular and were indeed effective in inducing visions, in much the same way that fasting and limited diets had produced weird spiritual sensations in Fruitlands. Communion with Nature was encouraged on Haight Street and any events publicly celebrating Nature drew large and decorous crowds.

And finally, there was another tool for effecting the psychedelic revolution in the Haight-Ashbury, and this seemed the most effective, the most lasting. For want of a better term, I will call it *instant theater;* it emerged in the Haight-Ashbury primarily in the phenomenon of the Diggers. In my estimation, much of what the Diggers stood for in the Haight-Ashbury will survive—by word of mouth, by a picture in people's minds of what they did, by their example of simple kindliness and humanity, by their reaffirmation of the importance of every person and of everyone having his "thing," and by their emphasis on the destructiveness of property values in a society moving toward technological affluence.

There were, of course, many foolish and tragic excesses in the Haight-Ashbury. Fruitlands also had its own foolishnesses, its own excesses—only water was used as a beverage; tea, coffee, molasses, rice were forbidden as foreign luxuries; the land could not be manured because it would force Nature; the bread was made of unbolted flour, and meat, cheese, milk were forbidden, so that some of the members nearly starved to death; and one of the members of the community felt that "clothes were an impediment to spiritual growth, and that the light of day was equally pernicious," so that he stayed "in his room in a state of nature during the day, and only went out at night for exercise, with a single white cotton garment reaching from his neck to his knees."[5] Yet in the end, Fruitlands became a symbol of the search for a way to improve the life of the spirit, to right injustice, to escape from material accumulation; and it was the defeat at Fruitlands that in the end brought a new harvest as Bronson Alcott spent another thirty-seven years teaching and lecturing, traveling through the Midwest and communicating to a new generation of teachers and thinkers part of the American hope and dream. In a somewhat comparable fashion, the living theater of the Diggers as it combined eventually with the wisdom of the black man in the slum represents the significant survival potential of the Haight-Ashbury.

Audience participation in theater has, of course, a long and intricate history; and the young people who began the Diggers movement had knowledge of this, as evidenced by their publications and actions. But the instant theater that was developed by the Diggers was more spontaneous and politically sophisticated. This kind of living theater had an immediacy and a communication potential that bypassed the failure of the establishment to listen to the words of the songs sung by the young—even the civil rights songs. All the skill of the medicine man, as the young had witnessed it in the TV ads in their growing-up years, was brought to bear on the audience. The Diggers knew how to make a point without words. They also recognized that a commercial ad would do no good; there must be conviction and dedication, which also had some element of being quite willing to suffer for their beliefs, if that became necessary.

The effectiveness of this kind of theater was brought home to me when the writer Kay Boyle, a professor of English at San Francisco State College, began a lonely and dramatic vigil in

[5] As reported by Robert Carter in "The Newness," *The Pioneer* (1843), and as reproduced in part in Sears, *op. cit.*, pp. 39–40.

front of a San Francisco undertaking establishment on those days when shipments of bodies from Vietnam would arrive for the final housekeeping details before they would be shipped on to Ohio, Mississippi, or wherever.[6] Dressed in deep mourning, Kay Boyle would walk up and down in front of this mortuary on the appropriate days, according to a newspaper account. Her vigil sent a chill of horror throughout the city, for it evoked the memories of the young soldiers who had begun to appear in sizable numbers in San Francisco some months before on their last fling before being shipped out; from many hilltops throughout the city, rich and poor alike had watched the gray war boats slip out through the Golden Gate, laden with the young and the weapons of war. So effective was this vigil that subsequently the shipping of bodies home from Vietnam was rerouted, according to widespread gossip in San Francisco, to avoid the Bay area. This kind of living theater was of a different ilk from guerrilla theater or audience-participation theater. It was action on feelings, an unwillingness to conform to established behavior, in the face of great tragedy. It was informed with an artist's sensitivity and an awareness of the human response that would be invoked in thousands of people in the Bay area; and it obviously depended on the name of the artist and the fact that she was well known.

The Diggers' drama was a group effort, and it evolved out of the sensitivity of several young artists to a particularly tragic incident in the city; most of these artists were part of the San Francisco Mime Troupe. In the early fall of 1966, San Francisco had experienced a so-called race riot, and the city was upset and puzzled that it could have happened at all. On the afternoon of September 27, three young Negro boys were stopped by a policeman in one of San Francisco's slums, on the chance that the car they were driving had been stolen; the policeman was correct in his surmise, although his hunch was not based on any report of a stolen car—the owner had not even missed the car by then. The policeman was white, and the

[6] As I remember it, this must have been in the late spring of 1966, although Miss Boyle herself is not sure of the date. A colleague sometimes accompanied her in this vigil, according to Miss Boyle, but the legend in the city at the time always defined it as a lone vigil, and that is the way I heard of it.

boys were understandably scared; they fled, and continued to run after the policeman ordered them to stop. One of the boys, sixteen years old, with the same last name as the policeman but a different shade of skin color, was shot in the back and died almost instantly. Thus began the San Francisco riots of 1966, with three days of "racial turbulence," as it was described in the *Chronicle,* and six days of curfew in certain disturbed areas of the city, including the Haight-Ashbury. In the slums of the city—and in this instance this included the Haight-Ashbury, which was not primarily a slum area at all—many people were caught without food because of the curfew and the rioting. Some members of the Mime Troupe, calling themselves Diggers, began to prepare food and serve it free to all comers. There was no formal organization; it was more a state of mind.

The name "Diggers" was somewhat obscurely derived, and different people had different theories about its meaning. Some of the members of the movement clearly connected the name with the Diggers in Cromwell's England who began to dig and plant the commons in towns throughout the country, distributing free the food produced, as a protest against a government insensitive to the hunger of some of its people. These early Diggers were a branch of the group in England known as the Levellers, who, like the Quaker movement begun in the same general period, had as one of their main tenets the idea of leveling all differences of position or rank among people. At the same time, the word Diggers in the Haight-Ashbury had other connotations, some of them continuous with the Negro culture, for instance, where the term "hip" had long implied that one really "dug" what was happening; and I heard various sympathetic puns on this usage in the Haight-Ashbury coffee houses. There was a free frame of reference for words on Haight Street, as there had been for James Joyce, and it would be restrictive to think that the word Digger meant only one thing in that rapidly changing culture. The use of the word was undoubtedly enhanced by the fact that a North American Indian tribe had once been known as Diggers because they lived chiefly on roots; and Ruth Benedict's book *Patterns of Culture,* which was well read by the young, had as its epigraph a "Proverb of Digger Indians": "In the beginning God gave to every people a cup of clay, and from this cup they drank their life."[7] The seekers had an affinity for odd pieces of information floating around which coalesced in remarkable ways from time to time, and they were considerably influenced by the romance and lore of the American Indian. For some of the young people, the name Diggers was connected with grave-digging—a macabre association in light of the young boy's death. They pointed out that the original Diggers in England had been Levellers, that they had acquired the name Diggers when they had to dig the graves for their own dead on the commons in the morning, after a night's encounter with the local officials; altruism has always been a peculiarly red flag for the establishment of whatever century or country. At any rate, the word "Diggers" captured the imagination of many people throughout the Bay area, and the concept eventually stirred up as much anxiety in the San Francisco establishment as it did in Cromwell's England.

My first formal knowledge of their activities and their name probably came from Ralph Gleason's columns in the San Francisco *Chronicle*,[8] but I had been aware of the phenomenon for some time. Early in my sojourn, I would see from time to time groups of monk-like costumed people distributing bread, or heavily laden with packages on obviously important missions, or moving steaming milk cans on to a yellow jeep; and I recognized that other costumed people in the area treated these monks with respect. In time I learned that they basically focused on two objectives: that every man had his thing—comparable to the philosophy of the Quakers and the Levellers in seventeenth-century England; and that there should be a free movement of goods in the society. They conveyed this philosophy by acting upon it, in a continuous and impressive morality play.

As I have already noted, many of the early Diggers were members of the Mime Troupe; the more formal presentations

[7] Ruth Benedict, *Patterns of Culture* (New York: Mentor Books, 1959), p. xvi.

[8] Ralph Gleason's columns focused on the music of the young, but they included much more than that; of all the material written on the young in the Bay area, I consider his evaluations and insights the most "beautiful," as the seekers would say; they were also unerringly correct and perceptive in the eyes of the young people themselves.

of that Troupe, in which audience participation was also encouraged, focused in true Swiftian fashion on the political and sexual hang-ups in the square world, and much of it was amusing and lusty. The combination of these two strands—the altruism of the Diggers and the sharp satire of the Mime Troupe—fused in a remarkable way on Haight Street, so that literally thousands of young people learned to use these two basic styles of behavior in ingenious ways, sometimes quite provocatively. Every hung-up square, venturing on to Haight Street in its heyday, would feel at some time or another that he was being "put on" by some curiously garbed person. In effect, everyone was included in the play on stage; if a person was not participating in the action, he was hastily enticed on to the stage by some action or other of a seeker already initiated into the culture. When the sight-seeing buses in the spring of 1967 began to bring tourists through the neighborhood, the young people began to walk beside the slowed-down bus as it went along Haight Street, holding up a mirror so that even the tourists could become part of the act, could see themselves peering with dropped jaws at the scene on Haight Street. And the new young seekers coming into the neighborhood would be "put on" in the same way. The impressive part of this phenomenon was that as far as I could see this teaching largely went on without exposition, simply by being.

Thus the new Haight-Ashbury society was but another facet of the continuing concern of the advantaged young students and ex-students in the Bay area, as elsewhere in America, over the great moral issues of the day. Some of the seekers had been deeply involved in student activism at an earlier period, so that there was a personal continuity in some instances. More importantly, the young people in the Haight-Ashbury were in continuous dialogue with the student activists in their midst as well as those at Berkeley. They were as continuously concerned with the plight of the leaders of the Free Speech Movement at Berkeley as the students at Berkeley were concerned about what the people in the Haight-Ashbury were doing. When I was on Haight Street, particularly in the Psychedelic

Shop, I would often hear a chance word of worried concern about the legal status of Mario Savio or one of the other student activists at Berkeley; and when there was a new crisis at Berkeley, the seekers in the Haight-Ashbury were often as depressed as I was by the punitive nature of what was going on. In turn, there is considerable evidence that the Berkeley students were concerned about the young people in the Haight-Ashbury. Allen Ginsberg once reported in a dialogue sponsored by *The Oracle*, the most important newspaper in the young community, that Mario Savio had expressed to Ginsberg some concern over "whether the Haight-Ashbury people would survive because he's facing jail."[9] There was a considerable legend on Telegraph Avenue that the hippies were babes-in-the-wood when it came to knowing how to take care of themselves; and I heard one Berkeley activist lament the "pitiful" naïveté of the flower children in dealing with the police during a particular bust on Haight Street, in which the Berkeley activist himself had also been inadvertently arrested.

The Diggers had been in existence a little more than two months when some of the activist students at Berkeley began their own instant theater, called the Yellow Submarine Movement. On the night of December 6, 1966, student activists at Berkeley voted unexpectedly at one of their meetings to suspend the latest strike on campus. Mario Savio—present at the meeting and only recently denied reinstatement at the University because he had refused to remain aloof from the current student struggle for political rights—talked about a coalition of hipsters and political radicals which would, in his words, "get the University, not by beating them down, but by blowing their minds." According to the San Francisco *Examiner*, the students then "broke into song for the first time in six days of demonstrations. They did NOT sing 'We Shall Overcome.' They sang 'Yellow Submarine.' "[10] The date December 6 is important, for it was the second anniversary of the sit-in in Sproul Hall. On the next day, a leaflet appeared at a noon

[9] Untitled dialogue (no date) between Alan Watts, Allen Ginsberg, Timothy Leary, and Gary Snyder, sponsored and published by *The Oracle*, 1, No. 7 (1967): 35.

[10] Story by Lynn Ludlow, San Francisco *Examiner*, December 11, 1966.

rally in front of Sproul Hall called by the "Campus Friends of the Lone Ranger," which announced that the song, "The Yellow Submarine," was "an unexpected symbol of our trust in our future, and of our longing for a place fit for us all to live in":

And we live a life of ease
  Every one of us has all we need
Sky of blue and sea of green
  In our yellow submarine.[11]

At the rally, students were urged to wear masks to their classes; and a fair number of them wore the mask of the Lone Ranger—an action pun on the administration's charge against the students of mass coercion (maskoercion).

One of the speakers at the rally proposed that Bob Dylan be made a Regent for the University. For many of the students, the reference to Dylan must have evoked a feeling of nostalgia. It had been just two years since Joan Baez and Mario Savio led the students into Sproul Hall singing Dylan's song.

Retrospectively, it seems to me that the Yellow Submarine Movement, no matter how absurd and brief, marked the end of an epoch in the student movement in the Bay area—an era of political innocence in which students stood up bravely and non-violently for what they believed in. Subsequently, their political convictions were tempered with the realization that the establishment would not listen, could not listen—not even to the words of civil rights songs that they sang. Nor did the establishment understand their courageous actions patterned in many ways after the model of Martin Luther King. Now the same conviction remained, but the avenues for finding the way toward the goals had changed. There would be new ways, and in the nature of things, some of the ways would turn out to be more strident. Periodically the establishment would wonder why the young appeared bewitched and demented in actions and appearance; and people would talk more and more about the generation gap, pointing out from time to time that there were really only a very few students who were intent on "making trouble."

[11] John Lennon and Paul McCartney, "The Yellow Submarine."

On both sides of the Bay, and indeed throughout the country, the yellow submarine became the symbol of new hope, tempered with the need for watchful waiting, for reorganization of one's values. The Diggers had their own yellow submarine —their yellow jeep—in which they delivered soup to the Panhandle in the late afternoon. As the spring of 1967 wore on, I, too, wore a yellow submarine button, with the peace symbol on it, this particular device emanating from the young in New York City. I came to think that the color yellow was a joke of the young, and that the Beatles, who know the young well, were in on the joke. *We may be yellow but we want to live,* the yellow submarine song says to me. *We want everyone to live and to be free. We may have to disappear for a while, underground or undersea, and we may be called cowards, but we will not participate in the aimless kill and overkill. We will, as we can, struggle for a way of life in which "every one of us has all we need."*

The reform of the institutions was no longer the only focus in the Bay area. From time to time, there would be fateful encounters and increasingly dangerous skirmishes with school authorities. But for many advantaged young people, the belief that allies in the broader society and in professors and administrators were effective resources in these attempts at reform was dissipated. Instead, the task had to be undertaken by each man; in a continuing dialogue of personal action, the truth would emerge. Perhaps the most monumental significance of this choice by many students on both sides of the Bay was that finally a new generation had, like Bronson Alcott and Charles Lane, tackled the paranoia of the society—the idea that the fault lies elsewhere, always in somebody else. These particular young people were beginning to think that the solution lay within each man, and "the most potent hindrances to goodness abide in the Soul itself."

CHAPTER 4
The Harmless People of the Haight-Ashbury

"Listen, father, I will never kill another. . . ." —*from "The Great Mandella" (The Wheel of Life) by Peter Yarrow*

In many ways, the seekers in the Haight-Ashbury had much in common with the young people in New England in the 1840's who seemed to the adults of that period to move in frightening and exotic directions, following the music of the transcendental drummers in Concord.[1] Yet, in one particular, there was a difference of great moment—the young seekers in the Haight-Ashbury, like young seekers in the 1960's everywhere, grew up with the certain knowledge that the actual survival of mankind was at stake. As Harry Stack Sullivan formulated it: "The bomb that fell on Hiroshima punctuated history."[2] The young seekers in the Haight-Ashbury had grown up in a world in which history had already been punctuated: The earth as

[1] See, for instance, Chapter IX, "The Younger Generation of 1840," in Van Wyck Brooks, *The Flowering of New England* (New York: Dutton, 1936), pp. 179–202.

[2] Harry Stack Sullivan, "The Cultural Revolution to End War," *Psychiatry*, 9 (1946): 81–87; see p. 83.

the natural home of man could become uninhabitable, and mankind could be destroyed. A kind of Noah's Ark syndrome emerged—a concern with symbolic survival and an identity with all the creatures and the flowers that could be seriously damaged or destroyed by a thermonuclear accident. Their writings and their songs reflect this concern; in their writings, as seen in their purest form in the early issues of *The Oracle*, there is a continuous search for wisdom from the stars, from the American Indians, from Buddhist teachings, from the widest spectrum of mankind's precise knowledge and of his uninformed speculation.

Certainly part of this burgeoning interest seems very much like what Van Wyck Brooks has termed "the flowering of New England" at an earlier period—an occasional generation of the affluent young who can afford to explore in relative freedom the world around them. The fifty "Orphic Sayings" that Bronson Alcott published in the first issue of *The Dial* in 1840 implied the same sense of revelation and inspiration as the title and contents of *The Oracle*, published between 1966 and 1968, in the Haight-Ashbury. And the young people of the 1840's in New England were almost as wound up in esoteric studies as the young people in the Haight-Ashbury in 1966–1967. Brooks takes note of the fact that the young New Englanders of whom he writes talked of "spiritualism and mesmerism, phrenology and animal magnetism, all the dark problems of the human mind over which the sun of hope seemed to be rising."[3] But the young people in the Haight-Ashbury were less hopeful that the sun would continue to rise, with good reason; they yearned for an instant Utopia, again with good reason.

For the young in the Haight-Ashbury, death had a different meaning; it was spoken of as an old friend and as more final than I had ever realized it, other than as an intellectual conviction. I suppose that I still cannot believe that the world as I know it could ever be no more. I grew up in a world of crisis, but it was still for me a world of sunlight and flowers that would continue. As a child, it was difficult for me to digest the fact of personal mortality, as it is for most people of my generation in Western society; but I was consoled by the knowledge that

[3] Brooks, *op. cit.*, p. 192.

people who came after me would enjoy sunsets, the first snow, the coming of spring. After Hiroshima, there was no such emotional solace for the young. It is no coincidence that one of the favorite rock bands in the Haight-Ashbury was named "The Grateful Dead." Nor was it strange that so many of them felt that the chief virtue of taking LSD was to be able to experience death; in this way one could be reborn and perhaps learn to live.

There was another influence on these young people in their own growing-up years that earlier generations of Americans—including my generation—had escaped: the instant pictures that came on television and captured the child for long hours in a net of inactivity. Two central messages seemed to emerge from Hiroshima, followed so shortly by mass television: *Unless something is done,* we shall all perish by a thermonuclear accident and there will be no more world, no more life; *and there is nothing to do about it,* except sit in front of the picture box, cocktail in hand when you get older, and have a ringside seat for that destruction. I would suggest that it was the frustration of this historical double threat that finally forced the young to try increasingly drastic measures, some frantic, some philosophically sound, all edged with the tragic sense of absolute urgency if the world was to survive. In the process of trying to escape this double message, the young in the Haight-Ashbury disavowed television as the focal point of their interest; practically none of them watched television at all. Yet in another way, the television screen had taught the young the power of a symbol, the importance of pictures without words, and the significance of a few words of truth, well chosen. Each of them seemed instinctively to know the meaning of his own individual action and to have a sense of being the focus of the camera.

In the continuing morality play that began in the Haight-Ashbury, the flower became an early symbol of the seekers' central value—the wish to shelter life itself, to be harmless. I remember the precise moment when this idea first occurred to me, some two months after I began to observe the young seekers. A day or two before Christmas, 1966, various church groups and citizens' organizations conducted a vigil for peace in Union Square in downtown San Francisco. The vigil was held on a rather chilly evening, and people of all ages, colors, and walks of life lit candles as they came in to the Square and stood quietly while a brief program was held on a raised platform at one end. There were a goodly number of young people, most of them dressed in the costume of the hippie, wearing the traditional flower on their hair or clothing. Various church groups came to the platform and sang Christmas carols, but the audience did not participate in the singing, as far as I could tell. Then four nuns came to the platform and, accompanied by a guitar, began to sing Pete Seeger's song, "Where Have All the Flowers Gone?" Suddenly there was a soft swell from the audience, and everyone in the Square seemed to be singing gently along with the nuns in a single strand of voices and feeling:

Where have all the flowers gone,
Long time passing,
Where have all the flowers gone
Long time ago,
Where have all the flowers gone,
Young girls picked them every one,
When will they ever learn,
When will they ever learn?

The song goes on inevitably to its own futility: "Where have all the young girls gone, . . . Gone for husbands every one. . . . Where have all the young men gone, . . . Gone for soldiers every one. . . . Where have all the soldiers gone, . . . Gone to graveyards every one. . . . Where have all the graveyards gone, . . . Gone to flowers every one. . . . When will they ever learn, When will they ever learn?" Suddenly I had a clear idea of what the flowers meant. After that, whenever I saw the young seekers with flowers, I would hear the song again, echoing softly in the chill of that night, and I would feel the answer acted out, innocently and sturdily, with no real necessity for words:

"Where have all the flowers gone?" And the answer, *They have not gone. They are right here. See, I hold them in my hands, and I want you to have a flower, too.* "When will they ever learn?" *We are learning, please understand, we are trying to learn, we want to learn: "I will never kill another."*

Unless this dialogue is understood as a living belief of the young people who costumed themselves and were called hippies, then it is indeed very difficult to understand what they had in common. In almost all other ways, they seemed to be experimenting in a variety of directions, to be eternally seeking and in motion; but there was this central hope and belief: *We shall learn a new way of living with others. There is yet time.*

Because I have come to understand this as their central passion, I think of these young people as the "harmless people," following Elizabeth Marshall Thomas' book of that name.[4] According to Elizabeth Thomas, the Kung Bushmen in Southwest Africa describe themselves as "*zhu twa si*, the harmless people. *Twa* means 'just' or 'only,' in the sense that you say: 'It was just the wind' or 'It is only me.'" So, too, the young people in the Haight-Ashbury seemed to me to be saying the same words, over and over again: *It is just the wind. It is only us.* At first, when one of them came up to me on Haight Street and offered me a piece of candy—a blond, blue-eyed girl, swaying on the sunny street in a brisk wind from the ocean—I reacted in the old way, saying "No thank you," fearing somehow that I was being "put on," that the candy no doubt contained some dread drug. But after a while I saw it as a gesture of ingratiating humanness, an asking for my acceptance of them; and I began to sense that I was overly suspicious, so caught in an older and sicker society that I could not even accept simple kindness, simple friendliness. In the end I came to feel that I had to respond in kind, that to be mistaken was less dangerous than to be so suspicious, so afraid of the young life around me. I came to accept gifts, and nothing bad happened to me. Other squares who went into the area have reported to me on the fact that they, too, felt afraid of proffered gifts of food and realized how strong was suspicion in our society.

The harmless people in the Haight-Ashbury propitiated with

[4] Elizabeth Marshall Thomas, *The Harmless People* (New York: Alfred A. Knopf, 1959). See p. 24 for derivation of title.

food and developed attitudes around the giving of food that bore a marked resemblance to its use as propitiation in so-called primitive cultures. Elizabeth Thomas writes of this use of food in her study of the Bushmen, who are at certain times of the year in mortal danger of starving to death or dying of thirst. On one occasion, when the author had accompanied the Bushmen on an expedition in her jeep, she was able to witness the elaborate sharing techniques accompanying the picking of about 300 pounds of tsi, a kind of nut, which is one of the three most plentiful foods in their diet. In loading the jeep with the various containers of nuts, they began immediately to give and receive presents of the nuts, which the author describes as an endless preoccupation of Bushmen. The larger gifts were not handed around, but were indicated verbally, with ownership often moving around and finally back to the original owner. Elizabeth Thomas suggests that these gifts are perhaps used "to cement relationships with each other, perhaps to prove and strengthen their dependence upon each other." This gift-giving continued for days, in smaller and smaller quantities as time went on and with the actual nuts now changing hands in "small piles or small bagfuls, after that in handfuls, and, last, in very small quantities of cooked tsi which people would share as they were eating."

Since the food in plentiful supply is often several days' travel away, by foot and over arid land, from the water holes where the band of Bushmen would be living, there has to be some provision for the old, the infirm, pregnant women, children, and so on, to have their share of the harvest. For this reason, the owner of the container in which the food is brought back to the water hole is the owner of the food in that container. In this way, a person too ill to travel may be in the position of sharing his food with one of the stronger members of the actual expedition.[5]

The Bushmen distribute food in this complex way in a desperate effort to keep everyone alive in a situation of short supply. Although there is no short supply of food in the United States, there are unsolved distribution problems—pockets of people who lack the buying power—so that a family living next

[5] *Ibid*, pp. 214–216.

door to a well-stocked grocery store can suffer from serious malnutrition. Indeed, the rats may have a better diet than the family living next door. The hippies and the Diggers recognized this, so that their division of food was also a complex phenomenon—an attack on the sickness in the method of distribution.

There were many instances in which the handling of money, goods, and food seemed to take on the characteristics of primitive societies in general and of the Bushmen in particular. Food was used as propitiation very often in the Haight-Ashbury. When the young people felt that the police at Park Station were harassing them at a new intensity, some of the leaders in the young community suggested at a Happening House meeting that the police and their families be invited to a picnic in the Park. There was a firm belief that the sharing of food would somehow dissipate the hostility of the police and that this sort of eating together would turn on the police.

Again, the Diggers served free lunch at the Civic Center to the Mayor and his assistants in the spring of 1967, with an eye to reassuring the Mayor and lessening his animosity toward the hippies. I myself became caught up in this effort in a kind of contagion that was evidence to me of the increasing level of my own acculturation. One morning, I ran into one of the leaders in the Digger movement. I paused to greet him, but he was in a hurry and seemed upset. Things were not going well that morning, he explained; they were supposed to serve lunch to the city officials at the Civic Center, but there had been a crisis and there was no immediate wherewithal for food. "Would this help in any way?" I said, opening my pocketbook and giving him what I had. He nodded offhandedly and took the bill without a word. He was a person of considerable charm and dignity, and his offhand manner gave me a feeling of some basic acceptance of my right to participate. That night I saw the Diggers on television carrying food into the Civic Center and realized with a start that however remote I was from the act of preparing and giving the food, I had been involved in a morality play that expressed my own basic values; and that this kind of event and my participation in it might be viewed as bizarre by most of my family and friends.

In another instance, I witnessed a more complex variation of sharing. One night as I was escorting some friends through the Haight-Ashbury district, I met a young Negro man whom I had previously met at the Black People's Free Store, which was in part an outgrowth of the Digger movement. I introduced Willard to my friends, all of us using first names, as was customary. We stood talking for a few minutes and then walked on. Later, that same evening, we met him again, and he asked me if I could spare a cigarette. None of us smoked, so we were unable to supply him. I opened my pocketbook, saying, "But I know where you can get some." Everybody in the group reached for some change and handed it to him while we all stood talking in a relaxed way. Our car was parked near where we stood, and as we turned to get in it, we heard the sound of change on the pavement. Willard was tossing the money to a group of hippies sitting in the entranceway to a darkened store, opposite our car. Everybody was gay, cheery, and laughing; most of the recipients, sitting back in the shadows where we had not noticed them before, seemed to be white. They all knew Willard, and his gift was greeted with a noisy affection. I sensed that Willard had arranged the incident so we could witness his gift. In essence, Willard, a black man, had gotten money from a group of white people to give to a group of white people. It seemed a joyous paradox in a "hung-up" world, and we departed feeling as delighted and merry with this encounter as the hippies had felt. The scene seemed again somehow reminiscent of the division of tsi by the Bushmen in Africa. And I understood that not all of the money given to Willard, or perhaps none of it, would be used for cigarettes—at least not the commercial variety.

CHAPTER 5

Instant Conversion

I read the news today oh boy
Four thousand holes in Blackburn,
Lancashire
And though the holes were rather small
They had to count them all
Now they know how many holes it takes
to fill the Albert Hall.
I'd love to turn you on.

—by John Lennon and Paul McCartney from "A Day in the Life" (*Italics mine*)

The desire to convert everybody to a harmless way of life as soon as possible became a consuming preoccupation of the young people in the Haight-Ashbury during the period of my observation. Many of them voiced to me their wish to turn everybody on, including the President of the United States. Although most of them felt that there were a variety of ways to be converted to a harmless way of life, they saw the psychedelic drugs as a form of instant conversion. Once a person was converted, he would only need occasional reinforcement of this process in order to remain harmless. Because the wish to convert was conceived of as a celebration of life, the psychedelic drugs were often presented as gifts and used, like food, as a form of propitiation.

The joy of the whole process of turning other people on is reflected in the Beatles' song, "A Day in the Life," with the final plea to the listener, couched in much the same words as those of the old-time gospel minister (and not even too different from Billy Graham today): "I'd love to turn you on." There is the joy of helping another to find the light, to escape from the aimless kill and overkill ("I read the news today oh boy") and the computer Alice-in-Wonderland depersonalization of our society (the number of "holes it takes to fill the Albert Hall").

If I seem to present the idea of the psychedelic drugs in a casual fashion, it is not because I feel casual about their use. There are, of course, inherent dangers in the use of *any* drugs that act upon the central nervous system—including perhaps the most dangerous one of all, alcohol.[1] Yet I think that the most dangerous part of psychedelic drugs is the fact that the core society continues to define all of them as being more dangerous than they are, in a kind of scare technique. In the beginning, the young people never defined them as an escape or as a path to destructive oblivion; and social definition is an important part of the effect of any drug. Very few Jews, for instance, become alcoholic, mainly because the Jewish child is introduced to small quantities of alcohol at an early age, in a family setting, usually in connection with a holiday, so that alcohol is not defined as a vehicle for escape and the release of unacceptable antisocial behavior, as it is in much of middle- and upper middle-class America. So long as the young people saw the use of psychedelic drugs as an act of conversion to a new set of ethical values, the drugs could be controlled by their own social definitions. Once the core society had managed to define them as dangerous, the use of drugs did indeed become more dangerous, in a kind of self-fulfilling prophecy. If adults are to retain any control at all over the use of the psychedelic drugs, they must begin to understand and accept a different basic meaning of their use—for conversion to new ethical standards.

I use the word *conversion* here in a religious and an American sense, thinking of the Chautauqua meetings that I attended as a child vacationing at my uncles' farms on the edge of Lake Ontario in western New York, watching the staid New

[1] I am defining drug here as any chemical that significantly affects the body and is not taken into the body primarily for food value.

England-like adults in that area respond with an unfamiliar enthusiasm and even joy to the stimulation of culture and religion brought together under the Chautauqua tents. Or again, I remember the gospel meetings held in a tent once a year in the small Maryland town in which I grew up; this town, on the edge of the nation's capital, had a large component of people who had come to work for the government from the impoverished farms of the Eastern Shore of Maryland and Tidewater Virginia, and the hill towns of West Virginia and Virginia—kindly people homesick for the bustle and jollity of clan and church gatherings; my own family did not attend the gospel meetings but I as a teen-ager went for the excitement of seeing neighbor women who were my friends caught up in the circus-like fervor of the preacher imported for the meetings, although sometimes I felt ill at ease with the display from some usually quiet, gentle person. Or still again, I recall the strange feeling of being an outsider to a meaningful and spiritual experience, when as a young woman I lived for a year on the Gulf Coast of Mississippi and occasionally went to hear the singing in a Negro church on the other side of the tracks; as was the custom there, I sat with the white townspeople on a grassy bank opposite the open church door and heard the beautiful voices winging through the damp night air and watched the graceful tired bodies transfixed for an instant as they moved up before the light on the altar to express their passion and their hope for some change in the nature of living.

This kind of need for conversion, for meaningful change in the pattern of living, was very much the concern of the harmless people in the Haight-Ashbury. For the most part, they avoided the formal religious techniques of rural America, but its values were often in evidence; like the American Negro, they often spoke of what they were seeking as "soul," and of being "beautiful." Because the young people in the Haight-Ashbury experimented with the idea of inducing soul in everybody by chemicals—by the psychedelic drugs—does not in any way lessen the nature or the seriousness of the actual goal of conversion of themselves and others to a new set of spiritual values.

My first awareness of the true meaning of the phrase "turn

on" came to me in a chance conversation after a meeting in the Haight-Ashbury community. The Diggers had met that evening at the parish hall of All Saints' Episcopal Church to discuss the influx of young people expected in the summer of 1967. Various interested social workers and social scientists from surrounding institutions had been invited, and some members of the San Francisco police force were in attendance. The city had refused to make any meaningful preparation for the influx of summer visitors, and the young leaders in the community, most of whom called themselves Diggers, presented the problem in a sober fashion. One of the most influential Diggers spoke of the whole tradition of the camp meeting in America in the summer, and several other Diggers wondered why the city fathers could not sanction the pitching of tents in Golden Gate Park. The police representatives reiterated the necessity for arresting "runaway" kids under eighteen years of age and of notifying their parents of their whereabouts; in the meantime, they stated, these youngsters would have to be housed in the Youth Guidance Center in San Francisco, an already overcrowded and scandalously administered facility.

One of the Diggers noted that some of the young boys, not yet eighteen, who would be coming to the Haight-Ashbury in the summer of 1967 might well be celebrating their last summer; in another year they would be old enough to die for their country in Vietnam. The Diggers thought that the younger kids should be encouraged to go back home, but that they should have a moratorium of a few days in the Haight-Ashbury so that they could discuss with sympathetic and more established members of the young community their problems with the adults at home. My notes for that date read in part:

> [The Diggers] wondered why they couldn't pitch some large tents in the Park for sleeping and set up some kind of eating place, perhaps in the Armenian Hall, which they said they could get for free. Someone said that there was an enormous circus tent in one of the city's warehouses and that would sleep a lot of kids. Someone else mentioned the fact that the National Guard had used Kezar Stadium in the fall of 1966, at the time of the so-called race riots, and why couldn't private citizens use the Stadium, too, that there were proper bath and toilet facilities there and that the center field

would be an ideal place for sleeping any number of kids with sleeping bags. There was no answer from the police representatives to this proposal.

Four of us (a well-known Digger and his wife, a reporter from the British Broadcasting Company, and myself) left the meeting before it was over to attend the first program of Happening House held that same evening in the Print Mint, a short walk away, and we all expressed disappointment at the rigidity of the city officials as we walked along. The BBC reporter noted that he was confused about the police policy of arresting kids under eighteen years of age, if they could not establish that they were living with their parents or appropriate adults. "Why, they're all over Europe on bicycles in the summer," he said, referring to kids under eighteen, "trying to find a free place to sleep. Nobody pays any attention to them."

The two men moved ahead as we walked along the rather crowded street, and the other woman and I walked alongside each other. I asked her how she and her husband had happened to get involved in the Haight-Ashbury scene, and later that evening I recorded what I could remember of her answer: "She spoke of the fact that she herself had 'turned on' in the second year of college, that she was from the East, that her own family were upper middle class, but that her husband came from a 'proletariat' family, implying that he therefore had been 'turned on' for a much longer time." Our walk to the Print Mint was sober and sad, and I was struck forcibly with the tone of the young woman's voice as she spoke of being "turned on." The words had a Biblical solemnity to them as if she were reporting on Paul's conversion on the road to Damascus. She did not reveal whether or not her turn-on had been aided or abetted by drugs, but she certainly implied that her husband had been turned on as a child because of a class factor. I suddenly realized that it was completely unimportant as to *how* a person turned on: What was important was the conversion to being harmless people, the turning aside from evil—"the unwarranted interference with life," as Sullivan had defined it. Within that definition, the attitude of the city fathers was evil, and it was this that created the barrier and the challenge: I, too, found myself beginning to wonder, How could one turn on the establishment efficiently and quickly?

That this experimental community with the missionary need to convert a whole society to a new set of values should have sought a chemical solution seems entirely natural and understandable, whatever the weakness of that effort turned out to be. Bronson Alcott had peddled many of the same ideas by foot and on horseback through the Atlantic seaboard, converting his listeners exclusively by his own wit and the magic of his voice and bearing, without benefit of chemicals; and the ideas had blossomed and borne fruit in schoolrooms throughout nineteenth-century America. But the Republic was small then, and the survival of mankind was not in question. In the spring of 1967, the stakes were high in a life-and-death game, centered some 10,000 miles westward in a small country inhabited by people of color; some efficient method for turning on the American society to a new set of moral values must be found, else all of mankind would disappear in a massive immorality emergent from the Republic itself.

In opting for a chemical solution, the young people had the strongest of continuities, of course, with the central society, which for some time had depended on the intake of all kinds of non-food products for escape from dissatisfaction, boredom, tension, and so on. But in another particular, the young people had clearly broken with their parents' values: They did not want to *escape;* they wanted to be turned on to life, to the excitement of living. Many of the non-food products used by their parents had been declared exceedingly dangerous by qualified researchers, particularly those researchers who had somehow managed to remain independent of the increasing power of the great industries involved—the cigarette, liquor, and pharmaceutical interests. One of the most bitter complaints of the young against their parents was the continued and, as they saw it, cynical use of cigarettes after it had been established that cigarettes were dangerous to survival. To the young, the adults seemed to be saying: *Life is such a mess that we really do not want to live out our lives. What does it matter?* The most frequent specific criticism by the young of their elders that I heard in the Haight-Ashbury was the dependence of the adult on cigarettes and alcohol. Some of the young people with whom I spoke felt that the adults could give up cigarettes and alcohol, if they only experienced just once the turn-on of the psychedelic drugs. It was useless to point out that marijuana was usually smoked, too, and that that kind of smoking might also affect the lungs; that would be a major task of researchers, they thought, and besides hadn't Alice B. Toklas reported efficient use of hashish in fudge?

The original shift from the use of pot to LSD took place among the young in the Bay area probably early in 1966, when the Psychedelic Shop opened its store on Haight Street and began to sell LSD legally. The possession of marijuana was a felony, so that its legal dangers were clear; in addition, there was a general feeling against smoking cigarettes of any kind; thus LSD became popular for a while. Over the period of my study, many recipes for the use of marijuana in cookies evolved; but the general consensus was that the kinds of marijuana available generally in the neighborhood did not particularly lend themselves to oral ingestion; it took a tremendous number of brownies, for instance, to produce a turn-on, and there was a time lag of several hours before the effect of eating them was felt. Sometime in the last part of 1966, LSD was also made illegal, but its possession never became a felony. Thus there was a clear shift to the greater use of pills that emerged from the legal definitions of the society. Marijuana continued to be the drug of choice for many reasons; but it was difficult to dispose of in case of a raid, and the penalties for possession were much greater.

This movement from pot to LSD and the amphetamines was, in my estimation, a fateful one, in that pot was so cheap and so accessible that it did not attract the criminal syndicates. Once the psychedelic drugs were available in pills, the opportunity for dangerous innovation in chemical content and the involvement of big money was much greater. In addition, pot continues to be, on the best authority we have, one of the least dangerous agents on the central nervous system of any of the armamentarium of such agents. Yet the central society must take the responsibility for pushing the young toward more dangerous avenues for turning on.

Incidentally, the establishment argument that pot is the first step toward the hard drugs is one that the adult population should abandon, if they wish to have any communication at all with their children. Most heroin addicts in this country have used cigarettes, alcohol, and, earlier, mother's milk or some substitute; but no one has seriously suggested these as determining causes for addiction. The young are much too smart to accept this simple kind of cause-and-effect reasoning about pot or the psychedelic drugs; in this particular as in others, the young have lost faith in the warnings of their parents and the establishment, and there is a dangerous credibility gap.

In the beginning of my observation, I assumed that the use of drugs was mainly an adolescent rebellion, but the more I became acquainted with the young society the more convinced I was that no such simplistic explanation was possible. Certainly some of the young runaways or new residents in the area tried the drugs in a spirit mainly of rebellion. But the core carriers of the culture were more concerned with a crusade than with rebellion: *There was a continued and valiant effort on the part of the young people to find a legal way to turn on,* in contrast with previous generations who have considered some kind of illegality as the preferred way of growing up. I think of the bright spring days in 1967, when the young people sat against the buildings on the sunny north side of Haight Street, busily scraping the inside of banana peels in the hope of finding a legal way to turn on; the young man behind the counter in the Print Mint smiled when I asked him about it and told me that someone had discovered a recipe for this in a book on American Indians and their lore. At the very time when the young people were frantically experimenting with some kind of legal method for turning on, pot and LSD were readily available, often free, on Haight Street, and the police busts were usually advertised in advance. Indeed the young of the Haight-Ashbury generation seemed considerably *more motivated to be law-abiding and less in need of rebellion than my own generation.* They were clearly on a crusade to save the world; but they were, perhaps under the mediate influence of Dr. Spock's book, in much less need to rebel than earlier generations in America. They had a sense of power and strength, and their sense of destiny was clear and impressive for those who stopped to look and consider. I believe that the establishment will understand the young better if they hold their minds open to the dichotomy of *rebellion* vs. *crusade* in examining the behavior of the young.

In particular, the older and more established leaders of the community continued to recommend that other avenues for turning on must be explored, so as to overcome the legal dangers of marijuana and the physical dangers of LSD and speed. The Beatles, who often reflect accurately the moral dilemmas of the young, suggested by example that meditation as practiced in India and sitar music were other alternatives. At the same time, most of the young people clearly recognized that the drugs might in themselves offer a new hope to mankind; they had grown up in the midst of the twentieth century, and they knew that good could come from scientific discovery based on chemical research. In brief, the most responsible attitude of the young might be summarized like this: *The psychedelic drugs should be explored and studied, should be distributed legally, and should be a resource for anyone who needs them; at the same time there must be a state of awareness and fulfillment beyond drugs.*

Throughout my stay in the Haight-Ashbury I saw all kinds of attempts to turn on—with drugs, without drugs, with food, without food (that is, by fasting), by contemplation, by acts of good will—and usually in conjunction with music or light shows. The goal was the same: to be harmless and to render all other people harmless—to struggle for the survival of mankind.

Over time, I recognized that I myself was learning to turn on without benefit of drugs, that I had begun to experience some emotional vitality that I could only describe as an experience I had known at eighteen, of feeling the beauty and brevity of life and of yearning to make it meaningful for all the people that I touched in any way. My middle-aged cynicism was vanishing—a frightening event for the middle-aged. For most of the adults in the society, cynicism is the chief defense against annihilation; and one is scared and lonely when the cynicism is gone—hope is bared to the quick, and life becomes almost intolerable as a record of lost opportunities and lost dreams.

After my first visit to the Fillmore Auditorium,[2] I had a strange physical reaction unrelated to any intake of drugs. The light show at the Fillmore and the beat of the music, the young lovely bodies dancing in fluid hope and caught in quick flashes of light as in the jerk of an old movie produced something in me akin to a conversion phenomenon; actually it seemed related to the conversion movements in the Mississippi Negro church. One could not systematically take in what was happening at the Fillmore; it invaded all the senses. I remember keenly a few sensations, the most poignant of which was the picture of a young boy flashed on the corner wall of the huge room; his face and air were of "the rose in the deeps of my heart," as William Butler Yeats has so aptly described hope; superimposed over the young man's body, the full length of it, was a large test tube. The strobe lights flashed on the young dancing below the picture, the music beat along with its hint of the great words, unheard in the swirl of sound and color, but known past knowing—the celebration of life, the turning aside from the very concept of killing. I stood on the dance floor, overcome with the movement of thought, the collapse of old standards of morality, the impulse of life, the movement of bodies and feet caught in the dance of life. When I left, I literally stumbled along the pavement outside, and my companion had to help me to stand. He reported the same kind of reeling of senses. We had had no semblance of chemical stimulation. I went home to sleep in the soundest and most restful way that I had known for months. I had been turned on to the hope still left in me for a better world than any I had ever known.

I am talking of turning on here as if it were completely unrelated to the use of psychedelic drugs, and I think that this is indeed true; at the same time, I think that the drugs are a very important part of the great revolution of values that has

[2] The Fillmore Auditorium, near the Haight-Ashbury, was a favorite place for light shows and psychedelic bands. It was run by Bill Graham, who was in tune with the young and was at the time of which I write the manager for the San Francisco Mime Troupe.

in part already taken place in this country, that without the psychedelic drugs it seems unlikely to me that the idealistic young could have withstood the genuine hostility of their surrounding environment in the last few years. I see the widespread use of drugs as declining over the next five years, if the society is able to pull itself out of the immoral morass in Asia and can begin to treat with respect and dignity all of its citizens. Whatever the chemical effects of the psychedelic drugs, they have had a social definition for the young—of making all people harmless, of survival. To the extent that the young can maintain that definition, they will be able to ride through the drug crisis. But the establishment has bent every effort to make the hippie movement in general, the Haight-Ashbury phenomenon in particular, into something reprehensible and ugly, focusing their attention on the horror of the drugs; and to some extent, they have made the whole issue into something potentially dangerous beyond the original situation.

There is no doubt that the young go through a tremendous crisis in Western society. Harry Stack Sullivan once made the statement that the danger of mental illness in the teen-agers in our society is practically ubiquitous and that most of us ride through it by a fortunate set of circumstances, often fortified at critical moments by alcohol; he was, of course, writing of an earlier period in this century, since as of now psychedelic drugs are preferred to alcohol. We have a tremendous number of troubled young in our midst; if they were not deeply troubled, they would be less than human. They see clearly the decay of values in the adults, and they yearn to build a new social order that is meaningful. In order to begin to build anew, they must make a break with the values of my generation of a magnitude completely different from the break that I had to make with the generation before me. Again, in order to encompass this kind of break with the mores and customs of the previous generation, and survive psychologically, it was natural and inevitable that they would need some chemical crutch. But they could not accept the chemical crutches of their parents for the very reasons I have given, reinforced by the obvious corruption in the whole drug industry in this country, by the fact, for instance, that only one person in the U.S. Food and

Drug Administration saved this nation from the production of an unprecedented crop of ill-formed children.

It is no coincidence that the young found the pattern for their drug use emerging from two groups of oppressed peoples in this country, and that in both instances the drug was derived from plants. I speak of the use of peyote by the American Indians; and the use of marijuana by jazz musicians, jazz having emerged primarily from the American Negro, of course. In both instances, these psychedelic plants were used by these oppressed peoples to achieve joy and peace in the midst of great travail and suffering, as a way of releasing the soul from its sorrow. If the young of this generation wanted to find their own chemical, their own path toward acquiring soul in the materialistic, immoral America of the 1960's, then it seems inevitable and natural that they should have found their models in the American Indians and the American Negroes.

The influence of the black man on the young white people in America and beyond came from a variety of experiences. Certainly the stories that were told and retold on American college campuses about the visits of students engaged in the civil rights movement to Alabama and Mississippi were crucial in uncovering the tremendous vitality of the rural Negro who had managed to maintain his human dignity and kindliness in the midst of an oppressive system of local government. But long before these young people knew anything about the oppression of the Negro in the city slums or in the rural South, they had known the soul of the black man by way of the hi-fi sets and transistor radios that gave out night and day the Negro jazz and spirituals that had sustained the spirit of an oppressed but not broken people. In many ways, this music became for the young after Hiroshima the illuminated manuscripts that preserved the soul of America through the Dark Ages of the mid-twentieth century. They listened to it, they revered it, the words spoke to them. When in the early sixties, the words "We Shall Overcome" burst upon their ears, they took it as their own. We shall overcome the apathy, the materialism of the middle-class world, they reasoned. If war had been going on "for ten thousand years," as Peter, Paul, and Mary sang, that is no reason to give up on changing that and changing it now; we shall overcome that, too, and within our own lifetime.

The best of Western society had been revived and kept alive in Negro music; even the young working-class boys across the sea in Liverpool had responded to that beat, to that demand for joy and justice—values that the older White Anglo-Saxon Protestant society had often forgotten or overlooked along the way. The Beatles had begun their own spiritual revival on the strength of the same illuminated manuscripts—the music of the American Negro—and they were clear about their dependence on that beat and that soul. The young knew that the Negro jazz musicians—or other jazz musicians—turned on with marijuana: That was a general consensus. And the young decided at some level that they would rather have their awareness expanded by the chemical of the Negro jazz musicians than to depend on the cynicism of alcohol so well exemplified in what they considered the real-life horror movie of the century: *Who's Afraid of Virginia Woolf?* In time, the conversation on drugs in the Haight-Ashbury focused on new varieties of amphetamines, but this kind of lore never achieved the romance of the feeling about pot. Pot and jazz and rock-and-roll and the Beatles were all rolled up in one package in the romantic legend of the particular generation in the Haight-Ashbury that I speak of here.

Although peyote and its derivatives were never used widely by the young people in the Haight-Ashbury, as far as I know, peyote had its own lore within their society. Its use by the American Indian, mainly in the western tribes, as part of their religious ritual in the Native American Church of North America, has been approved by the federal government, and in this respect it is unique among the mind-expanding drugs. All other such substances, natural and chemical, can only be used legally for research purposes and all distribution is presently controlled by the National Institute of Mental Health and the U.S. Bureau of Narcotics. The fact that peyote has been legalized for use in a religious rite was often commented on by the young people in the Haight-Ashbury. Since they felt that they used psychedelic substances in the same way and would like to develop spiritual rituals for their use, they felt a strong kinship with the American Indian.

Part of this kinship was of course related to the role of the oppressed, again. The American Indian, like the American Negro, had been treated brutally by the white power structure, although the young in growing up had been told otherwise, and this was one of their early disenchantments with the legends of the culture. These young people, growing up with television, were thoroughly indoctrinated in the role of the bad Indian through the Wild West stories. But as they grew up, they had come to understand, probably from the same television medium tuned in as they grew older to news stories, more serious drama, and particularly to educational channels, that the American Indians had in fact been the good guys and that the French, and particularly the English, had been the bad guys in the settlement of America and the gradual destruction of the dignity and beauty of the American Indian. I always felt that the strong influence of the American Indian on the dress and the thinking of the hippies was related to their first contact with the credibility gap in the values of the American society as dished out to them in the legends about the "bad" American Indians, and I found support for this in *The Oracle*, for instance.

Again the music and the dancing of the Indians—the vibrations of the spirit—had a kinship with the beat and the beauty of jazz music and the history of the American Negro. The hippie music was obviously more directly related to the Negro culture. But the hippies' clothing and their sense of dress and color showed the influence of the American Indian—the soft doeskin boots that were popular with the girls on Haight-Ashbury and the headbands and feathers that the men wore, for example. On almost any day on Haight Street one could find the beautiful and colorful trappings of an Indian girl or brave; the other costumes in the ever-changing live TV drama on the Street were much more difficult to identify and were often synthesized from several historical periods and ethnic groups.

The American Indian also had another hold on the young people—he was the only *native* American; in the Haight-Ashbury, this was said over and over again. So his drug, peyote, had the additional power of his own natural sacrament, given to him by the Great Spirit himself. The hippies' perception of the meaning of peyote and its *power* was similar to what is reported by the University of Chicago anthropologist J. S. Slotkin in his field notes. One of Slotkin's informants, Dewey Neconish, reports as follows:

This is how we were first shown pity by means of this medicine: That was when they killed each other, when our elders were doing away with each other. All the different kinds of tribes were killing. Some of our elders, among us Menomini, also killed those of different tribes. That was the way our elders used to be, long ago. When they found this medicine, they learned from it that all of us, from all the different tribes, should be like brothers and sisters. . . . Well then, all of us are now brothers and sisters; we think well of each other; we cooperate with each other; we have pity on each other. That is the way we have found out through it; the way He has taught us, our all-in-all father, Great Spirit. That, then, is the way everyone has learned, even until today.

. . . ["out west"] they have used it so long that they have grown old using it; therefore, they have discovered all about it. They know that they are all one; no one is different from another; they are all brothers and sisters; that alone is what they now know. Great Spirit placed them on this earth which he made, that alone is what they now know. Give thanks to the Great Spirit. . . .[3]

Slotkin himself was accepted as a member of the Church—an unusual honor; and he partook of peyote with the Indians in their religious rites. "While under its influence I felt neither tired, hungry, nor thirsty," Slotkin writes. During his second observation of the rites, Slotkin did not use peyote, and he notes that the participants "are certainly neither stupefied nor drunk. . . . No one has acted in an unseemly manner; in fact, they are all quiet, courteous, and considerate of one another. I

[3] J. S. Slotkin, *Menomini Peyotism: A Study of Individual Variation in a Primary Group with a Homogeneous Culture*, Transactions of the American Philosophical Society, 42, Part 4 (1952): 572–573.

have never been in any white man's house of worship where there is either as much religious feeling or decorum." Slotkin felt very strongly that

> the doctrines and rites of Peyotism can be learned only through taking Peyote oneself. Much emphasis is placed upon the necessity of direct revelation. What one learns from others is but second hand knowledge about the subject, rather than actual acquaintance with it; a matter of great importance because it is one's inner experiences which are believed to be fundamental. This is borne out by my own experience. Among the notes I wrote at the meeting at which I took no Peyote is the following: "I've never had such a sense of superficiality, if not futility, of the usual ethnographic accounts of the externals of a rite."

The young people in the Haight-Ashbury who had used psychedelic drugs for an actual expansion of their spiritual awareness expressed the same feeling, of their inadequacy of communicating what they had felt. They, too, recommended that everyone should have at least one experience with this sense of oneness with the world, as they described it. And they felt that this way lay a potential for an end to killing, to the endless violence, and to the meaningless search for material possession.

The influence of Asian cultures and thinking on the young people in the Haight-Ashbury was also extensive. In general, the young people most interested in the meditative techniques saw meditation as a substitute for drugs. At the same time, some of the more advanced thinkers held in greatest respect by the young people felt that drugs might well be used in conjunction with meditation as a kind of sacrament. Gurus from Asia had had their own followers on the West Coast for a long time; and the synthesis offered by Aldous Huxley, for instance, between the chemicals of the West and the meditation of the East was often cited and discussed in the coffee houses.

Many of the young people had a knowledge of Asia and its cultures that left me feeling ignorant and provincial. Again I surmise that part of their focus emerged from the same powerful identification with oppressed peoples and from the horrendous calamity of Hiroshima. There was an important intellectual influence here also; the high caliber of Asian scholarship in the Bay area generally and the new collection of Asian art objects in the De Young Museum in Golden Gate Park were important sources for the young people. It was rather commonplace for the young people to make fun of their professors—particularly sociologists, psychologists, even philosophers focusing on Western society. But in general they revered the scholarship available to them on Asia and its culture, as they did any knowledge of the American Indian.

In general, I would surmise that the new generation—that is, those now approaching ten years of age—will synthesize many of these influences and evolve some gradual *rite de passage* into adulthood, and beyond, that will delineate stages of growth, of awareness, of adult responsibility, and that these will not exclude chemical agents to initiate the experience; that some chemical agents will be used intelligently at times of crisis and physical pain throughout life; and that the drugs will be used delicately and sensitively to make the awareness of approaching death a rewarding experience for those leaving and those staying behind. At the same time, I think that the dependence on psychedelic drugs will tend to decrease as the old values give way toward the values of truly harmless people, who gradually learn how to live wisely and without killing.

In many ways the hope of the harmless people was but an echo of the American Indian tribes who turned to the Ghost-Dance Religion in their despair over the violence of the white man, believing that there must be a time when "the whole Indian race, living and dead, will be reunited upon a regenerated earth, to live a life of aboriginal happiness, forever free from death, disease, and misery. . . . all believers were exhorted to make themselves worthy of the predicted happiness by discarding all things warlike and practicing honesty, peace, and good will. . . ."[4]

[4] James Mooney, *The Ghost-Dance Religion and the Sioux Outbreak of 1890*. Extract from the Fourteenth Annual Report of the Bureau of Ethnology (Washington: Government Printing Office, 1896), p. 777.

But the harmless people in the Haight-Ashbury had included all of mankind in their ghost-dance religion. A poem "Plea" by Bob Kaufman, which I first saw in *The Oracle*,[5] encapsulated for me the essence of this new religion that was developing day by day before my eyes:

Voyager, wanderer of the heart,
Off to
a million midnights, black, black
Voyager, wanderer of star worlds,
Off to
a million tomorrows, black, black,
Seek and find Hiroshima's children,
Send them back, send them back.

Tear open concrete sealed cathedrals, spiritually locked
Fill vacant theaters with their musty diversions,
Almost forgotten laughter.

Give us back the twisted sons
Poisoned by mildewed fathers.
Find again the used up whores,
Dying in some forgotten corner,
Find sunlight, and barking dogs,
For the lost, decayed in sorry jails.
Find pity, find Hell for wax bitches,
Hidden in the bowels of male Cadillacs.
Find tomorrow and next time for Negro millionaires
Hopelessly trapped in their luxurious complexions.
Find love, and an everlasting fix for hopeless junkies,
Stealing into lost nights, long time.

Voyager now,
Off to a million midnights, black, black
Seek and find Hiroshima's children,
Send them back, send them back.

[5] From *The Oracle*, 1, No. 8 (1967): 29. Published subsequently in Bob Kaufman, *Golden Sardine* (San Francisco: City Lights Books, 1967). Used here by permission of City Lights Books.

CHAPTER 6
"The Beginning Is the Human Be-In"[1]

Afterwards I knew that there was an actual day, January 14, 1967, on which I was initiated into this new society, this new religion, as surely as if I had been initiated into the Ghost-Dance Religion of the American Indians. For some days before January 14, notices of this new event—the gathering of all the tribes, political activist and hippie, young and old—appeared throughout the Bay area, in shop windows, on bulletin boards in the coffee houses, and in the various so-called underground newspapers; the *Berkeley Barb* carried the announcement on the front page with a banner headline. By this time, three months after I had begun to be acculturated into this new society, I knew that I could attend the Human Be-In only as a potential initiate. The request for participation was very simple: If you feel sympathy, wear a flower, bring a musical instrument, wear bells. Two days before the event, I went into a shop on Haight Street and purchased a silver chain with a bell at each end—from India, the young woman in the shop told me approvingly; and I had a sensation of having taken some monumental step, unknown in import to anyone but myself. When I got home and showed my husband the bells, he smiled and decided to go himself. I suggested that he wear a flower; and he found an old gray-green floppy Panama hat that made him look like a sheriff somehow and stuck a flower in it so that he

[1] The headline on page 1 of the *Berkeley Barb*, announcing the first Human Be-In in Golden Gate Park, January 14, 1967, Vol. 4, No. 1.

did not look like a sheriff. Thus garbed we drove into the neighborhood and parked.

The gathering was scheduled as an all-day affair, "come any time," so we began our trek at about noon from Stanyan Street on the edge of Golden Gate Park and walked into the Polo Field where the gathering was to take place—some thirty blocks from the center of the neighborhood. By that time, there was a steady stream of people walking in, winding over the hillocks and through the glades as far as the eye could see. And facing us as we moved along with this human stream of communicants was a stream of people who had been there and were winding their way home; they all seemed enchanted, happy, and smiled like a welcoming committee upon us, as they trundled along with baby carriages and picnic hampers. It would seem almost as if they had been to early morning mass, which had turned out to be a huge picnic. Their costumes were varied and imaginative, or again they wore ordinary street clothes; but each person had his sign of participation somewhere upon him—a young boy with a nasturium stuck behind his ear, a gray-haired woman with a flower tied on her cane with a ribbon.

But it was the Polo Field itself that presented a new world. It was a medieval scene, with banners flying, bright and uncommitted; the day was miraculous, as days can be in San Francisco at their best, and the world was new and clean and pastoral. Children wandered around in the nude. People sat on the grass with nothing to do, sometimes moving up near to the small platform where a poetry-reading might be going on, or where a band might be playing. There was no program; it was a happening. Sounds and sights turned me on, so that I had the sensation of dreaming. The air seemed heady and mystical. Dogs and children pranced around in blissful abandon, and I became aware of a phenomenon that still piques my curiosity: The dogs did not get into fights, and the children did not cry.

To my amazement, there was a good deal of picture-taking going on, some of it obviously being done by the mass media; nobody noticed or objected. A young medical student had told me a few days before of his intention of going to the Be-In and taking some pictures; and I had warned him that picture-taking would probably be unwise. At a recent meeting between hippies and old residents, some of the hippies had requested that all cameras, TV or otherwise, be removed before the meeting proceeded; and when this request had not been complied with, some of the young people had attacked the cameras. My firm opinion was that the seekers did not take kindly to cameras. But the vibrations were good at the Be-In, so the cameras were no problem. It was the flexibility of these young people that caught the establishment, including me at times, off guard. They evaluated a situation as it happened and they responded to it appropriately; without voting or speech-making, they seemed to have the ability for quick consensus on behavior.

We sat on the grass most of the afternoon without any knowledge of what particular band was playing, what poet was reading his poems. Clusters of people would move up toward the platform at the east end of the Polo Field to listen to some favorite performers and then drift back again. From time to time, the loud-speaker on the platform would be raised in volume and everyone would become quiet, while an important announcement was made. These announcements concerned lost children. "The Hell's Angels have a little girl here behind the platform and she has curly hair. She says her name is Mary. She wants to see her mother." For that particular tribe of young men on motorcycles had also appeared at the Be-In, replete with a station wagon, bearing apparently all kinds of refreshments, liquids and solids. They were well equipped for the task of serving as a clearing house for lost and strayed children, since they had walkie-talkies and were well organized. Whether their services had been sought in advance, or whether they were commandeered on the spot, no one seemed to know; in hippie language, it happened. When a call would go out for "Timmie's mother," we all smiled and watched until finally from the huge throng a young woman would be seen moving serenely toward the Hell's Angels caravan, whereupon we would all settle back to our task of being. Late in the afternoon, when we walked by the caravan, we felt as if we were looking at a heavenly nursery, that indeed the formidably dressed young men were angels; and the children looked so happy and admiring of their benefactors that it was difficult to imagine that any of the mothers were urgently needed that afternoon.

In the midst of the afternoon, out of a clear noiseless sky, a man attached to a billowy parachute that looked like a huge cloud drifted down from the sky above; no one announced it but the message seemed to go soundlessly throughout that huge crowd of tens of thousands of people; and we all looked up into the sky with a single ripple of turned heads and eyes. No airplane was heard, there was no sign of where he came from, and we all treated it as a latter-day miracle. Slowly people got to their feet in awe and wonder, mixed with absolute delight; and no one asked, "How did he do it?" or "Wasn't that a clever stunt?"—remarks that people who did not attend the Be-In asked later, for the event captivated the entire city. Those of us who were there when it happened were children again: We wanted to believe in magic that would match the day; and the man floating down on a white cloud was clearly a fairy-tale happening.

Beyond that, it was difficult to sort out what happened. It was a religious rite in which nothing particular happened. And yet it was a day that marked for me at least the end of something and the beginning of something else. There was clearly a renewal of the spirit of man, unplanned, non-political. But then what do we mean by political? For at the end of the day, as the sun was sinking into the ocean beyond the Park, someone from the loud-speaker suggested that it would be nice to leave the Park clean, to practice kitchen yoga, and that is what happened. The litter of so many people, all the sandwich wrappings, the wine bottles, and the endless paper products so characteristic of the rubbish of our decade, disappeared, so that the police reported afterwards, with a sense of wonderment, that no other group of people of such a size in the memory of any living person had ever left an area so clean before, whether stadium or park. It was another miracle—and in some ways this was more disturbing to the square community than a ton of refuse would have been.

Wine, incense, food, and pot clearly intertwined that day; but none of these was necessary, as I can testify. We had not planned to stay so long, so we were without food; and we had no drugs. But it was the people that turned me on—the spectacle of people from so many walks of life, some come in curiosity, some in search of something, some in worship of the idea, some to be initiated into a new rite: It was people being together, unprogrammed, uncommitted, except to life itself and its celebration.

Afterwards, walking slowly toward the car, we did not have much to say; we did not walk back through the Park, but along the street bordering it, hoping perhaps to board a bus for the long return trip to where the car was parked. Half of the city seemed to be waiting at the bus stops, so we abandoned that attempt. Most of the people looked tired and droopy, but our eyes met in a secret delight. We had in common the sound of a different drummer.

In a few days, an original poster appeared in the window of the Psychedelic Shop on Haight Street, celebrating the Be-In and signed by Sister Maria Pacifica. This was but an early signal of a genuine acceptance of the young in the community, for the Human Be-In had somehow appealed to everybody, square and hip, young and old, who had been in any proximity to it. In a divided sick world, this was a new and exciting idea—that all people should just *be*. The religious organizations throughout the neighborhood began to show a new understanding of what the harmless people were saying. It clearly marked a high point in the period of my observation and my own full acculturation into the society.

Retrospectively, I feel quite certain that the Be-In also marked the beginning of nation-wide attention. Many people ascribe the failure of the Haight-Ashbury to the mass media which promised something to the young, encouraged them to come to San Francisco wearing "some flowers in your hair." But the word-of-mouth excitement of the Be-In, its imaginative character, met a deep need in the Republic. It was life-giving and it was freeing—it was, in short, a creative process, and it moved people toward the hope of a better world. In a jet age, the young move swiftly and can spread a contagion of hope in a matter of a few days throughout much of the world. The jet age has a potential for spreading hope and joy, just as much as for spreading some dire disease around the world. In this rare instance, it spread hope.

Vast numbers of students and ex-students, graduate students and young faculty had come over the Bay Bridge from Berkeley for the Be-In. Many of them came to scoff, but most of them were positively affected by it. Yet their criticism of the seekers remained—they were non-political in a political world; and how could any reform be accomplished? So it was that the peace march scheduled for April 15, 1967—three months after the Human Be-In—became an opportunity to clarify where the seekers stood on the great cause of peace that both activist and hippie agreed on. By a coincidence, the San Francisco Spring Mobilization was to have as its destination Kezar Stadium, in the heart of the Haight-Ashbury neighborhood and adjacent to the Park; there the notables would speak. Such mobilizations were taking place in large cities throughout the country. Martin Luther King was speaking in New York City; and his wife was to be the last and most important speaker at Kezar Stadium.

For weeks before the Mobilization I heard a good deal of discussion, largely in the established community, as to whether the hippies would participate in this peace march; but the young leaders in the Haight-Ashbury community always stated quite flatly to me that of course they would be in the march. Still, as the day approached, I found myself puzzled about what might happen.

I joined the march on the northern rim of the Panhandle and walked along to Kezar Stadium. There were hundreds of people with flowers; the costumed people were there in abundance. Indeed, the parade was headed by a truckload of musicians from the Haight-Ashbury, the Jug Band.

The actual march to the Stadium was, I felt, a celebration for peace. But the program in the Stadium was, very simply, a disaster, so that when the star speaker, Mrs. Martin Luther King, arose to speak, hours after the program had begun, only a handful of survivors remained; I myself had long since expired, cold and despairing. A variety of dissident groups had collaborated for the Mobilization, and each facet claimed its right to present a dreary catalogue of particularized grievances. Even more disastrous was the handling of the audience by the dignitaries on the platform. In the beginning, the Jug Band on its gay truck had begun to drive around the Stadium track to a burst of enthusiasm from the young audience, but the officiating dignitaries on the platform had asked them to back up and leave. From then on, the event seemed to deflate like a tired balloon, and the spirit was gone. The loud-speaker warned people about intruding on the center grass in the Stadium, pointing out that the authorities would charge the arranging committee for any damage to the grass; and some rebellious youngsters *and* adults of course proceeded to do just what they were asked not to do. Otherwise, it was simply another rally in which the faithful heard what they already knew.

Some days later I saw a poem tacked up on the door of Wild Colors, a hippie store on Haight Street. It was written in script—an original copy. I asked the storekeeper who the author was (he did not know) and whether I could make a copy (sure, he told me, go ahead). I include it here, since I think it is an excellent statement of how I, too, perceived the Spring Mobilization and represents an astute formulation of its shortcomings in the eyes of the harmless people:

Spring was not mobilized
at the spring mobilization
in spite of Comrade Beardshout,
who welcomed the New Youth
to their old home. I know, for
I was there; I, the son of old
Fyodor Freakpoet, who sniffs vodka
(do you not think I am laughable?
I am indeed laughable, as
my father was laughable before me).
But Spring was not mobilized she stood
in the park as they went rightfully by
until young Ernest Callow (a dedicated

student) handed her a pamphlet as
his roommate, Gristle (somewhat less
dedicated) sold red, white, & blue
hot dogs to the infinitely children
who are somehow able to consume
such things without being consumed
(in spite of which none of them
were asked to speak at the Rally).
Spring strolled naked through the
park caressing her friends & squirrels
while inside the stadium the forces of
Good Man Handled the Evil & I
wept & left early to walk through the
park & give Spring a loving pat on
her infinitely mobile & unmobilized ass.

The criticism here is precise and philosophically meaningful for the harmless people: Good Men can become ineffective by trying to Handle Evil, can in fact destroy the Good. We must celebrate the Good, and turn men toward it. It exists in children, in squirrels, in the park, and *it is Spring that must be mobilized.*

The Human Be-In and the Spring Mobilization encapsulated the drama that was taking place among the young in the Bay area. In a sense, it seemed clear that a more basic change was necessary in the society than the one advocated in the reform movement that had begun so long ago in Berkeley, that indeed the spirit of man must be revived and changed.

The Spring Mobilization had turned away the Jug Band, had warned the audience about walking on the center grass in the middle of Kezar Stadium, had evoked the specter of unless-we-can-all-respect-the-rules, it-will-cost-us-money. In the end the marchers, as they appeared in the Stadium, were unruly and dissident, although the planning of many well-intentioned people had gone into the event. The unplanned happening of the Be-In had achieved, without rules, much more hope for peace than could be found in Kezar Stadium.

Indeed as it turned out, the peace marches in the spring of 1967 seemed to have accomplished very little. President Johnson went on in his accustomed way, and the Pentagon stood strong and dominant in the world of power and destruction that lay heavy over all of us.

Nor did Spring put in an appearance at the March on the Pentagon in October of that year. I was near the steps that day, though I lacked Norman Mailer's conviction and temerity and I was not arrested; yet for the first time I had the impulse to storm the citadel. Afterwards I walked back to the city, spent with my own anger and feeling by then only a tired compassion for all the weary people, whether fighting in faraway lands, or being fought over, or hiding nervously behind the façade of the White House, or armed with bayonets and tear gas still waiting for some imagined violence from the bewildered harmless people in the huge parking lot at the Pentagon. Ah, yes, I agree: There were the potentially violent ones there, on both sides of the wall. But the tragedy was that the children were missing, so that no one had to take care of them or keep them happy. If the harmless people could have given a lesson to the Pentagon, the March would have been a Human Be-In; and we would have planned wisely to take care of the children of the world. But the military police, who were also potentially angels, were not socialized at the Pentagon, and the children remained lost.

CHAPTER 7

The Haight-Fillmore and the Haight-Ashbury

My dog love-a-your dog
Your dog love-a-my dog
I'm talkin' 'bout a black dog
I'm talkin' 'bout a white dog. . . .
My little doggie was playing one day . . .
Down in the meadow by a bundle of hay . . .
Another little doggie came along . . .
Said let's get together and eat this bone . . .
Why can't we
Sit under the apple tree?

—from "I Love Your Dog, I Love My Dog" sung by the Freedom Singers (from Albany, Georgia) at the Newport Folk Festival, 1963

By the time of the Human Be-In, I was already involved with an initiation of another ilk. This initiation was more gradual, and I could scarcely understand how it was happening, but I felt as if I were being freed from the curious concern with color of skin that haunts most of us who are raised in this country.

To my surprise—and I realize that this is at variance with what most observers have reported—there was a meaningful interchange going on between the white flower children in the Haight-Ashbury and the poor and largely uneducated black people living in the adjacent area of the Haight-Fillmore. There were tensions, of course, for when have people brought up in separate but related subcultures ever eased from mutual isolation into intimacy without some friction? But more and more, these two groups of people were in sharp and clarifying dialogue. Under the influence of the flower children, I, too, was engaged in a meaningful dialogue with the Negro in the slum, and he was teaching me more about my values and his than I had ever learned before, although I had grown up on the edge of what is basically a Southern city (Washington, D.C.) and had subsequently lived, as a young woman, for a year in a small town in Mississippi.

As I have gone over my own observation and that of others of the so-called disaffection between the seekers and the black people, I have finally reached the conclusion that the main friction was between the flower children and the middle-class adult, whether white or black. Thus Negro parents who were struggling to give their children a good education have told me how much they resent the example of the white middle-class kids abandoning the philosophy of "strive and succeed" as it has been revered in white middle-class America. By contrast, the poor Negro of whatever age was apt to understand the young flower children, often better than their own parents or teachers.

The growing relationship between the black people in the slum and the flower children took place, again, by using the techniques of the Diggers—the continuing and unrehearsed morality play. In this drama, the black people were changing before the white man's eyes from stereotypes to living people. The black man had always suffered from these stereotypes, which emerged in part from the white man's actual lack of information on black people's way of life. The white middle-class civil rights workers who had gone into Mississippi and Alabama in the first half of the decade had begun to glimpse for the first time the values of the poor black man in his own abode; some of these young people spoke to me of the humility and awe with which they watched poor people sacrifice in order to express their appreciation to the white civil rights workers, sharing what they had with grace. This legend lived on in the Haight-Ashbury, and the flower children in part adopted a voluntary poverty and even some physical privation in order to gain soul as they had seen it in black people in the rural South. Thus for the first time, the people furthest down on the American scene were suddenly and legitimately elevated into a source of wisdom. Like oppressed peoples of all times and lands, the black man had had ample time to study his oppressor, and his awareness of where the trouble lay was acute.

In general, the young Negroes who frequented the Haight-Ashbury and became interested in the philosophy of the Diggers, for instance, came from the Haight-Fillmore area and were uneducated and poor. The white flower children were in general trying to escape from the racist values of the white core society, and the young Negroes who came into the Haight-Ashbury recognized this extraordinary state of affairs at a glance. Since the young white people admired many of the values of the poor Negro and wanted to emulate them, the Negro Digger often found himself a genuine mentor of human conduct: "Do your thing," "Tell it like it is," and "Don't put me down" were new commandments evolved out of the history of oppressed people and used by the young black people to jack up me and the flower children, often and tellingly. Thus it was the black man who taught the white flower children how to gain soul, and in the process gained a new valuation of himself. In this manner, there was a new beginning in the often ruthless and dehumanizing process by which the dispossessed person in this country moves into the middle-class core society, forgetting the people still on the lower rung of the ladder. One well-known Negro leader in San Francisco—who, although he was a member of the educated upper middle class, had maintained his identification with the poor—expressed his hope that as poor black people began to move into the core society they would maintain the human values developed in the slums; he noted that the young white people in the Haight-Ashbury and earlier in the civil rights movement had been of considerable importance in giving the poor black man a new view of himself. For this reason he had hope that the poor Negro could avoid the conformity and the dog-eat-dog philosophy of middle-class white suburbia that had so obviously failed the young seekers as a meaningful way of life.[1] In order to find soul, the young white people were coming back into the city and trying to live like the dispossessed in the slums. In this way the hippie and poor black people were gaining a human consensus.

While there was a growing knowledge on the part of the seekers of the poor black people's way of life, and an increasing number of communes in which young people of whatever skin color lived together, other inroads on the stereotypes about the black man in the core society were being made, mainly without words. In general, they might be summarized as follows: The eccentricity in dress and behavior of the young white people in the Haight-Ashbury became a more dramatic reality than the color of skin and perceptually drew attention away from the major apple-sorting criterion of skin color in the Republic.

Moreover, both the white hippies and the white political activists, who looked more and more like what we have come to call hippies, were fast becoming the negative counterpoint for the paranoia of the society. Thus the black man was suddenly competing *for the first time* with the hippie for the lowest place in the rank ordering of human beings that had always been the sickest part of the Republic; in this way, black people were unfrozen from their traditional and absolute position and began to be looked upon as human beings, since they were, perhaps, *better than* hippies.

And finally, the Diggers in particular challenged without words, but with a knowledge of the intellectual underpinnings for their actions, the whole Protestant ethic of the Republic which had gradually won out over the equally important strand of pioneer neighborliness that had flourished in the early history of the country; thus the necessity for establishing *eligibility* in

[1] As E. Franklin Frazier wrote in *Black Bourgeoisie* (New York: Free Press, 1957), the Negro middle-class group has made the same mistakes, at least up until recently, as the white middle class had made earlier; that is, the black bourgeoisie had developed its own considerable rigidities, conformities, and eventual disappointments in the meaning of middle-class achievement, just as the white middle class had done.

order for human beings of whatever age to eat had become a religion in the Republic by the 1960's, while the TV ads, in prime time, discussed at length the proper diet for various categories of pets, dogs, cats, and even goldfish, none of whom was eligible for food stamps in terms of welfare requirements and the Protestant ethic. The black people had known for a long time the injustice of having to meet eligibility requirements in order to survive; but it was now taken up at another level by young white people who had full knowledge of the fact that socialism was as much a part of nineteenth-century America as it was of the Communist Manifesto. They were not afraid of words or labels; but they changed the stereotyped meaning of those words by action.

My indoctrination into what was happening between the Haight-Fillmore and the Haight-Ashbury came about not as an intellectual conviction but out of experience that I could not explain or that shook me out of accustomed ways of observing and required some re-examination of what was happening to me. Thus, early in my study, I became aware of a strange new perceptual phenomenon in myself that I can only describe as *color blindness.* As a good observer, I prided myself on being able to reconstruct after an interview careful detail and whole passages of conversation that could be verified by other persons who were present. But in the Haight-Ashbury, I experienced a blurring of certain relevant information that was different; and for a while, I felt that I had lost my ability to observe. For instance, one day someone asked me whether there were more girls or boys among the flower children, and I had not the vaguest notion. Afterwards, I was able to focus more sharply on this aspect and decided that there were clearly many more boys than girls in the neighborhood. Or, again, I found my ability to focus on physical handicap sharply diminished, although I was ordinarily sensitive to any kind of physical affliction because of my own family history—a younger sister had been crippled in an accident as a child. I would sometimes be abruptly startled to find that a person whom I was keenly aware of in some encounter in the Haight-Ashbury would stumble slightly in stepping off the curb; and I would then see that the person had a serious handicap that I had not noticed before.

In particular, I seemed to have trouble in being able to write field notes on any experience I had in the Psychedelic Shop, which was in many ways the center of the community during this period. There was a kind of dizzying quality about this shop, no matter how many times I entered it. In a period of three months, for instance, I did manage to count four definite changes in the actual architecture of the shop—the arrangement of stock, the décor, the location of the counters and the tables for stock, and so on. But the human arrangements changed even more swiftly. Each time that I went into the store, I was confronted with a sweep of new sounds and colors and movements—a kind of psychedelic experience comparable to the effect at the Fillmore. There were so many stimuli to eye and ear that one had either to try to catalogue them on the spot or else give oneself over to the emotion of the moment and lose the ability to reconstruct the details later. One day when I was busy responding to a young man dressed as a gypsy, to a box of beautiful avocados free on the cash counter, to strange new music that I had never heard before coming from the loud-speaker, to a beautiful young girl who leaned over the counter to kiss gently the man behind the cash register, to new varieties of beads and amulets on necks and wrists, to different words of gentle greeting, to a serious discussion of paranoia in the society coming from a small group sitting under the side shelf counters, I somehow managed to pull myself back from the scene and notice a man under the shelf who was clearly Negro; and I said to myself: It is strange I have never seen any Negroes in this shop before. In this way I deliberately focused on color of skin and then counted six people in the shop who were at least partly Afro-American in origin. *But it was difficult to focus on skin color.* There were too many other stimuli, too many interesting events taking place. It was primarily a human scene, and in this was its enchantment.

Several outsiders who visited with me in the Haight-Ashbury recognized the cogency of this experience—if one were truly able to give oneself over to the urgency of the stimulation—so that I feel assured that this was not an isolated phenomenon.

There was a blurring of so-called racial characteristics, so that what was happening and a variety of sensual stimulations became the focus of attention. In a racist society such as ours, it is difficult to achieve the forgetfulness of differences in color of skin even between close friends; it has happened to me several times in a lifetime, but I am always happily amazed when it occurs.

There were other, more negative, instances of this phenomenon of color-blindness, which involved a change in the rank ordering of human beings. Quite independently, my husband, who was doing a study of garbage men, mainly Italian-American, in San Francisco, reported that those who worked in the Haight-Ashbury district complained about conditions there, blaming it on what "they" did; although he spent several hours on the garbage trucks in the Haight-Ashbury, on different occasions, he could not determine whether "they" referred to the hippie residents or to the poor Negro residents; after a while, he felt that it was quite clear that it referred to both, that there was a blurring of these two groups.[2] It was as if the scavengers, as garbage men were called in San Francisco, couldn't decide which were worse in their crowded living conditions and their excess of garbage.[3] So in a negative way, the question remained: How do you tell the poor Negro from the hippie? Which is worse?

Again, the same question of *Which is worse?* appeared in a conversation that I listened to in a newly opened restaurant at the corner of Haight and Ashbury in late December. In this instance, I was having lunch with Mrs. X, an old resident of the area, who was upper middle class but supportive of the hippies. The store was crowded with hippies and old residents that day, and we sat at a table for four. My notes read:

[2] In the main there were very few residents in the Haight-Ashbury who were both hippie in costume and Negro; the Negro hippies were mainly only day residents, coming in from the Fillmore.

[3] The property owner contracts privately for garbage pickup in San Francisco. If a given flat in the Haight-Ashbury were overpopulated, the landlord's contract for a limited number of cans to be emptied each week would often prove inadequate for the actual number of people living in a building or a flat; both the landlords and the tenants tended to want to avoid looking at the overpopulation and the overspilling cans that made the conscientious scavenger's job so frustrating.

A man sat down at the same table who has had a business in the area for a long time, say, twenty-five years, although I don't remember exactly how long. He began to rant about the hippies. When Mrs. X spoke to him sharply and suggested that the hippies had rescued a dying neighborhood [speaking of the commercial part of the area], he agreed. He said that stealing was not done by the hippies but by the "colored." He then proceeded to stand up for the colored who are buying their own homes in the area [making a distinction between those who own their own homes and those who rent]. Again as with the garbage men, I felt the real confusion between the hippies and the Negroes. The middle-class Negroes in the area have now found their own group for disparagement—the hippies—and the white old-timers are confused as to who is lower on the totem pole.

In spite of the fact that these two instances showed *confusion* as to whether the Negro or the hippie was lower on the social totem pole, the actual confusion seemed to represent the beginning of wisdom. Even confusion was an improvement over the strict hierarchy of racial status that the society has imposed on itself. The hippies' influence over that hierarchy of status showed itself, I felt, in changed newspaper reporting. For example, in the Watts disaster of 1964, the press reported the losses suffered by the Negroes last on any list. Thus the Associated Press and United Press story for August 16, 1964, in the San Francisco *Chronicle* contains the following summary sentence on the deaths: "The 32 dead included two law officers, one fireman, one other white man, a Japanese, and 27 Negroes." In another newspaper story of the same general period, the rank ordering was basically the same, although a Mexican-American had been identified and his name inserted *before* the name of the Japanese-American and the Negroes. Yet as time went by, and stories on the Haight-Ashbury about pot raids or other disturbances between police and the new community began to appear, rank ordering was not used—those arrested were usually identified merely as hippies.

As these stereotypes began to be tackled and began to give, no matter how little, the possibility of all of us sitting together under the apple tree seemed more possible and more natural. For if one could be blind to color, then the human race could live together and love together without any painful realization of some insurmountable obstacle, some stigmatized barrier that maintained the power of the apple-sorting machine. Color-blindness in human love was suggested to me one day as I took a bus on Haight Street:

As I was getting on the bus today to go back to work, I saw a family group, the mother white, the father a dark-skinned Negro, the child a small light-skinned girl, with tight braids and blue eyes. They were a handsome-looking, startling family group, and I watched them intently out of the corner of my eye. Just as the bus turned the corner to pick us up, a well-dressed very light-skinned Negro woman came up to me and spoke quietly, "The Bible says that love is blind. Do you believe that?" smiling at me quizzically (obviously referring to this family group). I fortunately didn't have to answer her because she greeted a white friend and they started talking together as we got on the bus. I don't know what she meant exactly by her question, but she had seen me studying the group and she was testing my reaction in part I felt.

This note was made on November 8 of that winter. At that time, I was puzzled by her comment, but by now I have a clearer idea of what she meant: I would assume that she, like the Freedom Singers, was saying: Wouldn't it be nice if we in the human species could accept each other as the little dogs do, sharing our bones and our friendliness and our love?

While I was well aware, from the beginning, of the emphasis on the leveling of all human beings in the philosophy of the Diggers, it was the black people in the Haight-Fillmore who first made me conscious of another necessary change that the Diggers were dramatizing by their activities—the doing away with human *eligibility requirements* as a prerequisite for living and eating. My first full-fledged introduction to the meaning of no eligibility rules, as opposed to the dehumanized objectivity of organized charity, came shortly after Christmas of that year when I visited a store-front organization on Haight Street in the heart of the Haight-Fillmore district. This organization was called GROUP, the initials standing for Grass Roots Outreach to Underprivileged People. Some time in 1965, a few

Negro women, most of whom had been on welfare at some time themselves, joined together to try to help people who were *not eligible* for help under any welfare rules. Their objective was to try to do something for people who fell in the gaps between categorical aids; for instance, Negroes who came into San Francisco from the Southern states, looking for jobs, often had no resources at all and they had not lived in the Bay area long enough to establish any kind of eligibility for welfare. The members of the GROUP literally took such people into their own overcrowded homes and attempted to find other places for them to live until they could get jobs, and they tried to supply them with food and clothing until they could find a way to survive on their own. The members of GROUP rapidly became very competent in their appointed task; for instance, they literally learned all the jurisdictional eligibility rules for getting official welfare in the entire Bay area, so that in effect they became eligibility brokers. They knew the minute a particular person became eligible; and they knew how to place people geographically in the best spot for getting on welfare as promptly as possible.[4]

The notes on my first visit to GROUP actually give some preview of the themes of this book, for in essence much of what the flower children were trying to establish in the Haight-Ashbury was already a daily occurrence in the lives of these women. It is no surprise to me now that these women felt an affinity for the flower children, although at the time I was astounded by their acceptance of them.

I was finally able to make significant contact with the GROUP. When I have been by before, they have been too busy to talk. By going when they opened, I was able to talk to them. Had to wait sometime for Mrs. P., who is in charge apparently. Although she knew I was coming, she was late in getting in, because they couldn't get away from work last night, too much "suffering"—you can't just walk away from suffering. In the interim before Mrs. P. came, I had an opportunity to observe the patrons. I sat near the door,

[4] After GROUP had been in operation for some time, the American Friends Service Committee heard of their work and offered to pay for the rental of a store front and for telephone service; before that, the women had operated out of their own homes.

where I was told to sit, so I was not visible immediately when people came in. When they saw me, they all startled, cultural shock, since in that place, of all places, they did not expect to see a white face. I was impressed again by the gentleness and politeness of these people to each other. It was like a lobby in a Negro church in Mississippi, calm and peaceful, kind and really loving, in the best sense. Each person as he left wished everyone there a Happy New Year. Most people were looking for shoes, because there was a sign on the door that said "free shoes." Someone had sent shoes to them—they were mainly women's high-heeled shoes, all too small for feet that had splayed out into deformity from too much hard physical labor. . . . The sadness on their faces as they looked at the shoes (which they couldn't wear), which were actually almost new and quite nice-looking, was overwhelming.

There was a Christmas tree in the window and standing beside it what looked like a Negro angel, all in shades of bronze. Underneath the tree were seven or eight stockings filled. One woman came in with three children to see if any of the shoes fit her; she was quite young-looking and the children were quiet and well mannered. Under the tree was a small play electric iron, about three inches long, with a cord that looked real and had a plug on the end (although of course not usable). The little boy came over and fingered it gently and then went back to get his sisters to come and look at it; it must have been worth no more than a quarter but the wonder in their faces was great. I kept thinking of the story by Katherine Mansfield about the poor children allowed to come in and inspect the doll house of the well-to-do children; and one of the poor children saying, "I seen the little lamp," when she left the house of rich children. Anyway, when the children were leaving, they were each invited to help themselves to a stocking from under the tree; the youngest took the biggest stocking, but the two older ones took the smaller stockings, as if they were politely leaving the fullest ones for other children. I felt anew the feeling that I get so often that the poor are often socialized and civilized in superior ways, and that they do not act like pigs at the trough, as so many of the middle-class children do in supermarkets, for instance.

When there were no patrons in the store, the two women on duty would talk excitedly to me about what they were trying to do, of how people cannot be sorted out and told: You don't belong here. Mrs. P. reported that her nephew told her about a lovely woman who was just sick in the head from what wine she could get and trying to keep her children fed; that she just sat in her room, that she did "bad things" to get money, and so on. Mrs. P. told her nephew to bring her down to the store front, that she didn't have time right now to go to the woman's house. Her nephew asked, "What would you do for her? She can't get money, she's tried, she's just going down and down." And Mrs. P. told her nephew, "Well, I'd begin by brushing her hair and braiding it; when I don't know anything else to do, I always do just that for women. That's what their mothers used to do for them, and that is always a good beginning."

There was an old Singer sewing machine there, and one old sick-looking woman looking for a pair of shoes remarked on the sewing machine and said that her mother used to have a machine like that in Alabama (they all told certain information to the women running the store front, the state they came from, the name of their social worker, who had sent them there, because they didn't fall under "nothing at all" right now and they needed help right away); and Mrs. P. said that she could use the machine *anytime*. The patron got very excited, and said, "Why, I could make clothes for some of these children around here," but then she commented on the fact that she would have to wait until she got some glasses because she couldn't even see now to thread a needle.

They told about a young girl who was running around getting into trouble, was pregnant at thirteen, and someone had given her a slip to go to Mt. Zion Hospital for "psych help." But she was afraid to go, "I'm not crazy," she said, so Mrs. P. just talks to her when she comes in. And her mother says that it's helping, that she's not so wild. They reported to me that when they can't do anything else, they can just let people talk. And when they have time, they follow some of the poor kids home and it is just as if the mother is waiting for someone to come to that door, she talks as if they were her best friends, even though they've never met before. "She's just waiting for someone to come to that door, she's lying in wait for help." . . .

They understand the hippies, volunteered the fact that they approve of interracial marriages, in a roundabout way, telling me of one they had seen of a debutante from an upper-class family who had married a Negro artist; they have a baby and they understand the meaning of love. As they talked of love, I suddenly began to get a real feel for the close relationship between the Negro church (as I knew of it in the rural South) and its emphasis on simple human love, and the significance of the word "love" among the hippies. The hippies owe much to Negro culture, not the least of which is the religious emphasis on love (as evidenced by the non-violence of Martin Luther King), sexual expressiveness, and the acceptance of illegitimate children as full human beings, denying the legitimacy of the term "illegitimate" for any child. The music, the lights, the dealing in the illicit, and so on, are all part of the Fillmore and of Harlem, as they are part of Haight-Ashbury. The recent Glide church service for all people (including hippies) made use of hippie talk, which is really cotton-field talk—"man," "get with it," and so on, all terms I heard in Mississippi thirty years ago, no different.

In essence this is the first place I have ever seen in which no one is turned away. Just talking, if nothing else can be done. The telephone goes all the time, and there are words of encouragement, directions as to what to do now. The GROUP feel indebted to the Catholic sisters at a nearby convent who go out to supermarkets and solicit food. "A chicken and a box of rice give people courage to do miracles sometime, to begin to move ahead," Mrs. P. told me.

What is so significant here is the dropping of categorical definitions of people, so that *all* are eligible. "Sure some people are irresponsible," they point out, "but how did they get that way? What chance did they ever have? Now they suffer. It's no time to turn the cold shoulder." Again I am reminded of Makarenko's *The Road to Life*[5] and of how this was the important ingredient—no culling of people like apples, just the taking of everyone who came by. Total responsibility begets total responsibility. There is a contagion in caring which makes it possible for the ones who are cared for to turn around and care for someone else. This is not a simple-minded altruism, but a social process that does work. The people at the GROUP report that it happens for them, and I have seen it happen many times in a [mental] hospital, when a patient began to get well—he then had tremendous contributions to make to other patients.

As I left the GROUP office, one of the women there asked me whether I had attended the service at Glide Memorial Church on Christmas Day, three days before. "There were quite

[5] A. S. Makarenko, *The Road to Life* (Moscow: Foreign Languages Publishing House, no date). This book describes one of the great social and educational experiments in our century—the Gorky Colony, founded in 1920 to take care of the homeless children (including adolescents) who were wandering through the Russian countryside as an aftermath of the 1917 Revolution.

a few hippies there," she said, with evident pleasure, noting that several GROUP people had gone, too. I had clipped the story out of the paper, so I went back and read it again, more carefully this time. The story by Bill Boldenweck, titled "Glide's Hippies Turn On Christmas, Man," had appeared in the San Francisco *Examiner* for December 26, 1966, and read, in part:

Big Black spoke a sermon on the Congo Drums.

The Reverend A. Cecil Williams responded.

And the congregation of 850 hippies and squares who packed the Glide Memorial Methodist Church yesterday seemed to love it.

"It" was San Francisco's—and possibly the world's—first hip Christmas service.

From the moment organist Richard Judd and alto saxist John Handy came down together on the first note of "God Rest Ye Merry Gentlemen," until an hour later, when the Rev. Williams shouted from the rear of the church "Lord, thy spirit we praise, and we thank thee for Bach, and Handel, and Handy," it was a moving —and swinging—service.

The "Liturgical Jazz Worship Service," as Rev. Williams had previously explained, was an effort to preach the Christmas message in the vernacular of today. . . .

After Handy and his concert ensemble had filled the cavernous church to its heavily beamed ceilings with variations on the post-Medieval "God Rest Ye," lay reader Larry Mamiya sailed into the Call to Confession (an invitation to be who we really are):

"I say it and you feel it in your hearts:

"You and I, behind Merry Christmas smiles, are afraid to be alone.

"You and I, behind the presents we give, are afraid to love.

"You and I, behind our friendly words, are afraid to stand beside one another.

"You and I, behind our Christmas hymns and prayers, are afraid to stand before God.

"I say it and you feel it in your hearts: Let us humbly confess who we are before The One who comes today."

Behind him Big Black's soft drumming and the muted bowing of a bass fiddle provided a beat for the rhythmic reading.

Then lay reader Victor des Marais launched the congregation into a reading of poet Lawrence Ferlinghetti's poem "Christ Climbed Down." . . . as Handy's alto rose in an anguished, pulsating vibrato. . . .

Then, in almost startling contrast, lay reader Walter Lorenz read Christmas texts from both the Old and New Testaments, with Handy variations on "We Three Kings" sandwiched in between.

Then it was time for the Rev. Williams to explain it all; to deliver the message. Without batting an eye at the hirsute, sunglassed young man who sat in the third row with his straw hat square upon his head, he began extemporaneously:

"Christmas means, uh, it means that this is a happening, man.

"The thing that's happening to all of us in the 20th Century is that we have forgotten the meaning of Christmas.

"It means that a certain man came on this earth 2000 years ago, man. . . .

"Christmas, if it's going to be a happening, has to be able to get the message through without rules.

"A lot of people left the church a long time ago because it wasn't coming to grips with what it was talking about. Now some of them come back and talk about how the church was. And I say, 'Man, it's not like that anymore.' . . .

"It's like being on a stage, man, and when we get on a stage we want a script, because it gives us security. But there are people who are trying to take away that script. Life is not lived that way these days in the cities, the urban centers.

"Some of us want to take away that script, to yank it out of your hands, just as the author of the play did.

"He came on stage and took the script away. And a lot of people didn't like that, in fact they killed him. They put him on a cross.

"New life means getting along with each other," he said, shaking hands with a bearded man in the first pew. "It means that we can be alive with each other, be human with each other. God is acting in history to make and keep human life human.

"There's a happening in this place, I know there's going to be a lot of complaints, and a few people are going to be worried.

"But it's happening, man," he said as he walked back to the pulpit and his ever more softly repeated "Yeah, man" was snatched by the rising of Handy's music.

As the congregation moved forward to hear nearly an hour's concert by the Handy group at the end of the service, many left to attend other services or to go home.

The Rev. Williams shook hands with each as they left. The Rev. Charles Lewis, pastor of the Methodist North Beach Mission . . . explained that his small congregation had met at the mission, then decided to go in a body to attend the Glide services.

Father Basil, a Dominican at St. Albert's in Oakland, said, "I thought it gave a lot of people a profound sense of unity. As the Rev. Williams said, we must find the unity between what is essential and what is worth saving and the variants, the elements of change.

"As to the jazz, I might suspect that within 25 years it would become the true music of the church. There will be protest, and opposition, but I think it will come." . . .

Whatever it was that happened, happened. There were the believers and the disbelievers, the curiosity seekers and the jazz fans who came for the music. All heard the message; perhaps not all accepted it.

But they may have been in on the beginning.

After my visit to the GROUP office, I looked at the sign on the door of the Diggers' store front in the Haight-Ashbury with new interest. It read: "When you enter this door, you are a Digger." When I had seen it before, I had felt it as a warning against the casual trespasser. Now I began to feel that it was a double-edged invitation to all people: No matter how far any of us had strayed into the inhumanity of affluence and indifference, we were all eligible to come back into the condition of humanity once again.

CHAPTER 8

The Real Hang-Up

And the people bowed and prayed
to the neon god they made.
And the sign flashed out its warning
In the words that it was forming
And the signs said, "The words of the
prophets are written on the
subway walls and tenement halls"
And whisper'd in the sounds of silence.

—from "The Sound of Silence" by Paul Simon

Most of the adults in our society act as if the psychedelic drugs were their real worry about the ways of the young. But in my own observation, this is a cover for their central concern—the disrespect of the young for the property and status values as these gods are served in Western society in our time. The middle-class adults in American suburbia have labored long and lovingly for the Utopia promised by the soap ads, the car ads, the toothpaste ads—a Utopia that has been abandoned by the young as sterile. And many of the adults are frantic; for, tragically, they feel that they have lived in vain.

The *as if* quality of this whole performance reminds me of Harry Stack Sullivan's description of one of his cocker spaniels. Now this dog had a fear of the trash man, a common malady of many dogs. But this particular dog, timid from puppyhood, had an inordinate fear which she expressed by digging furiously in the yard. When the trash man came, she barked furiously at him more or less like the other dogs; but at about every third bark, she would go off and dig furiously in the yard. And it was the preoccupation with digging, which had nothing at all to do with the trash man, that saved her from her overwhelming fear. The dog acted *as if* she were entirely concerned with the hole in the yard. In much the same way, the core society's preoccupation with psychedelic drugs has been a way of avoiding their real hang-up: the attack of the young on middle-class values, particularly status and property.

In brief, the harmless people in the Haight-Ashbury had begun to discover that the values by which the dispossessed peoples in the world lived were in most ways ethically superior to the values of the adult middle-class world that they had known. And in this wise, the flower children spread all the values of the world out on a large sward of green in the sun and began to look at them, honestly and dispassionately. Once James Joyce had separated words and feelings from their usual syntax, and in so doing he had freed the language by smashing some of the old patterns; and people who had never read James Joyce would be affected in their language and their ideas from then on, for the process was revolutionary. In much the same way, the flower children were freeing behavior, for they separated all the values and the actions of the core society and spread them out on their huge work table alongside the values and the actions of various peoples from every corner of the earth and from all periods of history; and in the process of separating out all these pieces and trying to fit them back together again, they smashed some of the behavior of the middle-class society, and all of us have been affected. For the values-by-words and the values-by-action of the core society did not fit together when one looked at them closely, so new action was necessary to fit some of the revered values from the past; and some values from other cultures were found that seemed superior to some of the values of one's own culture and that required further experiments in new action. And bending over their huge work table, still sorting, still fitting, the seekers sometimes seemed disorganized and their task chaotic, for they had literally scrambled hundreds of huge jigsaw puzzles. But a new and often beautiful pattern was slowly emerging; and some of the old pieces of the puzzle, which had once seemed to form such a polished and unbroken unit, now seemed only tawdry and misshapen pieces in the bright light. And this was the procedure that frightened the adults.

Because the reappraisal of values undertaken by the young people was so catholic in its scope, jigsaw pieces from the Haight-Fillmore and rural Mississippi lay side by side with pieces from Cromwell's England, nineteenth-century Russia, and so on. Thus Father Leon Harris at All Saints' Episcopal Church in the Haight-Ashbury pointed out to some of his critical parishioners that the disciples pictured in the windows of the parish house bore a striking resemblance to the Diggers preparing food in the kitchen of the parish house for the multitudes on the Panhandle.

In general, I found myself rereading books from nineteenth-century Russia—Turgenev's *Fathers and Sons* and more particularly the writings of Tolstoy and accounts of his life. Leveling and sharing had gradually become often painful convictions for Tolstoy by 1898, when there was a famine in Russia; he was then seventy years old, but he personally manned the soup kitchens. When Tolstoy began his voluntary poverty, he was nobled, famous, rich, and loved throughout Russia, so that the authorities could not arrest him and had difficulty in controlling his activities, although they were apprehensive and fearful of his influence and his teachings. He adopted the dress of the peasants, and spent most of his time talking to them near the end of his life. In 1897, Tolstoy was described in the surveillance record of the Security Department in St. Petersburg as follows: "Count Tolstoy was dressed in an open-necked, lined sheepskin coat, patched in places, held in by a gray belt, dark colored trousers, worn outside his boots, with a dark gray knitted cap on his head, and he had a cane in his hand. . . ."[1] Such a description sounds very much like a description of a Digger or a hippie on a foggy cold day in San Francisco. What were young people who had access to money and/or jobs doing going around in torn and dirty clothes? the authorities in San Francisco asked nervously. In the same wise, the authorities in St. Petersburg wondered what Count Tolstoy was doing wandering around that city in his seventieth year, when he had already reached the peak of recognition and wealth, attired in a *patched* sheepskin coat. Tolstoy had his followers among the

1 Alexandra Tolstoy, *Tolstoy: A Life of My Father*, tr. by Elizabeth Reynolds Hapgood (New York: Harper & Brothers, 1953), p. 376.

rich of his time, just as the Diggers did; and "an unkempt appearance to some [of his followers] was one of the necessary attributes of Tolstoyanism."[2] In the same way, the hippies and the Diggers felt that their appearance was a badge of honor, an affiliation with the poor, if only in spirit.

Tolstoy found his relationships with the peasants increasingly rewarding, for they were shrewd and psychologically aware in a different way from the elite society, which became increasingly repugnant to him; the white flower children had much the same feeling about black people. Only a few people from the elite class sided with Tolstoy, but the advantaged young in America today who yearn to do away with status and property hang-ups are large in number. Many of them are upper middle class in origin; and their opportunities for travel, education, the comforts of life are impressive, although most of them do not occupy the socially elite position that Tolstoy did in his growing-up years. Like Tolstoy, the advantaged young in America today have considerable political power. Tolstoy's power was personal and derived from his family's position and his writings. The dedicated young today have power arising from their numbers and their access to mass communication, particularly through music. In many ways, the flower children, as exemplified by the Diggers, and Tolstoy seem to have much the same historical function: In both societies, of course, there was or is a wide disparity between the poor and the wealthy; and in both instances, the affluent person who is sensitive feels the necessity to identify with the poor and to actively misidentify with the wealthy in *a visible way*. Tolstoy's wife complained that he smelled like the peasants with whom he spent a good deal of time; and the same complaint about the dirt and smell of the hippies was ubiquitous in the square community. Tolstoy ate the black bread of the peasants; the hippies and the Diggers often ate the food of the poor. In several visits to one of the chain food stores on Haight Street, I noticed that the purchases made by black people using food stamps were similar to those made by hippies: rice, dried legumes, and chicken necks, cheap pieces of meat, or soup bones often appeared in both baskets.

[2] *Ibid.*, p. 337.

However many historical influences could be connected with the experimentation in values taking place in the Haight-Ashbury, it was the effect of the Haight-Fillmore that was paramount in the task of attacking the real hang-ups of the core society—status and property values; and it was the Diggers and their techniques, as vitalized by the example and the language of poor black people and taught to the novitiates of the new society, that began the cure of the sick society. My earliest encounter with a group of Diggers immediately mobilized an issue of status, without my being aware at the time of what was happening. I had been invited along with several other squares —representatives of the police department, social workers, and so on—to attend a meeting called by the Diggers to discuss the coming summer crisis, particularly in terms of housing. The meeting had no appointed leader; but a Digger began by introducing himself. We sat in a large circle, and each person in turn announced himself: "John, Digger"; "Mary, Digger"; "Steven, Digger"; and so on. The squares, seated for the most part near each other, squirmed as their turn came; most of the squares avoided titles (Mrs., Miss, Dr., and so on) but they gave their profession. I felt a paralysis creep over me as my turn came, but I found myself saying, "Helen Perry, Langley-Porter," avoiding the words "social scientist" in a swift, almost unaware decision. At that moment, I sensed that I really did not have a "thing" in that setting, that I was only part of a remote and not very well-esteemed establishment. But I also perceived as the meeting progressed that each Digger had potentially his own expertise, recognized by the group, so that there was no competition or argument, only a swift movement from one person's thing to another's. By contrast, the professional was trapped by some sense of loyalty to his own particular establishment, so that he could not uncover whatever special thing he might have as a human being.

In this instance, confrontation effectively challenged the status of representatives from the establishment. But words were a more usual method for tackling a status hang-up, and confrontation was generally reserved for tackling the property hang-up. I shall cite only a few examples of the expressions used to counter status, all of which were in common use by the black community long before the advent of the Diggers.

The question that most effectively threatened the professional person who encountered the new society was some variant of "*What is your thing?*" The word "thing" immediately levels all persons, for one can have education, wealth, a formal title, and yet not have what the Negro-hippie society calls "your thing." It directly challenges the definition of work in Western society. To care for the sick, to be concerned with the happiness of one's self and others, to deliver a message to someone who is lonely—all of these were important human tasks in the new society. For instance, most seekers did not like to work for the establishment any more than was necessary for survival, yet one of the acceptable tasks was to be a mailman, for he often brings hope in a letter and in this way helps to shatter the silence that "like a cancer grows," as Simon and Garfunkel sing.

The impact of this word "thing" was borne in on me in the spring of 1967, when another group of social workers and other people involved in mental health and welfare met with some of the Diggers to discuss how the professional people might help the Diggers in counselling the runaways then coming into the Haight-Ashbury district. The Diggers had been trying to take care of all of them, but the problem was growing by leaps and bounds. The Diggers' usual solution was to offer bed and board for a few days and someone to talk with; they made an attempt to see what was troubling the runaway at home or at school, let him talk it out, and then gently suggested that his best chance was to return home and try to manage until he was of age and could make the break on his own.

In this encounter between, mainly, social workers and the Diggers, there was a good deal of well-intentioned prodding by some of the social workers. Using certain non-directive kinds of procedures, particularly common to the mental health profession, several of the social workers present were trying to get the Diggers to define what they wanted the social workers to do. In a philosophical sense, it could be viewed as the encounter between the pragmatists and the existentialists; the social workers wanted (a) a clear-cut program for (b) a clear-cut group with (c) clear-cut goals; and all of this, they thought, should be succinctly outlined by the Diggers, so that there was a clear-cut client-social worker relationship. The Diggers did not operate that way, and there was an impasse on the resolution of this dilemma.

Finally one of the Diggers, John, who happened to be a Negro, asked one of the more articulate social workers: "What is your thing?"

"What did you say?" she asked.

"What is your thing? What do you do?" he again asked.

"I am a social worker for the —— Agency," she said.

"Yeah," John said wearily, "but what do you do—when you come to work in the morning, what do you do?"

"Oh, I interview people," she said. "I talk to the person in trouble or to his family."

"Yeah," John said, "but what do you talk to them about?"

"Oh, when I see them for the first time, I ask them questions," she answered.

"Nuh-uh," John shook his head negatively. "That won't work with these kids. I tell them, 'Look, whatever trouble you're in, it ain't all that bad. When I was your age, I fucked up everything. I just messed around, and it looked as if I had ruined my life. But you find your way after a while.' And then I just explain to them some of the ways I messed up."

In addition to the fact that this kind of conversation indicates a good deal of therapeutic sophistication about how to relate to teenagers, it also clearly demonstrated that John, uneducated and poor for most of his life, knew that he had a thing in which he was expert; that, in fact, he was more expert than the social worker. This encounter was conducted by John with dignity and assurance, for he knew that degrees and jobs were not determining skills: There was a human skill that transcended these paper qualifications.

Another expression, "*You're putting me down*," tackles the condescension and hierarchy of the establishment directly. It was also used by young black people to train novitiate Diggers; this charge could be implied sometimes by a glance, so that the serious novitiate would hasten to defend himself by saying, "I wasn't trying to put you down"—before the attack, "You're putting me down," could be made. For one person to try to lower someone else's status was unacceptable and showed a lack of humility and humanness.

The care with which this expression was reserved for a real act of condescension is illustrated by the following example taken from my February 4, 1967, field notes:

Went with E. and G. and E.'s friend, M., to the Haight-Ashbury. E. and G., both social scientists from out of town, were excited about the Haight-Ashbury and accepted the culture. G. was very thrilled by the acceptance and the gaiety on Haight Street, said it was just like the Left Bank in Paris; E.'s friend, M., lives in the Mission District, comes from a wealthy family in Mexico City, told us that she had taken about twenty out-of-town guests through the Haight-Ashbury—"they all want to see it." But she despaired of the young people in the Haight-Ashbury and did not approve of their values.

We went to the Psychedelic Shop and a young hippie girl came up to M. and said, "Don't look that way at me; you're bringing me down." This interested me very much, since no one had ever said that to me or to anyone who had accompanied me; and this was the first person who had gone with me to Haight Street who actively disapproved. Later on, this same young girl came up to us in a store several blocks from the Psychedelic Shop and began to talk to M. again. And M. queried the young girl: "Why did you say that I was *putting you down?*" "I didn't say that," the young girl responded; "I asked you why you were *bringing me down.*" The girl went on to point out that there is a lot of difference between putting someone down and bringing someone down. An interesting interchange. I have observed before that these youngsters are very discerning of what is going on, that they are trained observers. I think that she understood precisely that M. was disapproving of her.

Or again, the admonition, "*Tell it like it is,*" is an attack on the kind of loyalty to the establishment that can force the individual to evade, to lie, and to cover up. Only as the person gives up his blind allegiance to his profession or his employer, or, even, his government, can he gain the only meaningful status—that of being a human being, responsible to his peers. No other challenge to our society seems more important to me.

Even a Chief Justice of the United States has stated that some of the information on the death of President Kennedy could not be made public in our lifetime. Thus even in a democracy, the government as an institution has a hung-up status need that transcends the right of the people to know. Thus the people are personified by their leaders as being incapable of understanding or accepting the truth about an important issue: as simple citizens we wouldn't understand the truth or we would be upset by it. *Tell it like it is:* the words sound like music to me now, although once I would have winced at the grammar.

The expression, "*You're beautiful,*" has long been used by the American Negro to indicate the condition of a person's spirit, his soul; a person did not have to have status or possessions or material success, or youth, or any of the advertising criteria for physical beauty, to be beautiful. One could be beautiful by caring for others, by being thoughtful and giving, by doing his "thing." For the black man living in a white man's society, it was necessary to find a definition for beauty that transcended the white man's criteria; and this was a word and a definition that the seekers accepted.

I can remember three times that this expression was directed to me in the Haight-Ashbury. In each instance, the other person was someone whom I had just encountered; and in each case, the other person had adequately judged the nature of my feeling—I was indeed moving out of older patterns of dealing with strangers and relating on a simpler and more human level. This kind of spontaneous appreciation from a stranger or even a friend is so rare in our society that each time was an unforgettable and emotional experience for me.

In accepting these expressions and others from the black man, the white flower children gained wisdom about the values of the middle-class society. At the same time, it is understandable that as the seekers moved away from these values, they encountered from the establishment the same epithets that the Negro had had applied to him for 300 years in America: The hippie was dirty, lazy, no-good, shiftless, a drop-out, unproductive, child-like, wore gaudy clothes, and so on. In time, crime would be the responsibility of the hippie, too, and in this way the black man had a brief and deserved holiday.

Yet no matter how much the core society resisted these words and phrases that interfered with status needs, these words and values were coming back into common usage once again and changing our perception of the world around us. I say once again, because many of the expressions borrowed by the white man from the black man in the 1960's had earlier been a part of the American language as it first blossomed in the first half of the nineteenth century. Thus Nathaniel Hawthorne referred to every man having his "thing" in his short story, "The Intelligence-Office": "I want my place, my own place, my true place in the world, my proper sphere, my thing which Nature intended me to perform when she fashioned me thus awry, and which I have vainly sought all my life-time."[3]

Or to give another example: Bronson Alcott's eldest daughter, Anna, in her thirteenth year, wrote in her diary at Fruitlands: "Beautiful is my favorite word. If I like anything I always say it is beautiful. It is a beautiful word. I can't tell the color of it."[4] All the transcendentalists talked of soul and beauty, and now these feelings and expressions were coming back into the language through the influence of the black man.

Even the so-called obscenities of the flower children, which in their own way might be discussed as another preoccupying concern of the squares, represented an attempt to "tell it like it is." Emerson also thought that the younger generation should have the right to speak freely, although one day the "Apostles of the Newness" entered into such resounding oaths on his front porch in Concord that he had to invite them to move round to the back of the house.[5] Obscenity was also a charge against Bronson Alcott on the closing of his school in Boston; at that time a Harvard professor said that Alcott's Conversations, which he used as a teaching device, were one third nonsense, one third blasphemous, and the rest obscene—the ob-

[3] I found this quote from Hawthorne in a footnote in Van Wyck Brooks, *The Flowering of New England* (New York: Dutton, 1936), pp. 179–202.

[4] Sears, *Bronson Alcott's Fruitlands* (Boston and New York: Houghton Mifflin, 1915), pp. 103–104.

[5] *Ibid.*, pp. 19–20.

scenity "consisting of a few lines in which Alcott spoke with a beautifully simple reverence about the physiology of birth."[6] Whenever mankind makes an attempt to open closed doors in the human mind, the question of obscenity seems to emerge, for what freedom can there be when certain subjects represented by certain sounds are forbidden except by certain people in certain places? It is notable that the soldier geared for killing is allowed absolute freedom in his use of so-called obscenities which would be forbidden in other situations. The seekers felt that the only obscene words used in the society were kill and overkill, war and napalm, and so on, and this was surprisingly close to Alcott's position. On March 2, 1848, he wrote that "the stalk and flower of our English speech is plucked only by boys. . . . The human body is itself the richest and raciest phrase-book; and it is at once a proof of the shallowness and indelicacy of our American authors that our rhetoric is so seldom drawn from this armory, and our speech partakes so little of the blood-warmth and the flesh-colours of nature."[7]

Words were a powerful weapon in the seekers' attempt to free the core society from its status needs and its hypocrisy. But stronger methods were needed for tackling the related and more entrenched hang-up about property and money. At Fruitlands also, "money was abjured as the root of all evil," although in the end, as Mrs. Alcott notes wryly, they could not live without money or means. Yet they made notable strides in that direction. When Alcott and Lane wanted to travel, they walked or begged the loan of a vehicle. In one instance, they got on a boat without any money. The boat was already under way when the fare was demanded, and the two men offered to talk for their passage. Some of the passengers took up a contribution after they had listened to them, and apparently enough was collected to cover the fare, with a considerable sum left over. When the captain offered the excess money to the penniless

[6] Odell Shepard, *The Journals of Bronson Alcott* (Boston: Little, Brown, 1938, p. 81. In a commentary for the 1837 excerpts from Alcott's Journals, Shepard gives an account of the attitude of the public toward Alcott that finally closed down his Temple School.

[7] *Ibid.*, pp. 203–204.

passengers, "the reformers proved that they were consistent even in their madness, for not a penny would they accept, saying, with a look at the group about them, whose indifference or contempt had changed to interest and respect, 'You see how well we get on without money'; and so went serenely on their way, with their linen blouses flapping airily in the cold October wind."[8] This kind of morality play is almost a facsimile of what the Diggers did when they first began to receive money from indulgent squares: they burned some of the bills (although later this action was thriftily revised) in order to make the point that the gift without the giver was bare.

In the Haight-Ashbury, the most usual way to initiate the newcomer was to ask him for money; and begging was used as confrontation in order to change the principal hang-up of the core society. Previously I have cited my own reaction to a request for cigarettes from a Negro hippie, which was actually a request for money; by that time, I was well in tune with what was going on, and the request and the incident did not trouble me. But initially I was puzzled and upset by some of my encounters on Haight Street and looked upon a request for money as close to an act of hostility. On one occasion, a beautifully dressed young girl came up to me, leaving her male companion standing off to the side, and asked me for some "change." Her soft doeskin boots and expensive silver jewelry and her well-dressed male companion standing so as to observe me made me feel angry. It was near a park, and the block was almost empty; I felt afraid and at the same time felt the necessity of refusing, so I shook my head negatively and moved on quickly. At the end of the block, I turned and watched them strolling down the street, away from me, and watched them meet other people and pass them without making an attempt to stop them or ask them for money. I became curious about the phenomenon, and began to try to study it more systematically. For a while, I was usually accosted at least once or twice each time when I went on Haight Street; then for several weeks I was not accosted any more at all, and I interpreted this second phase at the

[8] This is from Louisa May Alcott's fictionalized account of Fruitlands, "Transcendental Wild Oats," but it is essentially the same story as reported by Bronson Alcott himself. See Sears, *op. cit.*, pp. 164–165.

time as my acceptance in the Haight-Ashbury. Subsequently, however, there was a third phase in which I was asked casually for money and I accepted it as casually; in this third phase, I no longer cared about money in the same old way. At the same time, if I did not feel as if I could spare money, I could turn the request aside without anxiety. I became comfortable at a different level about money. Retrospectively, I believe that the second phase was an interim step in which the young no longer felt that I needed to be challenged, that they recognized at some level that I had a knowledge of their values *in re* money; at the same time, I was not completely one of them. In the final stage, I think that there was a clear recognition that I had become indoctrinated and could be trusted; that I would understand the standards of sharing and casualness about money.

It is very difficult to trace out this change or to document it convincingly. I can state that it has happened, but that I still feel trapped by money. If I were younger, I would want to have no necessity for money as security. At any rate, what is notable is that I have a different attitude about money and that undergoing this change was comparable to a psychoanalytic experience, which I had some twenty years ago.

A field note, dated February 4, 1967, traces out the evolution of some of my changing attitudes and my lack of assurance with this new value:

A young Negro man approached me on Haight Street today. He was sitting on the steps of a building with other young people, several of them I think Negroes, although I am again struck by the fact that Negroes fade into the background on Haight. . . . Anyway this boy came up to me, this Negro boy with psychedelic glasses (one red glass, one blue, Benjamin Franklin-like glasses), and asked me for a nickel to buy a battery for his little tiny auto that he held in his hand, and I had a Truman Capote feeling sweep over me, that it was important that his car run, that he was a little schizzy and terribly needful, and I opened up my pocketbook and we both peered into the change purse and there were six pennies there, and I took out all the six and said, "I don't have a nickel, but maybe these pennies would do," and he said, "You are a beautiful lady," and I felt somehow that he had sensed my simple kindness at that moment, and that somehow I had stumbled onto some feeling in this group and that the word "beautiful" is not always phony. Although even as I write this, I feel self-conscious as if I had perhaps been put on and didn't recognize it.

Actually I did not feel contemptuous of him as I was taught to be of beggars when I was young; and this was a very strange experience. I think of the time when I was ten or eleven and didn't have any carfare to get home from city school through a mistake on my father's part (failed to pick me up when he was supposed to) and I went along the streets crying and not asking anyone for carfare, but finding my way to a friend's house alone, quite an achievement, since I had only been there once in my life. And then later telling my family (when they pressed me as to why I didn't ask someone for carfare) that I had asked, and a woman had called me a beggar, and it seemed quite real to me, even as I knew that I was lying, that I had feared someone would turn me down and that is why I had not asked.

Once the old ideas of begging are tackled, other attitudes toward giving and receiving are challenged and must be met. The concept of *generosity* is but the obverse of begging. This was brought to my attention in a visit to the Black People's Free Store in the Haight-Fillmore—a store which paralleled the original Free Store for hippies in the Haight-Ashbury. Some time in May, 1967, one of the psychiatric residents in training at Langley-Porter accompanied me on a visit to the Black People's Free Store. One of the Negro Diggers, Willard, had been taking us around the store and showing us proudly how the store was already operating significantly in the neighborhood. We went into the basement where there were a number of women with children of various ages looking through clothes that were really minimal for an affluent society—unpressed, rumpled, torn; indeed they looked like castoffs from the Fillmore district itself. Suddenly the trainee, knowing that Glide Foundation had helped financially in setting up the store, turned to Willard and said very quietly, "I hope that these people [meaning the customers in the store] understand who is responsible for this generosity." I felt unable to speak or to try to rescue the situation. But Willard, an uneducated, simple person, was very quick to answer. "We don't use *that word* any more," he said, with a great deal of dignity. "You see, it's just like electronics, you get this feeling, it's like a vibration and you know what's right to do and that's all there is to it."

I myself had a somewhat similar encounter with Willard on the other end of Haight Street a few nights later. There were five of us in the group, walking through the Haight-Ashbury. Suddenly a Negro man, with a feather in his hair, came up to me and spoke affectionately; I didn't know him in his hippie garb (he had had on work clothes when I had seen him previously in the Free Store in the Fillmore), so he mentioned the Free Store and told me that he was Willard. We all stood and talked with him for a while; he was very friendly and advised us where to go for coffee, since we had planned to go to the I-Thou coffee house that evening and it was closed for renovation. When we took our farewells from Willard, I told him to say "Hello" for me to Roy, one of the guiding spirits at the Free Store, and to tell Roy that I was coming down to the Free Store soon. Willard looked angry. "We don't want you there," he told me, and I felt rejected and unhappy. "Because of the color of my skin?" I asked him. "No," he told me, "that's not the reason. It's just that if you're coming, then just come, don't talk about it." Here again is the same criticism, this time of *my* condescension, for I had in effect said that I would be doing a favor and being generous to the Free Store to come and see them. I accepted the rebuke and I felt it was justified. Moreover, I had learned from Willard, a Negro, an important key to the hippie population.

If the white flower children and some of the middle-aged squares made some progress in this kind of self-examination, they did it under the sharp tutelage of the poor black man who began to interest himself in the ethical standards of the white man; and a great deal of this confrontation took place on Haight Street. An anonymous black man has cited his own experience in the teaching of whites that went on during this period:

I was on the street the other day. There was a white girl standing there. This poor white man stood there, and he was hungry. He asked this white girl for a dime to get him a cup of coffee, and she said she didn't have it. I'm standing there, looking at her. I said, "Girl, you should be ashamed of yourself, turning that old man down for a dime." I gave him a dime. I say, a dime won't make me rich. Poor's poor.[9]

By May, 1967, my own experience with the Black People's Free Store, with GROUP, and with the Diggers had made me sufficiently uncomfortable and searching of my own attitudes toward property that I felt the need to explore these feelings with someone else. I had tried to write about them, but I felt self-conscious and frozen, so I asked a particularly sensitive observer of what was going on—a young woman, Mary, who had been born and raised in San Francisco and who was then living in the Haight-Ashbury—to sit down with me and discuss some of my evolving philosophy about various values, including property values. At the last minute, I decided to make a tape of this encounter, since I found my own attitudes elusive and somewhat frightening. The following is an excerpt from that tape:[10]

H.P.: I have one other thing I'd like to talk to you about today, and that is the hippies' attitude toward property and ownership—"This is yours and this is mine"—and sharing. One of the things I feel is that their sharing is something that actually we all want to do, and that we're stuck on another thing. One of the things that I've had experience with in studying them is that I have become keenly aware of feelings that I had as a child and that I had forgotten, and this reminds me of my own experience with psychoanalysis. When you first start analysis, you start dreaming; and even if you have never remembered your dreams before, suddenly you do. And suddenly, also, you remember real events from childhood that you hadn't remembered before. I've had this same kind of experience by going in to the Haight-Ashbury; and that is why I think that the hippies have something which is akin to psychoanalysis. . . .

One of the things that haunts me lately has to do with property; and I want to try and tell you about it because it's hard to write it down. When I was a child we lived in a town on the edge of Washington, D.C., which was a sort of rural, working-class area. And although we didn't have too much, we had decidedly more

[9] From *Venture* (August, 1967), p. 9.
[10] This tape, dated May 18, 1967, has been minimally edited.

than most of the other kids in the neighborhood as we grew up. . . .

At Christmastime, we had access to various sweets that we didn't have during the rest of the year, and we were expected to share these with the kids in the neighborhood who came in to see our tree. There was a bag of walnuts, and a bag of figs, and another of chocolates, and so on, and they were placed in a chest in the dining room; and then there were small empty Christmas bags under the tree, and each caller would receive one of the small bags filled with some of each kind of sweets in the larger supply in the chest. When I was very small, I remember my mother saying to me, "Now you can fill a bag for Elinor," or whoever it was; and I would take one of the small bags and climb up on a chair to fill it from the larger bags, some of each kind. My earliest remembrance of this procedure is of how much I hated to do it. I would reach into the chest and just grab handfuls of each kind. My idea was that I wanted to give all of it away as fast as possible. So instead of doling it out so that it would last . . . I would put in great handfuls and fill the bags so they would almost spill over. After a child had gone, my mother would sometimes say to me, "You know, there are other children coming, and you really shouldn't give so much to the first ones." I could see the reasonableness of what she was saying, and yet I couldn't help myself, because I didn't want to be responsible for doling it out. I tried to get out of doing it because —and I'm using a grownup's word for a child's feelings—there was something immoral about my being in the position of giving largesse when they had nothing to give me. There was something wrong and embarrassing about it, and I didn't like any part of it.

I keep thinking about this incident when I'm down in the Haight-Ashbury, although I haven't thought about it for years and years. If anybody wants money, I find myself wanting to give him all I have at that moment. I've changed my whole attitude about money since I went to the Haight-Ashbury. When Roy told me they needed a truck for the Free Store, and I asked him how much the truck would cost, and he told me he needed $250, I had all I could do to keep from writing a check for the whole amount, because I happened to have $250 in my checking account at that time. I gave him $50. And as I talk to you now, I realize that one of the reasons I haven't been down there lately is that I'm scared that I'm going to give them the rest of what they need. In a way, money has no meaning to me any more.

Somewhere between the period when I was five, six, or seven, when I had this feeling of wanting to get rid of the Christmas sweets as soon as possible, and the period when I became adult, I had to learn not to give things away because I had to protect myself, maybe because of the depression. So I had to learn how to restrain myself, and finally I had just forgotten about ever having this feeling. But with the invasion into my life of hippie morality, what I once felt as so overpowering reasserted itself, and this is of course what Tolstoy wrote about near the end of his life. I realize now how powerful this feeling may be in all of us; I almost feel that in the beginning, we didn't say, "This is mine; and this is yours." We had the instinct of feeling that *the world was ours*, all of us, and that somehow or other this was beat out of us. This is what I feel is one of the most powerful moral concepts in the hippie movement—this thing of sharing and not worrying about money. If they get money, they go out and buy food and invite everybody in for a decent meal; they know that it's going to clean them out and that tomorrow they may regret that they spent their money. But the important thing is that hungry people be fed *tonight*. This is a powerful moral issue that confronts me at every turn, and I keep having this very clear feeling of what I experienced when I was five or six. Do you have any of this feeling in the Haight-Ashbury?

Mary: Yes, and it causes quite a conflict, too. I think, for one thing, that part of the attitude toward sharing is that most of these flower children have never really wanted for money or food before, and they've been tabbed as fakes, that it's going to come, and that they will be provided for. For me, this causes a very great conflict because there have been times when there was no money and no food; and when I got married and we had money to buy food, I bought so much food—you wouldn't believe it. [I finally realized it was] an obsession when I couldn't close the door of my storage cabinet—I really got carried away with this thing. And when I was asked for money in the Haight-Ashbury, I'd have a hard time giving it, even though I *wanted* to give it. I know it's *right* to do it, and I'd really want to. It really causes a deep conflict within me because I think I subconsciously or unconsciously have been afraid that if I start giving away money I can't give it to one person and not give to the next person. I'm always asked for money, constantly—every day. I walk down the street and I'm asked for money, and I can't imagine being able to give money to everyone, because I'm so concerned for me.... I'm not expressing myself clearly, but it is a tremendous conflict, because at the very same time that, as a child, you're being taught not to respect beggars, you're also being taught that

Christ begged for food and money and help, and so did all sorts of other prophets. And it's a conflict in values which is never resolved. If you add to that the personal conflict about whether this has been something that has been a problem, or whether it's something that one has never found to be a problem, then it really gets confusing.

I think that hippies *can* do this with less inner turmoil, because they feel that they are a part of the culture around them: If they take care of someone today, then someone will take care of them tomorrow.

In the course of my observation, I found that I was challenged more and more on this subject of property. As I became aware of my own anxiety and conflicts about giving away all I had (which, needless to say, I have not yet resolved satisfactorily), other people confided in me their own concern about property. One of the most revealing incidents that I heard was told me by a mature professional woman who lived with her husband and children on the edge of the area. She was very sympathetic with the philosophy of the hippies, and her children were eager observers and occasional participants in the action on Haight Street. She was enchanted with the work of the Diggers; and when, late in the spring of 1967, she first heard about the real shortage of bedding for sleeping the young runaways coming in to the Haight-Ashbury, she generously went through her own more than adequate supply of bedding and assembled a large supply of blankets and pillows to take down to the Free Store then on Cole Street and run by the Diggers for the flower children. In recounting this story to me, she said she was thoroughly disgusted with what had happened: She had gone in with her husband, each of them laden with a large box of excellent bedding. No one in the Free Store took any particular note of the "gift"; someone in the store told them where to put the boxes, and they departed. As they were going out the door, they noticed a nicely dressed Negro woman parking her car in front of the Store. They sat in their own car parked nearby and watched this woman go into the Free Store and walk directly over to the boxes of bedding that they had just deposited there; in two trips, she gathered up all the bedding, placed it in her car, and drove off. Both my friend and her husband were outraged. They were connected with several charitable enterprises in San Francisco, and they were quite firm in stating to me that in the future they would confine their good intentions to helping these enterprises, that they were through with the Free Store. They felt that the people who ran the Free Store should have supervised the distribution of the bedding; in essence, the Free Store should have established eligibility. I fully shared their anxiety, but at the same time I understood the philosophy of the Free Store.

To cite another example, this time of an eighteen-year-old girl who was visiting me from the East in the summer of 1967: She was disturbed and yet intrigued by the hippies and asked me many questions about them. She wanted to know all about the Diggers in particular, and I explained that anybody—yes, anybody—could get free soup from the Diggers in the Panhandle in the late afternoon. She explained to me that this would not work; although I assured her it did, she seemed genuinely upset and doubtful. She had just graduated from a public high school in one of the most affluent suburbs on the East Coast. She hypothesized to me a situation at her own high school in which, for instance, free Cokes would be made available to those who didn't have money to buy them; *all the students,* irrespective of whether or not they had money, would instantly line up for free Cokes, she insisted to me; she knew that this would be their attitude. Maybe they would the first day, I noted, but would the kids with enough money to buy Cokes continue day after day to line up for free ones? She thought that they would; it was just not fair, she felt, to have no standard for who should get the Cokes and who should not. Here again was the whole question of eligibility.

What is noteworthy here is that the question of eligibility, of sharing, the conflict about the ethical problems of property was the problem of the white society. When the SNCC Negro leaders in Mississippi had said to the white middle-class kids, Go back home and reform your society, they had been quite right; it was here where the problem existed. In general, the poor Negro understood the process of sharing; and it was the poor Negro who encouraged and applauded the hippies' attitude about property.

The following short essay appeared in a publication on the

Black People's Free Store in the Haight-Fillmore neighborhood. But it represents the combined wisdom of the two free stores—one catering primarily to the white flower children and the other to poor Negroes—and to me it seems a meaningful philosophy on giving and receiving for all harmless people everywhere:

SHARING & TAKING IS NATURAL[11]

"Do people take advantage of the store?" This is a question frequently asked when a free store is first encountered. The question is, do people take things they don't need, do they take more than they need, do they cheat on the store?

This is rather like asking of a businessman, "Do you have much trouble with shoplifting?" Such questions turn out to be more mirrors of the questioner's mind and attitudes than real queries about a store's operation. Taking advantage is an attitude grown from the money-and-profit culture. It is sister to such capitalistic rules of thumb as you get what you pay for. The questioner is speaking for himself, making it clear that if he were allowed to take whatever he wished from a store, free and with impunity, he would take everything he could get his hands on. With a free store, such questions become irrelevant, leftovers from the old way. When the profit motive is removed, people remain. It is a fact that some people come into the Free Store and take more than they need. . . . Some people believe that the Store is not real, that they had better get what they can while they can. Stock up, get ahead. These, too, are old ways. When a person realizes that he can always get what he needs when he needs it, that the store is not going to empty or disappear in a day or two, he usually begins bringing extra items back, feeling that other people, like himself, also need. Instead of a maze of fears about acquisition and possession, people find themselves feeling responsibility towards other people.

A free store is about people—now. Each person carries a vision of what he or she would like to be. But today—people need. It is natural to give, it is natural to take.

[11] From *Venture* (August, 1967), p. 9.

CHAPTER 9
The Juice from the Greens

It was a long road from the civil rights workers who went into Mississippi, to the Free Speech Movement in Berkeley, to the Diggers in the Haight-Ashbury, to the Black People's Free Store in the Haight-Fillmore; but beneath the surface, it was all part of the same process—a human reawakening that still throbs with promise as I write this book. The Black People's Free Store represented the completion of the circle of the journey that began on college campuses throughout the North and West and led to the South and then back to the city slums where the dispossessed people lived. In the end it was the Black People's Free Store that bloomed from the dust of the Haight-Ashbury and the lost dreams of the flower children. It is, I believe, important to tell this story, for the communication between the Haight-Ashbury and the Haight-Fillmore is the significant bond that must be tenderly and carefully forged over and over again in a thousand communities in the Republic before the society can be healed in wholeness.

What seems to me to be the key to the story here is the experience of mutual reward and exchange. In a relationship of equals, the white seekers learned and borrowed from the blacks and their subculture; and the blacks similarly found something important to adopt from the best of the white subculture.

I shall begin this story with a meeting held in the Civic Center of San Francisco on Friday, April 28, 1967, an open hearing in which the citizens of San Francisco were invited to present their attitudes about the hippies in the Haight-Ashbury to the Fire, Safety, and Police Committee of the Board of Supervisors for the City and County of San Francisco. In reality, the Board of Supervisors had called the meeting as a mere gesture, a *pro forma* indication that they had heard "all sides." Behind closed doors, the decision had already been made to do everything possible to stop the hippie movement in the Haight-Ashbury. There is some proof of this hidden decision in an event that preceded the hearing by only a few days—the abrupt dismissal of the only city official who could have at that point rescued the situation in a responsible fashion, so that the summer of 1967 in the Haight-Ashbury could have been other than a catastrophe. This public health official, Joel Fort, M.D., charged with the city's program for special problems in the use of drugs, alcohol, and so on, had been a voice crying in the wilderness of fiscal and civic irresponsibility that had constituted the official response to the influx of young people into the Haight-Ashbury.

In a deteriorating situation, whether it is police brutality in the ghetto or deliberate harassment of any particular minority group by the political establishment, one sign of the establishment's fear and its inability to cope with the situation may be found in the sudden desire for an absolutely monolithic consensus—the dissenter must be eliminated from the body politic. This rule of thumb, at least as old as Socrates, has to be constantly challenged and examined if a democracy is to survive. All too frequently, the only person with the clear-cut ability to save a deteriorating situation is put out of commission in some manner, so that the rest of the group can ride to disaster with a brief feeling of triumph and power. In the case of Joel Fort's dismissal, there was no one left in official San Francisco who had any modifying attitude toward the flower children in the Haight-Ashbury.

One public official after another arose during the course of the first part of the April 28 meeting to report on the negative results of the movement of the harmless people into the Haight-Ashbury. The head of the public health department reported on the increase of venereal disease in the Haight-Ashbury and mentioned in passing that this seemed considerably at variance with the hippies' avowed attitude toward love. Although this official should have had some sophistication about venereal disease epidemiology, he totally overlooked the fallacies in his statement. Venereal disease is not, of course, a moral problem; in fact, San Francisco, as one of the ports most used for the movement of men and supplies in and out of Vietnam, might well have had some access to new strains of venereal diseases at that time, more resistant to the then available cures. Furthermore, the rate of venereal disease is always higher among the young than the old, and the Haight-Ashbury had attracted into the city a considerable young population by then. Nor did any official mention at the meeting the fact that the newspaper published by the hippies in the Haight-Ashbury, *The Oracle,* had been carrying on a campaign of encouraging the young people to act responsibly toward each other by visiting the free venereal disease clinic in the city. Since it is generally accepted that education is an important variable in the reporting of venereal disease, it should also have been self-evident that the increase of young middle-class white people in the Haight-Ashbury would automatically increase the number of reported cases in the city.

Several city officials reported on the lack of cleanliness found in the Haight-Ashbury. One official reported on a recent survey of the area which had in fact been, he noted, disappointing in that it had not uncovered nearly as much filth as the city had apparently hoped for. Still, obviously, any further crowding of the area would make the conditions even more serious and that would be bad, several officials felt. The park official reported on conditions in the rest rooms in Golden Gate Park and noted that the city was using an unprecedented number of paper towels, soap, and other supplies; the young people used the rest rooms for bathing, he said, implying that this established a dangerous precedent. No one of the supervisors questioned him as to whether the problem might be that the city did not have any public bathhouses; nor did there seem to be any contradiction for the officials in the constantly reiterated supposition that the hippies were all dirty and the fact that they used the public rest rooms rather extensively for taking baths. The police chief gave, of course, an equally discouraging picture; shortly after this meeting, incidentally, the one police officer who had had some kind of meaningful contact with the young people in the Haight-Ashbury, a man who was in charge of community relations, left San Francisco to take a better job elsewhere; actually he had expressed in various ways the hopelessness of his task and the punitive philosophy of the Park Police Station (located in the Haight-Ashbury neighborhood). All in all, it was quite clear that the city officials had arrived at a powerful consensus that there was nothing good to be found in the young people in the Haight-Ashbury.

After the officials of the city had presented their side of the case, various members of the audience were recognized for the purpose of presenting the community's viewpoint. Some of the community, noticeably the older part of the business community in that neighborhood, spoke out against the young people. But other members of the settled part of the Haight-Ashbury community were positive toward the young people. The most notable defense of the flower children came from two members of the black community—Cecil Williams, one of the ministers at the Glide Memorial Methodist Church, and Roy Ballard, one of the members of the poor black community who had become a Digger in the Haight-Ashbury and was a leader in both the Haight-Ashbury and the Haight-Fillmore.

Throughout the winter and spring of that year, Cecil Williams had been a beacon of understanding for the Diggers and the hippies, and on that day he made an impassioned plea for the young white people in the Haight-Ashbury; he noted that they represented the soul of the white society, and that in fact the sons and daughters of the dignitaries assembled were involved in the hippie community. As he spoke, Bob Dylan's words came alive in a new way:

Come senators, congressmen, please heed the call
Don't stand in the doorway, don't block up the hall
For he that gets hurt will be he who has stalled
The battle outside raging
Will soon shake your windows and rattle your walls
For the times they are a-changin'.

Come mothers and fathers throughout the land
Then don't criticize what you can't understand

Your sons and your daughters are beyond your command
Your old road is rapidly aging
Please get out of the new one if you can't lend your hand
For the times they are a-changin'.[1]

Cecil Williams stood before the bar at the official end of the hearing room, with his back to the general audience and facing the Board of Supervisors seated at a raised table and the officials of the city ranged along the sides of the inner area. From time to time, he would turn and briefly face the general audience; and he was reprimanded for this by the chairman. The words of a black man seemed to make the white man anxious and guilty, particularly as the black man defended the white man's children. There was a turnabout involved in the scene, and it gave one a sense of a new locus for the conscience of the society.

Eventually, Roy Ballard was recognized and he, too, arose to defend the flower children. He began his presentation by asking the chairman of the Committee for permission to wear his hat during his address—a French beret of a rather nondescript color which he usually wore. He meant no disrespect to the Supervisors, he pointed out, for the hat was simply part of his religion. Roy had been a follower of Malcolm X in the Organization for Afro-American Unity, and his hat was perhaps related to that experience. But it was also related to his experience with the Diggers in the Haight-Ashbury, for as I have noted earlier, their roots were on an aware level connected with the Diggers in Cromwell's England and the phenomenon of the Quakers. The philosophy of Malcolm X and the Diggers seemed to coalesce when Roy Ballard made his request at the Board of Supervisors' meeting. After some brief and unhappy mutterings, the chairman acquiesced in Roy Ballard's request, and the black man stood before the high officials of the city with his hat on, like the Quakers of the seventeenth century.

Incidentally, there was another way in which Roy Ballard had impressed himself upon me as Quaker-like, and this requires a brief personal digression. For some time, I had subscribed to the philosophy that if a white person wishes to extract himself from the customs of a racist society in present-

[1] From Bob Dylan's "The Times They Are A-Changin'."

day America, he must be punctilious in his use of formal terms of address (Mr., Mrs., Miss, Dr., etc.) with a black person. This often delays my arriving at a mutual first-name basis even in a fairly close relationship with a black person, since for different reasons each of us is reluctant to make the initial move. Yet with Roy, I had always been comfortable on a mutual first-name basis. Of course, this was the Diggers' way, and I had first met Roy through the Diggers. But for me to be comfortable on a first-name basis with a black man from the first moment of meeting meant that I could sense his unique stature as a person—a stature that, as a child, I saw accorded to only one other person in my own family: When I was still quite young, I could identify all of my grandparents, great-grandparents, great-aunts and uncles—regardless of whether they were dead or not, or whether I had ever seen them—from their pictures in an album; and I always used their correct relationship title, with one exception. One of my great-grandmothers, whom I had never known, was always called "Sarah Haight," no title, and my mother told me that Sarah Haight preferred to be addressed that way, that even the children in the neighborhood addressed her that way when she was very old. This was explained to me by the fact that she was a Quaker and this was part of her belief; and I felt a special sense of awe when I said her name. As I grew older, I developed a respect for her sturdiness—a nineteenth-century farm woman who had felt equal to any person in the world as evidenced by her willingness to accord a real measure of social equality to a child. It was this quality that I sensed in Roy Ballard; by dint of hardship and painful development, a deprived black man in the twentieth century had arrived at much the same sturdy position as Sarah Haight.

In the course of Roy's presentation to the Board of Supervisors that afternoon, he made reference to the document that he formally presented. The document, under date of April 12, 1967, read as follows:

REQUEST

The following people [names of four people from the slums] from the Haight-Ashbury, Fillmore, Mission and Hunter's Point respectively, make the following request of our brothers and sisters who occupy the powerful coordinate points in the city government of San Francisco.

That the mayor and other properly authorized individuals give back some of the taxpayers' money in the form of a free warehouse located somewhere in the center of the city—that the free warehouse be filled with free things: fruits, vegetables, grains, dairy products, meats, and other foodstuffs—and that the foodstuffs be replenished as quickly as they are distributed.

EXPLANATION OF REQUEST

It is totally obvious on religious, philosophical, psychological, and technological grounds that such a warehouse be a reality. Technologically it is possible for machines to do at least thirty percent of the jobs now being done by people. The jobs would be done more quickly and more efficiently and the people would have more time to pursue the goals they wished. The only reason that this is not being done is the fact that the city government would not be able to support them in the present social structure. What the city needs is different social forms. That is, alternative forms. The free warehouse is an alternative form that has been proved successful on a small scale in the Haight-Ashbury. We invite the city government to support this new form.

Hundreds of pages of explanation could be written in and about the above request, but since the city government has of late been acting in bad faith, the above individuals wish to wait for some interest to be shown by the city government concerning this request before they go into further explanation.

Bad faith has been shown by the Park Department, in their demands for empty nighttime parks. Bad faith has been shown by the Police Department in their constant demanding of identity cards and in their vicious busts of people for no reason. Bad faith has been shown by the Building Department in their condemnation of houses used as free space by hundreds of people. Bad faith has been shown by the Health Department in their enforcement of restaurant and public assembly laws in places where free food is given. . . .

Early in his presentation, Roy Ballard related what was happening in the Haight-Ashbury to what was happening to the dispossessed and the poor throughout the world. I was impressed with the formality and restraint with which he spoke, for he was sometimes abrupt, direct, and sharp on other occasions; he was obviously making an effort to address the Supervisors with great respect. At one point, a member of the Board suggested to Roy that he should confine his remarks to the subject at hand—the hippies and the Haight-Ashbury and not talk about the rest of the world; and Roy Ballard, temporarily exasperated by the failure of the Board to understand the obvious connection between the hippies and the problems of poverty throughout the world, said, "I want to say to you gentlemen that unless you get off your asses . . ." His statement was cut short by the chairman, who requested the sergeant-at-arms to remove Roy Ballard from the hearing room, terming him a "communist." Several of us who were outraged by this treatment left the hearing room as Roy was escorted from it; he did not protest his removal. Outside of the hearing room, I went up to him to express my sympathy for his statement; he seemed on the verge of tears. Roy explained to me that he meant no disrespect by anything that he had said; that he had tried to be consistently polite and not to lose his temper. He felt that he had been a failure at communicating with the Supervisors and that there was much at stake in the meeting which was still going on. "Where do you live, baby?" he asked me. I gave him my upper middle-class address. "You had better get out of there before the summer comes," he told me, "the good and the bad will go together. Nobody is listening to what is happening." I realized that he was genuinely concerned for my safety in the summer months.

Contrary to Roy Ballard's prediction, there was no "rioting" in San Francisco that summer. And at the end of the summer, many parts of the community, including the San Francisco *Chronicle,* credited Roy Ballard and the Black People's Free Store as an important factor in the relatively quiet summer in the ghetto. In April the Board of Supervisors had not been able to grasp the relevancy of a free warehouse of food, but fortunately there were other people who did, notably the officials of Glide Memorial Methodist Church, and the Store was actually but a modification of the proposed warehouse as presented to the city by Roy Ballard.

I missed the rest of the statements after the ejection of Roy Ballard from the hearing room, but I subsequently obtained copies of several statements made, after I had left the meeting, by members of the audience in support of the philosophy and meaning of the flower children in the Haight-Ashbury. Yet it was Roy Ballard's statement more than any other that I heard or read that significantly connected the young people's movement to the world revolution in which we are now mortally engaged, although the Board of Supervisors had treated him as if he were a dangerous nut. That a black man with little formal education who had lived mainly in a series of ghettos should become the coherent spokesman for what was taking place represents an important coalition of experience and ideas between the Haight-Fillmore and the Haight-Ashbury.

As for the flower children in the Haight-Ashbury, nothing that was said or done by their supporters that day changed the inevitable outcome. Already the mass media had taken their story to all parts of the United States and beyond; and thousands of young people were determined to make their way to that part of the world that summer. Once the city had decided to allow police harassment, to make no plans for any kinds of hostels, not even to set up additional chemical toilets in the Park, to forbid the sleeping of young people in sleeping bags in Golden Gate Park, as they would be sleeping in national parks throughout the United States and in hostels in Western Europe—then the die was cast. For with the best will in the world, the Diggers and other leaders of the young community could not listen to all the sadness and problems of the thousands who would troop into the area that summer, to say nothing of supplying them with adequate sleeping space, blankets, bathing facilities, and food.

The outcome of the Board of Supervisors' meeting might be summarized in these words: *The Haight-Ashbury is dead; long live the Haight-Fillmore,* although certainly the Supervisors would have been shocked to think that any such outcome was possible, that the cancer of "communism" that had frightened them in the Haight-Ashbury had metastasized and would now appear in a new form in the Haight-Fillmore.

Up until this chapter I have avoided as much as possible any focus on the particular people who emerged as personalities in the Haight-Ashbury. I think that such a focus would be at actual variance with the philosophy of the founding fathers of that movement and with the conditions that existed there in the movement's heyday. There was great flexibility in the leadership function as it emerged in meetings called by Diggers and hippies, so that the leadership role changed smoothly during the course of any one meeting. Such meetings would have confrontations and dialogue, and sometimes actual tension and annoyance would be expressed—as, for instance, in the planning sessions for Happening House—but the problem of one person taking over and running a meeting or a particular venture was minimal; the community would not tolerate such a takeover. It was a society of no heroes.

Yet in talking about the Black People's Free Store, I am focusing in a different way on one person; to a very real extent this is at variance with Roy Ballard's philosophy itself, which is basically very close indeed to that of the white Diggers in the Haight-Ashbury; in essence, Roy Ballard was a black Digger and had accepted the philosophy of the non-hero. Glide has referred to Roy Ballard as the "guiding spirit" of the Black People's Free Store, in an obvious attempt not to violate the Diggers' principle.

For some time I have puzzled as to how to avoid this apparent discrepancy in my own presentation of material. I consider the non-hero philosophy a crucial contribution of the Haight-Ashbury society and one that actively affected the emergence of Eugene McCarthy in the 1968 election as a representative of the young idealistic segment of the American population. The stance of the non-hero, which I submit was partly hammered out by the Diggers in the Haight-Ashbury, is a new one in American political life, and it is bound to make radical revisions in our national scene in the next few years. The role of the non-hero clearly is built upon a working knowledge of interpersonal relations—the fact that each person is "a part of the maine" and has his own thing. The dichotomy is not between the individualistic concept of the right-winger and the so-called welfare state of the left-winger, in which individual differences and needs are supposedly met in monolithic programs. In hippie philosophy, each person has his thing and is continually in the process of rediscovering it; but he is in a moving sea of humanity in which his thing becomes a significant part of the general process.

Yet the black man, like other oppressed peoples, still has need of important role models for the emergence of his own dignity. Roy Ballard, like Malcolm X, Stokely Carmichael, H. Rap Brown, and others, became a role model for his own people and as such he required definition and separation. In a sense, he was perhaps in much the same position as Eugene McCarthy in relation to the advantaged young. McCarthy and Ballard both walked a tightrope; they had to be role models, guiding spirits, but at the same time they had to suggest the qualities of the non-hero. Since no other national political figure in our time has adopted the particular stance of Eugene McCarthy out of the need of the new generation for such a stance, then his role became sufficiently unique to evoke a mystique and a sense of unique individuality; yet McCarthy somehow managed to evade this fixed position of the unique person for the unique moment in history by hedging his expertise. When he was asked to predict how he might handle a particular situation if he were President, he usually began by saying, "Well, I don't know . . ." There was the implicit command in such a statement that there were others in his audience throughout America who would be needed to help him make up his mind; it was also the classic position of the Digger confronted with a new and critical situation in which he suggests that he has no magic formulas; at the same time, the person who begins with this kind of tack has clearly shown that he has an open mind, that he does not make snap judgments. Obviously this is the intellectual's pose; no one person is expert on *all* parts of a complex situation. *The non-hero stance allows for the correction of error and for change,* even in as complex a field as international relations. It also allows for the abrupt voluntary retirement of the non-hero, or for him to fade away. In the network of events that preceded the Haight-Ashbury movement, Mario Savio was another non-hero leader.

With that as preliminary, I should like now to focus on the Black People's Free Store and how it emerged largely through the guiding spirit of Roy Ballard, who was basically a non-hero. Its beginnings have been described as follows in a publication issued by Glide in August, 1967:[2]

In the Spring of 1967, Roy Ballard proposed to Larry Mamiya[3] that a *free store* be established in San Francisco's Fillmore ghetto. Roy had worked as a Student Nonviolent Coordinating Committee organizer in the Deep South and had become an ardent follower of Malcolm X in the Organization for Afro-American Unity. Living in the Haight-Ashbury in late 1966, he became involved with the Diggers who were soon to open a free store on Cole Street. Contrary to popular conceptions, there are deep social and political motives at work in the Haight, and Roy saw the possibility of applying Digger concepts and philosophy to the poverty and depravity of the black ghetto.

As Glide's Intern to Young Adults, Larry was in a position to seek the financial support necessary for such a project, having the potential backing of Glide Church and Urban Center. While Roy enlisted the help of other civil rights activists and people in the ghetto, Larry conveyed the excitement and importance of the idea to Ted McIlvenna and Cecil Williams at Glide. It was agreed to go ahead.

In April, then, Larry and Roy set out to locate and lease a large store-front which would become the Black People's Free Store. They discovered that most vacant, prime locations are owned by the San Francisco Redevelopment Agency and are thus unavailable. Such properties will be razed to make way for middle income housing. But at the corner of McAllister & Webster, a store was found and leased. With the necessary cleaning and repairs completed, the Black People's Free Store opened its doors in early May.

What is a free store? Its first principle is to give whatever can be obtained to those who will take. This means clothing, furniture, appliances, food. In a ghetto area where physical and emotional needs are critical, where American Opportunity is an outworn joke,

[2] *Venture* (August, 1967). I am indebted to Glide Memorial Methodist Church, to its staff, and to Roy Ballard for permission to quote freely from this material.

[3] Larry Mamiya was mentioned earlier in the newspaper story on the Christmas service at Glide; he was an intern at that time at Glide. As a Japanese-American, he seemed to have an unusual ability to relate to the two neighborhoods.

where the ravages of racism are as real as the pavement, a free store means revolution. Much more than the distribution of free goods is involved. In the case of the Black People's Free Store, the fundamental revolutionary function is to communicate *love* to fellow human beings. With love—feeling, understanding, respect, communication—people are allowed to believe in themselves, to love themselves, to *become* themselves.

Such communication happens in many ways. Each Saturday the Store prepares and serves a free meal in Malcolm X Park, Turk & Laguna Streets. Over a thousand people have attended this event, the primary function of which is to bring people together with a focus upon themselves. Creating this focus means affirming individual worth. Smaller quantities of food are given out at the store daily [the Ukrainian Bakery provides bread regularly] and the process of communication through a basic necessity is thus continued.

In another direction, a basement dark room has been installed, and volunteers are available to teach the fundamentals of photography. It is felt that the camera can become a means of profound expression for people denied almost all forms of public expression save violence. Also, Mitch the Drummaker is ready to begin instruction in the craft of drum construction. But these and other projects cannot begin until money is donated.

A one-ton truck was purchased three weeks ago, enabling the Store to pick up donated goods and to transport people into the country. Relief from the deadly oppression of ghetto living is literally life-saving. On the weekend of July 22–23, twenty-five kids and store workers camped in the Sierra Mountains. Upon returning, one youth, who had never seen the wilderness before, said the trip had been more fun than shooting up the city. Other trips are planned as money becomes available, and efforts are being made to use some of the extensive Methodist Church camp facilities later in the summer.

The Store's guiding spirit has been Roy Ballard, but he is the first to say that the people have taken over. It is their store. No one believes in the idea of *leaders,* and everyone seems to have had enough of leader-follower patterns. The Digger motto, *do your thing,* is the key to the Store, and black people are beginning to discover their thing at [the Black People's Free Store].

As reported in this account, Roy Ballard's life had some of the same progressions as the historical movement of the young white students outlined in the early part of this book. In a sense, Roy Ballard and his counterparts in SNCC had formulated the admonition to the young white civil rights workers, Go home and carry out your reforms. The Free Speech Movement, and its subsequent counterpart in colleges and universities throughout the country, had been an attempt to meet that criticism made by the black leaders in SNCC and CORE. When it became apparent that the institutions of the dominant society in this country were unable to make the necessary reforms, then the young idealistic white people had regrouped, had sought to make the reforms from within. In the meantime, Roy Ballard and other young militant Negro leaders had established their own identity and pride, moving away from the religion of Christian submission foisted on the American Negro by his oppressor; by the time of Malcolm X's death, Roy Ballard had arrived at approximately the same important insights as are incorporated in the end of Malcolm X's *Autobiography*.

When Roy Ballard moved into the Haight-Ashbury in 1966, and became a Digger, he had arrived at a new point of departure, just as the young white ex-civil rights workers had new insights and new attitudes. It was the *reciprocity of the interaction* that was the essential ingredient. In the human be-in that the world moves painfully toward, each man has his thing, and each man can teach and learn.

When Roy Ballard and other black men began the Free Store in the Haight-Fillmore, they carried in through the doors some of the lamps kindled in the Haight-Ashbury. The Fillmore Store had its meditation room, which looked for all the world like the meditation rooms that the flower children frequented; there was the intellectual conviction that religion was as broad as human beings, that it was not the property of the religious establishment.[4] The black man in the rural South, particularly under slavery, had depended on the sharing of the "juice from the greens," as Roy has put it; but the educated Diggers had given new stability to that concept, had elevated it to a working doctrine of love and human survival, with intellectual underpinnings gleaned from the world's knowledge of political and

[4] In this particular, the role of Glide Memorial Methodist Church was of course crucial, for it fostered a new role for the church in the inner city and moved sharply away from the conventions of organized religion.

social reform. The black man's contribution to the Haight-Ashbury thinking has already been presented, but again I would like to stress its basic nature, felt and experienced through the black man's words and turn-of-phrase. The challenge of the black man's language had created anew a conscience for the white man; and in the Haight-Ashbury, the black man had been given a chance to challenge the white man as an equal in the community of men. It is as if the Haight-Ashbury scene served as the common meeting ground for two co-equals to hammer out the shape of a new society, a new Utopia.

The white flower children who came to the Black People's Free Store in the Haight-Fillmore came as I did—with admiration and respect. This was in sharp contrast to the do-good-ism that had been in operation among white people earlier. Most of the young white civil rights workers who had gone into Mississippi and Alabama had gone as missionaries, carrying the proverbial white man's burden. But in the struggle at Berkeley—using Berkeley only as a particular example of an emergent struggle in American universities and colleges—and in the so-called dropping-out, or seeking-of-soul (as I prefer to call it), in the Haight-Ashbury, the young white people had learned a little of what it meant to suffer and of how little they had understood of the real plight of the oppressed. They had become outcasts, hounded by the police, witnesses to injustices and harassment. And they had often found the poor black man at their side, understanding and supporting. The middle-class society, including the black middle class, scoffed at what they termed the phony suffering of the flower children, pointing out that the hippies were not in the same boat as the ghetto Negro, who could not simply shave, clean up, and go out and get a job, as the hippies could always do. But the ghetto Negro who was in touch with the Haight-Ashbury knew that he had a new and powerful ally in supporting his charge of police brutality, for instance, that white flesh had felt the billy club and knew injustices in a way that only the inarticulate and powerless had known before. In general, there was a sympathy for the flower children among the oppressed, including the Japanese-Americans in San Francisco, who had themselves memories of concentration camps and injustices perpetrated in this instance by the federal government. The oppressed seem to understand that a Leo Tolstoy can never indeed put himself realistically in the peasant's shoes *but it is notable that he tried.*

While the white flower children in the Haight-Ashbury constituted a continuing threat to the materialistic values of the middle-class society and this was the real hang-up, as I have noted, it was the black people who made the major attack on these values and trained the white flower children in a hydra-like attack on the hang-up. For a very long time, the black people in America had had a chance to observe the reluctance of white middle-class people to give up their hold on the material possessions and the wherewithal to acquire more and more of these same possessions. Before the advent of the hippies, there was no group in white America with whom the poor Negro could share this insight into the real hang-up; certainly the dispossessed white man had insufficient self-respect to examine with the poor Negro their common plight, although that is to a limited extent now changing. And the middle-class person plowing along toward upper middle-class-dom, regardless of color of skin, had no interest in examining his flimsy moral position. But the white flower children were ready and willing to learn. The black man encouraged their students by a series of skilled devices to become aware of the way in which the central society had brainwashed them. He joked, he used invective, he challenged, he demanded a sharing of possessions. An illustration of this device is described in Glide's publication, *Venture,* under the heading "Don't Nod!"

Eight representatives of San Francisco-Bay Area foundations recently met with a group of men from the Black People's Free Store. The meeting was held in the Store's basement Meditation Room. Cushions are scattered on the cold cement floor, people lean against the brick walls. A psychedelic light-sculpture flashes changing colors, and the air is tense, heated. One of the black men, Mitch, has been arguing with the foundation people, among whom is Glide's Lewis Durham. The purpose of the meeting has been to familiarize the foundations with the Free Store program and to engage their support. Subjects at hand are black liberation, white liberalism, the problems of operating a free store, the philosophy of giving. Suddenly Mitch looks at Durham and commands: "Give me your watch, man!" Durham nods in agreement, understanding the point —property is things, people are human beings with immediate wants and needs; black people are owed these by white America. But Mitch continues: "No man, don't nod! Give me your watch!"[5]

With most of us, the challenge is too great. Like Tolstoy's wife, we understandably balk at the ultimate challenge to property; she felt that the royalties from his books should be held in a private account for the children, and this is an understandable position for a woman who had so unstintingly and anonymously worked to further her husband's success. But the challenge remains. It is notable that Martin Luther King is as far as I know the only American winner to give away all his Nobel prize money.

I had several experiences with this challenge from both the Diggers and the people in the Black People's Free Store, some of which I have already recounted. When I was moving away from San Francisco, some of the people from the Black People's Free Store came to my apartment to haul away some of the household goods that we were disposing of. One of the items was a well-worn rug. There was another rug, in good condition, on the living room floor. One of the representatives from the Free Store looked at the good rug and said, "What about this rug?" "No," I said, "we will take that with us." I did not realize until afterwards that I had been tested and failed. For I had had a chance to see their commune where they fed each evening a succession of poor people, tiding them over one day at a time, giving them a warm meal, a clean and comfortable setting for one evening, in the hope that the next day would be better. I wonder sometimes how many people would have sat on that rug by now, for there were not enough chairs to go round; and I know full well that it would be worn and enjoyed in a thousand ways beyond my knowing.

A conversation once took place in the Black People's Free Store that embodied the qualities of many conversations that

[5] From *Venture* (August, 1967), p. 3.

took place in the Haight-Ashbury throughout my encounter there—the constant seeking, the expressions of despair and hope, the full awareness of the violence in the society and the counter feelings of violence in the hippies and in the poor black man, and the hope for some way out other than counter-violence. But this conversation took place in the ghetto and many of the participants had little formal education. It was reported and published by Glide in *Venture;* more than any other document that I have seen it suggests the nature of the liaison between the white flower children and the poor black community, especially as it focused on the real hang-up.

[Reporter from] *Venture:* Who has been giving the store the goods being distributed?

Roy: So far it's been mostly white people, but we have people from the community here bringing things in on their own. But first of all, white people are the only ones who have got it. There's no one else that has it. You have the black bourgeoisie, but brother, they're not going to give it up and you know that. We know that there are liberal whites that'll give it, because they recognize that they owe it to black people.

Venture: What do you mean by *owe?*

Older man: The average girl of my time—and I'm in my fifties—could have an education, where the fellas had to get out and go to work because there wasn't no relief at that time. You had to work, you had to forget about an education. You had to get out there and dig ditches, make your living. Now how in the world you going to explain education with digging ditches? You can't read a book and dig a ditch at the same time. Their intention is to keep you low. Mop the floor and all. Then when you get as old as I am, then you go down and apply for some job and they say, "You got an education?" Where was I going to get an education when I was out there digging ditches? Here I'm about ready for old-age pension, you want to tell me to go to school for ten years?

Young man: White people ask, "Why should you get anything free?" That's the reason!

Arthur: I'm sick and tired of talking—I'm ready to do, regardless of whatever it costs. I'll pay the biggest penalty I got which is my life! That's where I'm at.

Young man: That's the way I feel myself. If my kids are going to be killed, I'd rather kill them myself than have them come up under something like this. Living as a fifth of a man. You know, jobs where you have to bend over and cop-out. It's the same with white collar jobs on Market St. They're copping out too. It doesn't matter what level, you're copping out on yourself. I'm teaching kids from nine to fifteen how to fire weapons. It's nothing but a suicidal matter, I know this. But it's a suicidal matter to be black!

Roy: Black people have always been castrated. We're being castrated in the jails, in Vietnam, on the damn street! You name it, we get the short end of the stick. Even the Mexican-Americans, who I consider equally poor with blacks, even that cat is two or three steps higher than I am. Therefore, the only thing we can do is ask for what's due us. We have to take it the best way we can.

Young man: Either we're going to get total peace and recognition and respect or else we're going to have to go down and die!

Roy: Our thing in the store is not the black and white issue—we're far from that. Here in the store we welcome everybody. The only way we're going to bring about change is people communicating. Once a person closes his mind, that's it. Things become one-sided. Brother, I'm going to have to keep my mind open! This store is bringing about a hellava lot of wisdom. It's helping a lot of young ones on the street who are coming in here. And it's opening their minds to where it's really at. That's our whole thing here in this store. Opening minds—to share, to make understanding, to feel for each other.

What I'm thinking is what would happen if black people could disaffiliate from money altogether. Black people by nature were born to understand each other and to share with each other. They did this even in slavery time when they was sharing the juice from the greens. They were sincere about each other. In Louisiana that's still the way it is. When I came up here to California, hell! I was surprised. I met some of the very same people I went to school with, but they acted like they didn't know me. I said, "Hey, buddy, don't you know me? I know you. Aren't you so and so?" "Ya, I'm in a hurry right now, I gotta go." But down in the South everybody shares with each other, because down South everybody's so poor they say that's the only way we can live.

Arthur: Let's face it, people say it takes money to live. If you look at money itself it's the money that causes confusion, man. Those that got want more, those that don't have want whatever they can get.

Older man: When I first heard about the store, I thought it was a whole lot of bull. I'll come truthfully out and say it. When I come here and pick up something, I walked out and nobody said nothing and I got to wondering is this true. Because it sounds so funny, walking in and getting something you need, and it didn't cost you nothing. And I really needed it. So I started telling my other friends about it. I brought different people here. A pregnant girl, she came down and got some baby clothes because she knows that Welfare won't help her get those clothes.

Roy: What I'm saying is that this whole store centers around this basic reality of understanding and sharing with each other. And you'll notice that there's a whole lot of black people from the community who know where it's at. They're not digging this stuff about black people—black people gotta do this, we gotta do that. No! None of that stuff! We're people from the black community who feel the poorness, who feel the poorness of being knocked down and slapped down every time we turn around. The whole store is a center of bringing about that kind of communication of understanding and sharing with each other.

Older man: In my apartment building I got an ironing board one day. I come over here and left it. Boy, I didn't even get out of the store before a woman comes in and takes the ironing board. She needed it!

Roy: Somebody said, "How long that ironing board gonna be here?" I said, "You just stand there and see how long." It wasn't hardly two minutes before that woman walks in and says, "Do you know where I can get an ironing board?" "There's one right there." She said, "Here's a dollar." But no! We don't accept no money here.

Older man: She just picked it up and ran out the door, afraid he might change his mind.

Older woman: A white lady came in one time, do you remember her? She needed things. I said, "Here, lady, you can wear these. Take them." We don't make any exceptions because of color. When the whites come in here we help them. Poor is poor.

Arthur: We got twenty keys out in the community. Many people have them. We have several prostitutes that stand out on the corner. They have a key too. Our whole basis is not only to be giving things away free, but trust and charity and truth. It's really getting down to it. A question was asked, "How do you know that people need these things they're taking?" Well, it's like this. People come in and take things. It's all free. Now, they have to suffer with their own conscience, because my conscience is clear. I know I let them get it. Now if they go do something else with it, that's them.

Roy: We got a number of people that come in and pick up clothes and sell them. We don't worry about that. But maybe that guy got to sell those clothes because he got two or three kids at home and he can't work. Maybe the guy's selling clothes because he wants to have some extra money in his pocket. We're not concerned about that. We got four or five cats that come over here and sit every day and take out two or three boxes of clothes. Good clothes. And we know that they're selling them. But at least that cat is not walking down the street to Littleman's Market, taking all the meat from the counter and then going to jail for four or five years.

Arthur: He ain't standing around no dark alleyway waiting for nobody to come by and knock him on the head.

Older man: Others pick up things because they have friends that are shame-faced and won't come into the store. I do quite a bit of that delivery. And I know girls who are ashamed to come in. They want it. On their own, they don't got the nerve to come in.

Roy: They're afraid to get caught. And when I say *afraid to get caught,* I'm talking about *caught* in the sense of getting caught in what's really happening in this store—brotherhood and communication and the whole bit. Because once you walk into this store and really start talking to the people, you finally get caught and you start coming every day. Before you know it, you come here every day.

Arthur: When Roy and them was first getting ready to open up, Roy walks up to me and says, "Hey, baby, I need you." I said okay. And I was working then on an eight hour job. I went down to pick up my check in the personnel office. Been here ever since.

Venture: What are some of the other ways you're communicating with the people?

Roy: We got some alcoholics. One man, we call him Pops—when he came in here, that man couldn't walk. People who knew that cat used to watch him drink down ten or fifteen bottles of wine every day. He walked in that door, sat down, heard what was going on. He was swollen up, could just barely move. You look at Pops now, Jack, Pops is down there poppin' his fingers. And done cut alcohol a-loose.

Arthur: He was sitting around telling me: "You know one thing, little brother, I used to be lonely. I'd sit up in my room, look at them four walls, and I didn't have no place to go. Since you came and opened up this store, I ain't lonely no more. I know where I can come, and I can enjoy myself when I get there." This, right here means more to me than all the money in the world. To hear him say this and know and see him standing up on his own. 'Cause I'm not doing it, he's doing it. All we done was just open up his mind and say, "You can do it, baby! It's not impossible. You're a man!"

Roy: We got little radio speakers outside the store. One night we were standing outside, playing around with each other. And the prostitutes are usually standing out there. They said, "How come you don't have no music out here for us?" Next day we had a speaker out there. And all the other prostitutes are beginning to come here. One by one, they're peeking in, coming in. We got hot coffee for them at night, any food that's here they eat. They even buy food for us—which is unusual. Prostitutes don't get up off any money, Jack, they take that money to their man. But these prostitutes get up off their money, Jack, so we can buy food for these people in here and them too.

Older man: Roy, I want to ask you one question. What makes a lot of prostitutes? Because they can't get the money they need to get the clothes and furniture that they need? You're cutting it down because the store's giving things free.

Roy: Right. You see, brother, first of all a prostitute becomes a prostitute because she fears the man who put her out there. That's the way he runs his game. To me, a pimp is nothing but another white man. A slavedriver. Driving those black sisters out there who are selling themselves. When you start cleaning it up, you got to start from the pimp on up. We got six women so far that wants to cut it a-loose, but they are scared of those men.

Arthur: I take and stand back sometimes, walking up and down Fillmore. I stand back and look at that pimp. Just like I'm saying, "O yes, baby, my time's gonna come when I blow out your brains too!"

Roy: And we got alcoholics coming here. They kept saying, "Man, we get tired of drinking on the corner." I said, "Look, man, there's room right there for you to come and sit, play cards or drink your wine—whatever you want to do, there's the place to do it." Now we got a whole bunch of alcoholics that come in, lie down there and do their thing. There's never been anything like this in the district before. Sometimes they get too drunk and can't go home —and fall asleep right there. And they feel free. We had one guy who fell in here and had $150 on him. When I looked up he was down on the couch. When he woke up, the first thing he looked for his wallet. He started counting the money about 3 A.M. He counted it out and said, "All my money's here! Where am I?" I said, "You're in the Black People's Free Store." "You mean nobody's gonna take my money?" "Hey, brother, we don't do no stealing in here. Whenever you walk in these doors here, Jack, you're protected, you're safe." That cat put his wallet in his pocket and laid right back down and went to sleep. Didn't wake up till morning. Got up and bought something like four dozen eggs, some bread and sausage. He said he never in his life been in a place where he could just lay down and feel like home. When you're at home, you know you can be at ease, nobody's going to take nothing.

We gave another man a refrigerator. He came in the store and said, "This here is a free store? You must be kidding. I want that refrigerator." We said, "You can have it." "I want the stove." "You can have it." "I want a couch." "You can have it too." He was playing, you understand. He went back home, got his wife, brought a truck. We helped load the stuff on. The man was crying at the same time and he tried to give us twenty dollars. We said, "No man, we don't want no money." That man cried more and more and went down and got a case of beer. He said, "I just got to get you something. I don't feel right. I got to get you something."

Arthur: Not only that, but Saturday night we got some teenagers who got [busted]. A couple of policemen stopped them and they came over here to the store and asked us to help them out. We said to the police, "Hey, man, any other young fellas that you see drunk or whatever, bring them here. Don't take them downtown." They said okay. Later on that morning, the police brought a couple of prostitutes by and dropped them off and walked them to the door and said, "We brought them home."

As I see it, what we're doing now is getting people back to basic realities and showing that there is still love and sincerity for our own. After the civil war they took the chains off our arms and legs. Sure we were free, but they put chains around our minds. Now the chains are breaking loose from our minds. That's what scares them, because we're thinking for ourselves and not letting somebody else do our thinking. . . .[6]

[6] From *Venture* (August, 1967), pp. 4–8.

CHAPTER 10
Loneliness

All the lonely people
Where do they all come from?
All the lonely people
Where do they all belong?

—*from "Eleanor Rigby" by John Lennon and Paul McCartney*

And when I touch you I feel happy inside

—*from "I Want To Hold Your Hand" by John Lennon and Paul McCartney*

In the city, even poor black people who knew something about community and sharing sometimes got caught in pockets of loneliness and isolation. So it was that both the GROUP and the Black People's Free Store acted to revive the neighborliness that had been so much a part of actual survival in the rural South particularly. In the Haight-Ashbury, loneliness was even more pervasive, and messages of loneliness crowded the bulletin boards in every gathering place for the young. Some of the messages sounded so vulnerable that I often felt concern for a person's safety; but over time I felt more relaxed about them, sensing that the request for companionship was far safer than the isolation that the young too often experience. I once voiced my feeling that loneliness was the main theme on the bulletin boards to the medical student mentioned earlier. "I don't call it that," he chided me, "I call it outstretched hands." His correction was subtle and precise: the request for friendliness as a cure for loneliness was a mark of the neighborhood. Being lonely was not something to be hidden—everyone was at one time or another; and the messages reflected all levels of education and life condition.

A good many messages were from young people who had had to leave the neighborhood for some reason and who wanted someone, anyone, to write to them. Occasionally, there would be a letter from Vietnam:

Hi there,

You may not remember me, but I remember thee. Well I used to hang out there before coming to Viet Nam. I tried to dodge Uncle Sam but he got me anyway.

If they're any swinging chicks who'd love to hear from one of the old fellows have them drop me a couple of lines. I'd appreciate it. I'm sending souveniocs and Vietnamese housecoats or a dress to all whom write and man it's the groovest silks in the world.

I was known there by Tommy. I was a regularly customer there. I only wished I was there now. To swing a expresso mug.

Yours truly,
Steven ———

Another letter might be from a runaway girl who had gone back home under some duress from parents or authorities; I would guess that the following letter describes such a situation:

Give sunshine give some love to someone alone. Write to [name and address]. She will be ecstatic to hear from the hip population as she just recently moved from S.F. and she is having difficulty making the adjustment to "straight" life in [Maryland].

Each message had its own poignancy, so that I still find myself wondering what a given message meant and how things turned out. Often there was a clear expression of the need for sexual companionship, usually accompanied by a statement of intellectual and artistic interests. The request for unusual sexual experience was a rarity on the bulletin boards, although of course the underground newspapers then and later often carried such messages.

However one defines it, the avenues for dealing with what I have called loneliness were effective and contagious among the young people. Strangers talked with each other in comfort, and after a few moments' conversation on the sidewalk might decide to move in with each other. A newcomer to the neighborhood in search of a particular address would be surrounded within a few minutes by a small cluster of people with information; the newcomer could be of any age, size, or complexion. Sometimes an older person would be confused by the attention and be dubious of the intent, but it was a sincere and earnest desire to enter into the neighborhood spirit.

In part, the freedom to express loneliness stemmed from the increased sexual freedom in the young community; and this in turn was clearly related to the sexual revolution taking place on college campuses throughout America, with the availability of "the pill." To oversimplify a very complicated process, companionship and intimacy could be achieved with or without sex, because sexual needs were more openly expressed and directly met. As a result, intimacy blossomed in new and rewarding ways; and the expression of loneliness was not an expression of vulnerability or an invitation to a premature and possibly unhappy sexual experience.

The same medical student reported an example of this kind of intimate expression. Sitting in a coffee shop in the Haight-Ashbury, he became engaged in conversation with a young girl, the mother of a six-month-old baby. "In the course of the conversation I told her my wife was pregnant—something few of our closest friends knew. . . . She suggested that she has some boy-baby type clothes that we could have that her son has outgrown, and one of her girl friends has some girl-baby clothes that we could have, so we would be covered in any case. I thanked her, saying that my wife was planning to sew some, but that she might tire of that scene, and that I would tell her of the offer. . . ." Later on, the student commented on the definition of sex in hippie culture: "Sexual relations are explicit in their sexuality, a fact which relieves other interactions of the stress of possible, surmised or imagined sexuality. The talk with the young mother, for instance, had no sexual overtones. [Later] I had a similar conversation with another young woman with equal freedom from any sexual content. Offer of help to a fellow by a gal has no sexual content—it is merely a person-to-person content." The expression "freedom from any sexual content" is an interesting one, coming from a person who appeared to have a rather relaxed attitude about sex. He is referring, of course, to a separation of intimacy from sex in such a way that one could be less lonely and could express needs for companionship in a more open way. This ability to separate out the need for intimacy has several profound implications in relation to the problems of adolescence as they have existed in the general society and to the changes taking place in the Haight-Ashbury society.

Part of the redefinition of loneliness that took place in the Haight-Ashbury stemmed from the young people's almost deliberate fostering of touch or *contact with the living,* as Sullivan has formulated it. This term implies that there is need for the touch of warm living things that appears early in life and is transmuted as life progresses into the need for tenderness and approbation, finally merging in the maturing person into the specialized need for sexual-touch-with-tenderness, unless there is some malevolent curtailment of the developing person.[1] In the Haight-Ashbury experimental period, the young touched the living—other young people, adults, children, and animals—and quite simply enjoyed it; they managed to make of touch an innocent act again, as perhaps it has not been since the Garden of Eden. By extension, they even began to make innocent the much more specialized need for sexual-touch-with-tenderness, which in our sex-ridden society is a major task.

In its most elemental form, this need for contact with the living is found in a favorite nursery verse of my generation, the lines of which came back into my head repeatedly as I wandered around in the Haight-Ashbury. In the first part of this poem, the father is telling his "little one" about a stormy night when he was lost on the "lonely mountain":

I crept along in the darkness,
Stunned, and bruised, and blinded,—
Crept to a fir with thick-set boughs,
And a sheltering rock behind it.

[1] Harry Stack Sullivan, *The Interpersonal Theory of Psychiatry* (New York: Norton, 1953), pp. 290–291.

There, from the blowing and raining,
Crouching, I sought to hide me:
Something rustled, two green eyes shone,
And a wolf lay down beside me.

Little one, be not frightened;
I and the wolf together,
Side by side, through the long, long night,
Hid from the awful weather.

His wet fur pressed against me;
Each of us warmed the other;
Each of us felt, in the stormy dark,
That beast and man was brother.[2]

One of my earliest memories is of the comforting feeling I had when this verse was read to me; other people of my generation remember this poem from their own childhood in much the same way. Even if one is caught in a storm, far from human beings, there are the animals of the forest, alive and warm, equally frightened of the elements.

In the gathering storm of possible total destruction and dehumanization in the mid-sixties, the young sought out the simple and uncomplicated touch of the living of whatever species. In particular, the young people in the Haight-Ashbury expressed a need to caress and touch young children regardless of whether they knew the children or whether the children were accompanied by adults. In the beginning, this interest in children on the part of young men was very suspect by the community. The police had a number of complaints from parents of schoolchildren in the neighborhood who feared that the young bearded men carrying flowers were really sex maniacs, trying to ensnare eight- and nine-year-olds on their way home from school. By now, most of urban America has had enough experience with the hippies that the sight of a long-haired man with beads and flowers stroking the head of a small child does not seem automatically dangerous. Nor does the sight of two young bearded men embracing each other when they unexpectedly meet on the street seem necessarily odd, particularly if

[2] Bayard Taylor's "A Story for a Child," in Burton E. Stevenson, *The Home Book of Verse* (New York: Henry Holt, 1926), p. 175.

one of them has obviously just arrived in town. But at the time of which I write, the cultural shock of such sights to middle-class Americans, including myself, was considerably greater than we perhaps want to remember now.

In white middle-class America of my generation, touch in public between two people was circumscribed and brief, except for very specialized situations. Babies and young children could be held and affectionately touched, as long as the parents gave permission. Two young people of differing sexes and near or after the age of consent could publicly engage in touch of some duration, but there were rules as to time, place, and nature; this indulgence did not extend to couples past a certain age, who were considered silly if they showed in public other than brief affectional gestures. Women could embrace publicly with impunity, but even this embrace should be brief and defined. In general, boys and men could not embrace in public, except under extraordinary circumstances and then only fleetingly. Indeed, preadolescent boys often became self-conscious about any public embraces from their peers and certainly from adults, including parents; yet a man or boy could pat and fondle a male dog with no self-consciousness. A young girl bordering on adolescence could not even hold hands with a boy publicly unless she were brave enough to risk public disapproval and censure; for the young girl, particularly, guilt and fear were associated with an affectional gesture from a boy.

Some time in the 1960's there seems to have been a genuine revolution in the rules for touch among the young who were white and middle class. I associate the time of this change with the appearance of the Beatles in this country and the speed with which their song "I Want To Hold Your Hand" swept through the ranks of the young, particularly young girls. The Beatles neither anticipate nor follow the young, but they are tuned in to what is happening. I take this date because shortly before this time I experienced a number of instances in which touch was made a problem for adolescents, by the adults around them. While this experience took place in a mental hospital program for adolescents, what happened there was a general reflection, somewhat exaggerated, of cultural attitudes in vogue at the time.

For eighteen months, beginning in 1959, I observed about forty adolescent patients intensively as they lived on six different wards with patients of all ages, in a 150-bed research and training mental hospital in a large city on the East Coast; I shall call the hospital Southside. In general, the hospital staff at all levels, most of whom were considerably younger than I, placed a sexual interpretation on any touching between adolescent patients and were fearful of it. Many of the adult patients had the same concerns and fears as staff about the younger patients. The staff was oriented toward classical psychoanalytic thinking about sex, and touch patterns between patients were often used as ominous indicators of a patient's permanent sexual adjustment. If the patient spent a lot of time alone, then he might be rather permanently narcissistic, and the prognosis was poor. If he sought out the company of a person of his own sex and made any body contact at all, then he was probably a confirmed homosexual. Or if he became overly interested in a patient of the other sex, he was perhaps a character disorder, acting out his impulses in such a way that he might reflect discredit on the hospital.

In one particular instance, I found that a sixteen-year-old patient, Maria, alert and attractive, and in good contact most of the time, had aroused fears in one staff member or another that spanned all the possible interpretations. A nursing supervisor had seen Maria holding hands with a young male patient in the main lobby of the hospital, and she recommended to ward staff that the patient be restricted to the ward; previously Maria had been considered well enough to be "off restrictions" and had moved freely about this relatively open hospital during the day. Later in a ward meeting, a psychiatric resident reported that Maria seemed to be developing alarming homosexual interests in another young girl on the ward; they had been seen dancing together in the day room. And one morning the nurses' notes relayed the information to staff that Maria must attend hospital school that day, even if she appeared to be ill; there was reason to believe, the note said, that she had not been really sick the day before, but that she had stayed away from school and in bed in order to masturbate. Needless to say, Maria could not be tolerated long in a relatively open hospital, once staff anxieties had coalesced on her in such a way as to deny her the touch of all living creatures, including specialized touch of herself; she was shortly transferred to another hospital where she could be supervised more carefully, although her presenting symptoms were not severe. While Maria's pattern of touch was within normal limits for the outside world at that time, she was under the careful scrutiny of many people with clinical concern in the hospital; in this way, there was a coalescence of adult fears, activated by the hospital's responsibility and the definition of the patient as having something wrong with her. But well-educated friends of mine have occasionally voiced one or another of these fears to me about their apparently well-adjusted adolescent children.

Two other young girls at Southside confided in me that they wished that they had been born animals, because everybody seemed to love animals regardless of what they did. One of these girls, Elinor, explained to me one day that she wore a pair of white gloves to bed each night because it was fun to pretend she was a cat. The charge nurse at night, who was incidentally Asian in origin, felt that Elinor wore the gloves to keep from touching herself when she masturbated, but that particular nurse was not disturbed by this behavior, and as far as I know never charted it nor reported it except to me. The day staff were considerably more concerned about Elinor's touch behavior. She was discouraged from staying away from school because of their fear that she would find the opportunity to masturbate. The clean gloves that she washed each day were regarded as a phobic illness, but I never heard them discussed by day staff as related to her masturbation and her fantasy. One day Elinor confided in the head nurse that she liked one of her schoolteachers so much that she was afraid she would touch her; and the head nurse suggested that she knit a shawl for this teacher and give it to her so that in this way she could express her feeling in an acceptable way; the shawl would "touch the teacher for Elinor." This suggestion was heralded by senior staff as a good way of handling the "impulse."

During the first year of my study, I began to go on the wards one evening each week, since in any institution this is the lonely time of the day and the atmosphere is quite different. Any significant visiting that I did took place in the girls' rooms or wards, or in the day room on each service, since I did not feel comfortable going into the private areas for boys or men when they might have already begun to undress for the night. Usually I had already seen the girls at some time earlier in the day; but the evening encounter had a different flavor. The girls were quite explicit in being glad to see me. I would visit them one at a time, stopping by a bedside or seeking one of them out in the day room and sitting beside her for a few minutes. They were wistful and seemed to cast me in a maternal role. This visiting seemed my most important contact with them. I found myself shortly making some slight physical gesture of a maternal nature toward them upon leaving. I kept the gesture minimal and casual, but I did not attempt to restrain myself from making it; within the heavily charged interpretative atmosphere of Southside, this kind of expression required some measure of courage. If a patient had already gone to bed—and many of them went to bed early in a kind of withdrawal—I might catch hold of her foot and shake it gently as I left, or rub her head gently, or press her arm. I finally became aware of what I was thinking when I made the gesture: "Look, not all touch will kill you; touch is not evil; touch can be friendly." There were some interesting confirmations of the significance of this kind of interchange. For instance, shortly before one patient, Dorie, was discharged from Southside, she was able one day over a game of cribbage to tell me that she was frightened of her feelings for some women, like me, the schoolteachers, and so on. I assured her that all teenagers got crushes on older women, that I had had such feelings for my teachers at her age, that these feelings would change and develop in the same way that all of life was a change and development, and that it was nothing to worry about. She went on to tell me that she had discussed this with her doctor, who was male, and that he had told her, too, that it was nothing to be afraid of. "But you're *really* not afraid," she told me with wonderment, "you're not afraid to touch people." This was a rather amazing communication for this shy, withdrawn girl, and I felt that my actually touching her had been of some use. One staff member reported to me on the therapeutic meaning of casual touch to young patients.

By contrast with Southside Hospital, physical touch in the Haight-Ashbury was easy and natural, and it was used extensively by the young people, already acculturated to the new Utopia, to calm the disturbed in public places, to reassure the frightened, to greet the newcomer. A young man, newly arrived from some distant part of the United States, would meet a group of friends originally from the same town; and they would pause on the street and embrace, warmly and casually, as people, with no distinction made between the sex of the individual members of the group. In fact, from a distance of a few feet, it was, of course, sometimes difficult to identify the sex of a given person, since levis and long hair were fairly commonly worn by both sexes during the daytime.

In a number of public places, I have seen young people move swiftly and efficiently to calm a person who had become upset; this care usually included some form of physical reassurance. Sometimes an old wino would wander into a gathering in the Haight-Ashbury and be disruptive; or a young black man obviously disoriented with drugs or alcohol might become wildly angry at some remark by a white man in a restaurant in the neighborhood, for instance. The costumed ones would move in quietly, as if on cue, speak softly and touch the disturbed person in some way, so that magically the scene would be over. A trainee attached to the program with which I was affiliated and doing some work in the Haight-Ashbury gave me an excellent example of this kind of intervention:

I went to a meeting one night at *The Oracle* office. This was a lecture by the high priest of the Zoroastrian Church. There were about 100–150 inhabitants of the area there, and one man from the south of Market. He was between fifty-five and sixty, in rags, and obviously very drunk on alcohol, very obnoxious and disrupting the meeting. At first they tried to ignore him but this didn't work, and finally a group of girls took him over into the corner and laid him down and began stroking his head and calmed him down; and he went to sleep.

One evening I stood and talked to a young woman in the doorway of the Print Mint, where a meeting was going on. She and I had both been at the meeting earlier, but she had left because her young infant, in a rickety baby carriage, had begun to cry. It was her first evening out since the baby's birth; and most of the people entering and leaving the meeting, as was usual in gatherings for seekers, stopped and greeted her. She told me something of her situation, and part of it gradually emerged from the brief interchanges between her and the people greeting her. The baby's father was in Vietnam, and I gathered that they were not legally married. She had wanted the baby and had refused to give it up for adoption, as the social worker at the hospital had wanted her to do; but she worried about the baby some, she told me, and she wondered sometimes whether she had done the right thing. Almost each one of the people who stopped to speak to her touched her or the baby's garments, unobtrusively and gently. Several people, in the brief period that I stood beside her, offered her food and shelter if things worked out poorly where she and the baby were staying. One young man gave her a sip of his drink from a paper cup as he greeted her. In the course of my periodic conversation with her, I discovered that she had never finished high school, had come from a small town in the Midwest, that her mother had died when she was very little, and so on. Some of the people who stopped and greeted her were well-known leaders in the new community, with considerable intellectual sophistication. I could almost feel her dignity and sense of worth grow as I stood and watched this stream of tender humanity flow by her. She seemed of a piece with most of the young women who had been labeled patients at Southside, and I found myself wondering then, as many times later, whether the patients at Southside might not have fared better in the Haight-Ashbury.

Several times when I saw some young girl, gauche with acne and gracelessly fat, touched casually and treated affectionately by a young man in the Psychedelic Shop, I felt close to tears. Slowly, as I have noted before, I became aware of the number of handicapped people who moved with dignity and naturalness through the streets, so that again and again I had the vision of another kind of world in which it was acceptable to touch with tenderness the bird-fallen-from-the-sheltering-nest of whatever species. As I thought back to my own childhood, I remembered the curious hardness with which a small child in my own family had been questioned repeatedly on street cars and in public places on the nature and manner of acquiring an obvious handicap—wondering even then why the little hurt animal on the farm was treated with greater naturalness and gentleness than a child of the human species.

Again, as with other values in the Haight-Ashbury, I felt the influence of the black people in effecting this radical change in the patterns of touch among the advantaged young. From casual observation of black children playing at recess in a schoolyard in Washington, D.C., as I write this book, I would suggest that a good deal of affectionate touching goes on between black schoolchildren that is not as apparent to me in the pattern of touch between white schoolchildren. Within my own ken, I can report that I felt remarkably lacking in self-consciousness when one of my new friends in the Black People's Free Store would sometimes greet me with a hug when I visited there; he greeted all of his soulmates of whatever sex or color that way, but it was clearly reserved for a particular moment of genuine feeling. Over the years, I have found that black friends of mine are able to be spontaneous in expressing their affection for me through physical contact and that I can respond in kind, although I have not always been demonstrative in other than the ways prescribed for my generation.

Neighborliness as a cure for loneliness, however expressed, was in serious competition with the formal procedures of psychiatry in the Haight-Ashbury. By mid-century, psychiatry was society's technical solution for problems of isolation and anomie in middle-class America. But the young advantaged seekers had developed a feeling of distrust for psychiatry; although the distrust came from a somewhat different direction, it was akin to the poor black man's fear of the mental hospital.

One key to the young seekers' distrust of psychiatry and the mental hospital could be found in their devotion to Ken Kesey's book *One Flew Over the Cuckoo's Nest.* He and his book and his gaily decorated station wagon were all familiar sights in the neighborhood. I once found a well-worn copy of his book in a rest room in the Panhandle, marked "Take it. It's good." It was an all too reliable account of what might and did go on in the state hospital system of California or in other states in the Republic—"the shame of the states," as Albert Deutsch called it.

Some of the seekers talked of their own encounters with the mental hospital or with a mental health clinic when they were children; many of them had parents who had spent some time on the analytic couch. They were sophisticated about the failure of psychiatry and psychoanalysis in a way that left me raw and miserable, realizing that I was still affiliated with two mental hospital establishments; and knowing full well that on the wards of any mental hospital the hapless patient could still be caught in the toils of officialdom and struggle helplessly with non-personal cruelty.

The black people had another kind of experience with the mental hospital, knowing that for most of them it was the end of the road; that once a family member had been transferred from the city hospital to one of the state hospitals at some distance from San Francisco, he or she practically never came back. Trips to see the patient were costly of time and money, and there was never an abundance of both at the same time in the ghetto. For poor black people, the idea of taking a relative back home for a period of recuperation posed a financial burden of insupportable dimensions; each day had its own burden of counting whether or not there were enough chicken necks and slices of bread to go round and did not allow for a non-paying adult guest who might stay in that position for years. And so the patient rotted in the hospital, all too often for years, while the social worker lamented the lack of interest that the family took—"No family member has visited her for three years and there seems to be no interest in Mattie," the record might read. But the family, lost in the jungle of the city, defined the patient as "mental," sadly and despairingly, as if she were already dead; once one had gone mental, all hope was abandoned in the ghetto.

Yet, from a variety of directions, the young advantaged seekers and the black people in the ghetto had some human consensus about the dimensions of a truly preventive psychiatry. The young seekers balanced their distrust of most of the professional workers in the field with their sophisticated knowledge of the insights of the discipline. And these insights were reinforced by their beginning awareness of the way in which black people had through the wisdom of experience arrived at a pattern for survival in a hostile land. Without benefit of any explicit knowledge of the formal tenets of psychiatry, the black people in the rural South had over the centuries of oppression arrived at certain insights that supported, negated, refined, and helped to make American some of the more sterile formulations of psychiatry that had depended too long in America on translations, literally and figuratively, from the German. Thus the black man from rural America had celebrated life for some time and had usually defined a baby as good in much the same way as Bronson Alcott did; despair and oppression were transmuted and dignified by song into the experience of the human condition; love and soul were words touched with meaning; and, finally, neighbors were necessary. Without knowledge of the term "interpersonal relations," the black people knew the necessity of moving from the rural South into the city under the umbrella of neighbors or relatives who had already made the move, in order to overcome loneliness and homesickness.

Throughout the Haight-Ashbury, this sense of American villages transplanted to the city was a reality. One spring day in the Psychedelic Shop, the girl behind the counter explained to me that they were remodeling the shop in anticipation of the influx of young people that summer, so that there would be a calm center where they could get off the street. "A whole bunch of my friends from Rahway, New Jersey, are coming as soon as school is out," she explained to me; and I had a moment of pure panic when I looked at the small dimensions of this calm center and thought of all the bands of young seekers from Winesburg, Ohio, from Vicksburg, Mississippi, and from a hundred other towns and villages, who would need rest and sustenance, a place to sleep and a shoulder to cry on in the coming months. I knew then that there would not be enough room at the inn, nor would there be enough wise seekers to initiate the newcomers into the new Utopia. At the same time, I had the clear recognition that at some level the bread and the fish would miraculously feed more than could be realistically expected, that these young people had the kind of vision that might conceivably spread in time to the establishment, to the whole of society. Over and over again, neighborliness bloomed, moving from the tribal formations of small units of seekers—in one case, all the members of the board of a literary magazine at a small college—to a sense of oneness, of being at home in the world, of a human be-in.

There was another tool for combating loneliness and isolation in the Haight-Ashbury that had its more surgical counterpart in psychiatry. Over and over again, the young people introduced themselves by giving a thumbnail case history of themselves; and in turn the recipient of this information would counter with the points of similarities and dissimilarities from his own experience. Some of these communications became almost rote-like at times, almost a parody of the classical case-history presentation given by the psychiatric resident in training: the seeker might explain how he had missed out on some important ingredient in growing up—Mary's father had died when she was five; the family had moved when Tom was eleven and he had never found another friend like Jerry, so his ego had been broken; the family had decided that John would stand a better chance of making it to Princeton like his old man if he went to a private instead of a public school and he had never felt he belonged in the private school; Alice had had trouble with stealing in high school, even though she had charge plates everywhere—she had just not believed in the life that her mother and father were living, cheating on each other, you know; and so on.

Even more significant and ubiquitous was the wish on the part of most initiated seekers to tell the stranger how he differed from the American myth of conventionality in his ethnic background. The WASP tradition had its biggest put-down in the Haight-Ashbury; and Tocqueville would have been shocked by the zeal with which the young American refused to hide beneath the cloak of conformity. The seeker had been caught between his mother and his father, he might tell you; his father ran his mother down because she came from the wrong side of the railroad tracks; but the old man had his troubles, too, you see he was part Jewish, and he was really passing, changed his name and all that.

The stigmas of social differences, and failures of various kinds, were out in the open in the Haight-Ashbury. They did not exist in a closed conference room where professionals talked about a patient who was not there but whose life was spread out in surgical disarray before dispassionate experts—some of whom, as consultants, would never see the patient. In the Haight-Ashbury, the patient was present; and he usually talked with a person who frankly admitted that he, too, had been a patient in this sick society.

An example of this kind of case-history report is found in the poem quoted earlier, "Spring was not at the spring mobilization." The writer speaks of himself as "the son of old Fyodor Freakpoet, who sniffs vodka (do you not think I am laughable? I am indeed laughable, as my father was laughable before me)." Here is swift and specific joking about one's name and one's national origin—the hilarity of being a foreigner in a society so intimately concerned with the WASP tradition. In addition, the father's occupation—his last name is Freakpoet—indicates a deviant in the American scene, an unsuccessful artist, a poor poet perhaps, a ne'er-do-well. By one stroke, the writer has punctured the myth of conformity in America—the shifting sands of American respectability and nativism that have so tragically supported inadequate standards of justice for the obvious foreigner—the Saccos, the Vanzettis, the Rosenbergs.

The elder statesmen of the hippies, none of whom were ever complete heroes in the electronic movement of values in the Haight-Ashbury, also tried to grapple with this problem of conformity and the hidden stigma. An illustration of their concern is found in an issue of *The Oracle:*

Snyder: My grandfather was an I.W.W. and he played a silver flute.

Leary: I think it's important to know who everyone's grandfather was. Your grandfather was a "wobblie."

Snyder: He was a wobblie, a homesteader, and he played a silver flute and sat in a black leather chair with a white mustache.

Watts: My grandfather was private secretary to the Lord Mayor of London.

Leary: Who is your grandfather?

Ginsberg: He was a black-hatted man with a black beard who came from Russia and walked down steps in Newark and said his prayers every day.

Watts: Tim, who was your grandfather?

Leary: Oh, he crawled out of a sludgy pool and learned how to breathe without gills.

—from (untitled) dialogue between Alan Watts, Allen Ginsberg, Timothy Leary, Gary Snyder, and others[3]

Or again, as I have already reported, the black Digger at the meeting of social workers suggested that the way to help the young runaways was to explain to the young person how you yourself "fucked up everything" when you were young. The act of being vulnerable, of telling how one had struggled with life, was a ticket to the Haight-Ashbury society. The vulnerability in and of itself was a part of the therapeutic technique of the street. At the same time, the seekers who had been around longer did not derogate their own expertise; having been in trouble and having emerged was the diploma. The painful idea of *unique* problems that had plagued each generation was magically transformed: problems were not unique, and in fact the most respected members of the community spoke of their problems in growing up, simply and explicitly.

Over time, I came to think of the neighborhood as a halfway house[4] for a sick society, considerably more sophisticated and effective than any such halfway house that I had ever seen. This house was open twenty-four hours a day seven days a week; and there was, of course, no eligibility requirement or time limit for remaining there, except the official stand of the city on runaways. The population of this halfway house was

[3] *The Oracle*, 1, No. 7 (1967): 34–35.

[4] That is, a protected residence for mental patients in transition from hospital to the outside world.

often more challenging in its pathology at all levels than that of any one institution in the country, whether jails, state hospitals, or youth detention centers.

Sometime in January of 1967 I was confronted quite by accident with an example of my own faith in the system at work on the street. Late one Wednesday evening, I was returning to San Francisco on a bus, after spending a couple of days as a consultant at one of the state hospitals 120 miles north of the city. The experience always left me exhausted and psychologically drained, as any intense exposure to patients on a back ward is apt to do. I vaguely knew that there were two young girls sitting in back of me; I had seen them at the station when I boarded the bus, and had wondered idly why in the middle of the week two school-age girls, probably no more than fifteen, would be traveling at night to San Francisco on an express bus. Almost automatically my mind had recorded certain information on their appearance and their probable station in life, for that is what I had been doing for two days with chronic patients who had more or less receded into incommunicability in the state hospital. I had seen that both girls had front teeth that were decayed and crooked; and both of them had new home permanents which, after the straight long hair of most of the girls in the Haight-Ashbury, seemed remarkably artificial to me. They chattered in back of me on the bus and giggled a lot, nervously and excitedly; beyond that I did not have the energy to focus on what they were talking about or to care, partly because I felt worried about them. I sensed that they were in some kind of trouble and that they had never been in the city before. When we stopped on the Golden Gate Bridge for the tollkeeper, one of the girls went forward and spoke to the bus driver, asking him in a rather high, scared voice, "Where do we get off to go to the Haight-Ashbury section?" The driver gave the girl some inaudible information which seemed to satisfy her, and she moved back to the seat beside her friend.

I had a moment of wondering whether I should, Digger-like, offer my assistance. Then I began to fantasy what would happen to them on a Wednesday night in the Haight-Ashbury, if all went well: It would be almost midnight by the time they arrived there, but the streets would still be busy and active. Somebody would have an idea as to where the girls might stay for the night, even though there would be some difficulty because of their youthfulness and the fact that the police were beginning to be quite precise about rules for the Diggers' hospitality. Someone might send them to the coffee house that I shall call St. Martin's; and the proprietor at St. Martin's, Ben, would find some way to put them up, with friends, or even on the window seats in the front windows; it would be taking a risk with the police, but Ben had taken this kind of human risk before. And in the morning, several people would scurry around and make some plan for them, would probably find some dental clinic where they could have some work done on the cavities, would find somebody to talk with them—to find out what had made them leave home. Over the period of a few days, someone would persuade the two girls to go back home until they were older; but in the meantime, someone would invite them to come back at a later time for a visit, informing their parents this time. In the meantime, they would be fed and listened to, and, with luck, the whole expedition would be of considerable value for them.

All of these events were well within the tradition of the neighborhood, when it was operating most effectively; and I realized the considerable trust I had acquired almost imperceptibly in the therapeutic effectiveness of this society for dealing with these two runaways. At the same time, I recognized that some of the concern I had felt for many years about the plight of the young had been met in the Haight-Ashbury on many occasions within my knowledge by wiser and in many ways more competent hands. Within a few days, a colleague, who was a senior consulting psychiatrist in the Bay area, made a point of telling me that he had recommended that a young patient, whose case he had been supervising for some time, try living in the Haight-Ashbury for a while; this patient had been in and out of hospitals for several months, making very little progress; and I told my colleague that his advice was excellent. It seemed obvious to me that the ingredient to be found in the Haight-Ashbury was a method for dealing with isolation and loneliness; in this way, the young seekers could offer to the lonely something that no institution or professional worker could offer with the same freedom or tenderness.

There was one coffee house in the Haight-Ashbury neighborhood that I came to know better than the others, partly because I had had a personal introduction to its proprietor by a friend; I have already mentioned it—St. Martin's and its proprietor Ben. Because this shop was somewhat out of the main stream of the central part of the neighborhood, it maintained for a longer period the essence of some of the original colony of seekers. I saw it first in the evening when there was a lighted candle on each table and most of the customers—if one could call them that—had settled in for a long evening of chess, with very few plans for purchasing anything. There was a guitar player in the back of the shop; and, from time to time, someone would have a coffee or chocolate or a pastry, or even a can of soup. My first reaction was that I had wandered onto a stage set depicting a Dublin bar as I had seen it in Joyce's *Ulysses in Nighttown*, produced by students in Cambridge, Massachusetts, some years before—it literally seemed impossible that St. Martin's was real and had simply acquired over several years of intense usage such dramatic feeling. The conversation was gently flowing, the light was soft on the walls covered with messages and pictures, the costumes were fanciful and pleasant. I sat at a table near the door and an elderly woman stopped by my table where Ben was talking with me to thank him in an English accent for such a "lovely" place, just like a London pub, she said. "I'll be back," she told him warmly, and he responded invitingly.

In the course of the evening, two policemen walked in, telling the proprietor that they just wanted to look around. For the first time in my life, I felt afraid of policemen, as they wandered around in the shop, peering into people's faces; their manner was insolent, and the firearms on their hips seemed menacing. Ben had a reputation in the Haight-Ashbury for running a "clean" shop—that is, no drugs could be brought into the shop or used there, and no deals about drugs were to take place there. The customers were obviously tense and upset while the policemen walked around. Afterwards, Ben seemed unhappy about the occurrence, explaining to me that the police had not harassed him for a long time.

Yet over time I came to at least partly understand the suspiciousness that the police felt for St. Martin's and other such gathering places. It was not too different from my own reaction when I was first offered candy on Haight Street; friendly spontaneity, an acceptance of all kinds of people, and a shop that was obviously not making money were largely unknown quantities in most big American cities by the 1960's. The belief persisted that something illegal must be going on if the proprietor obviously sold very little; how did he manage, what was he selling? In the beginning, I also wondered how Ben managed to pay the rent. In the course of a few hours, I would see quite a few dollar bills taken out of the cash register in response to a request from a "customer" for a brief loan. "Go and get a dollar out of the cash register and put in a slip," Ben would say. I never saw any slips removed in exchange for the return of money, but Ben told me that there was no problem, the debts would be made up somehow. Often someone would ask Ben whether he could get supper there that night in exchange for playing the guitar or reading some original poetry; and Ben always said "sure."

The secret of financing at St. Martin's was really quite simple: it did not pay for itself, but Ben supported it by working in one of the building trades. Although he was an artist of another generation—a holdover from the old North Beach artist colony—and could occasionally earn some money from his own artistic skill, he had learned long ago the wisdom of having a quick ticket to ready cash. Periodically Ben would not have enough money to pay the rent at St. Martin's (usually when the shop was very busy with newcomers to the area, paradoxically enough), and he would go out and work at his trade for a few days or longer to catch up with expenses, leaving the shop in the hands of a few young seekers. St. Martin's was his thing and his pride; and he managed somehow to support it.

On one cold rainy day in December, I saw a newcomer to the city literally take Ben's coat off his back. The young man came up to Ben and said, "Have you got something warm I can wear? I just got over a cold and I don't have anything warm to wear."

"No," said Ben with a worried expression, "I don't have any extra jackets around today; everybody seems to need them."

The young man eyed Ben for a moment and then asked, "Are you going to be going out soon?"

"No, not very soon," Ben said, rising from his chair and removing his jacket. He actually seemed relieved that the young man had thought of such a simple solution. The young man promised to have it back in a couple of hours, and Ben settled back in his chair.

By January, it is clear from my field notes that Ben was willing to take care of me, too, on occasion:

Went to St. Martin's, had an appointment with Ben. He was late, because he was engaged in various tasks pertinent to running a halfway house. When he finally came, there were several other people besides me waiting for him—he was behind in his appointments. There was a young couple waiting for him, dressed in typically hippie clothes; Ben took me over and introduced me to the young couple, while he did some private conferring in turn with several people who were waiting to confide in him about something or other—individual psychotherapy, as it were. The young couple that I saw turned out to be married, each had on a rather large wedding ring; they had an eight-month-old baby, they told me, and they had gotten a baby sitter so that they could come up to see Ben. The wife had not been in the coffee shop for some time, and she said with an admiring glance that it was much cleaner and all spruced up since she had seen it, although in daylight it looks quite run down to me. Her husband often came to the Haight-Ashbury, she told me, but she seldom got away from the baby, so she had persuaded him that they should get a baby sitter and come. Afterwards, they were going to go over to the Psychedelic Shop, since she had not seen it at all. They now live in another section of town, but the Haight-Ashbury is an important part of their past. The husband stops by St. Martin's quite often when he gets off from work; he works for the post office and has to get up at four in the morning. It was strangely sad to think that this little shop was looked back upon so nostalgically by this young girl. I had the feeling that Ben had helped this young couple significantly and that he was the only functioning parent they had known. Later Ben joined us, and as he talked with them, inquiring about the baby, seeing her picture, and so on, I got this feeling more and more. Ben insisted they have some mulled cider on him, and he got me some too, wouldn't let me or them pay for it. This again was a pattern. When they got ready to leave, it was raining hard, and Ben took them over to the Psychedelic Shop in his car, like a mother hen protecting chicks from the wet. Incidentally, when I left he took me to my car under an umbrella—I didn't have mine with me.

From many directions, loneliness was combated at a human and personal level in the Haight-Ashbury. The impact of the neighborhood as, in general, a positive force for mental health in the lives of the young seekers can be inferred from San Francisco's suicide statistics during the year of the Summer of Love. San Francisco has consistently had one of the highest suicide rates in the world; and it might have been expected that a large, swift increase and high turnover rate in the young population, who are as an age group prone to suicide in our society, would have been reflected in a rise in the city's suicide rate. Moreover, if one assumed that many of the young seekers were more psychologically prone to trouble than those who did not migrate to the Haight-Ashbury, this, too, would have led one to anticipate a further increase in the rate of suicide.

In fact, the overall number of San Francisco's suicides stayed almost precisely the same in that year as in the previous two years, according to official coroner figures.[5] I can only conclude that the tolerance of the neighborhood, the welcoming of the newcomers, and the general support provided them as they came into the young society had a truly therapeutic effect; and that the idea of a human be-in, enacted in daily living, might offer an undreamed-of solace for "all the lonely people" in the larger society.

[5] The stability of these figures is subject to differences in interpretation for a number of complex statistical reasons. It is possible, for instance, that the number of suicides did rise for the Haight-Ashbury age group, but that the rise was masked by a corresponding decrease in suicides for one or more other age groups. That interpretation is possible, but there are no grounds to suppose it particularly reasonable.

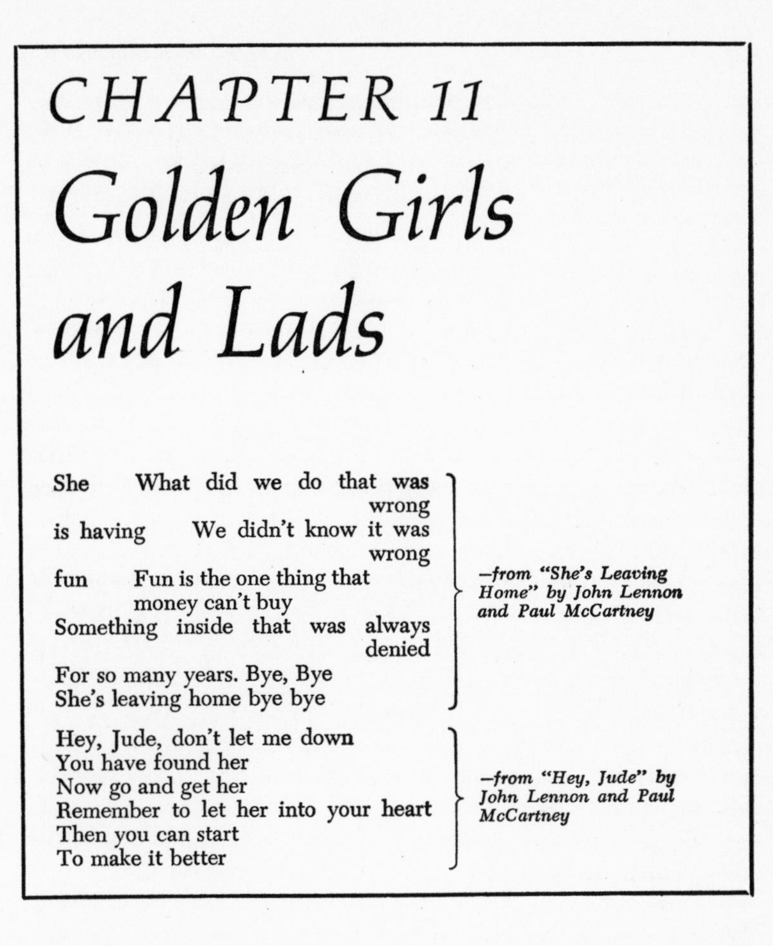

CHAPTER 11

Golden Girls and Lads

She What did we do that was wrong
is having We didn't know it was wrong
fun Fun is the one thing that money can't buy
Something inside that was always denied
For so many years. Bye, Bye
She's leaving home bye bye

—*from "She's Leaving Home" by John Lennon and Paul McCartney*

Hey, Jude, don't let me down
You have found her
Now go and get her
Remember to let her into your heart
Then you can start
To make it better

—*from "Hey, Jude" by John Lennon and Paul McCartney*

By a happy series of coincidences, a sexual revolution of some magnitude and long overdue has taken place in this country within the last several years, with its main impact probably on the advantaged young. As in any revolutionary attempt, there have been some exaggerations, dangers, and tragedies; yet the net result has been liberation that can touch even the elderly and the middle-aged. The seekers in various urban centers throughout the country and the student activists on most campuses have been in the forefront of many of these reforms. In a good many instances, the psychedelic drugs have probably been of crucial importance in helping young people to achieve a more integrative relationship between sexual contact and interpersonal intimacy—a considerable improvement on the use of alcohol by previous generations to deaden anxiety over initial sexual experience, often defined as evil, and to disconnect it from genuine intimacy. Although many critics of the new generation have focused on the so-called excessive sexual experimentation reported, for instance, in the personal columns of the underground newspapers, I would suggest that there is rather a surfacing and exposure of fears, doubts, and behavior that have been around for a very long time; the exposure itself constitutes reform and furnishes a common ground for communication in a society that Sullivan has aptly described as "sex-ridden":

> The lurid twilight which invests sex in our culture is primarily a function of two factors. We still try to discourage pre-marital sexual performances; hold that abstinence is the moral course before marriage. And we discourage early marriage; in fact progressively widen the gap between the adolescent awakening of lust and the proper circumstances for marriage. These two factors work through many cultural conventions to make us the most sex-ridden people of whom I have any knowledge.[1]

The danger of a nuclear holocaust and the concern over the immorality of the Vietnam war have given an unusual impetus to the speed of the sexual reform. As no other generation in the world's history, the young have intellectual *and* emotional knowledge that all of mankind must—perhaps permanently and all too soon—"as chimney-sweepers, come to dust." Both the seekers and the activist students felt that a satisfying sexual life was another tool in the development of modes for survival, for avoiding war: "Make love, not war" was a symbol of this concern and belief.

Most observers, including myself, have reported that there were many more young men than women in the early days of the Haight-Ashbury; and this was undoubtedly related, as I have already noted, to the crisis of the draft and the Vietnam

[1] Harry Stack Sullivan, *Conceptions of Modern Psychiatry* (New York: Norton, 1953), pp. 58–59. Lectures originally given in 1939.

war as it more directly affected the young men. But I have placed the girls before the lads in the organization of this chapter, with apologies to Shakespeare, out of a fierce identification with the young women in the Haight-Ashbury who had begun to achieve, often with considerable pain, a new sense of being people. In the beginning, most of the young women who participated at varying levels in the life of the seekers, as I came to know them, were already earning some kind of a living and/or were going to school at least part-time; the society still imposes stringent control over most advantaged young women, so that their freedom to drop out of college, for instance, was often less real than that of the young men.

As time went on, however, more and more very young girls, clearly under the legal age of autonomy in our society and usually referred to as "runaways," appeared in the neighborhood. These young girls came from every level of society. The very act of a girl's running away from home represented a courage beyond my own growing-up years, when a runaway boy was considered somewhat of a hero but a runaway girl was a tragedy, often representing a "disgraceful marriage" or an "illegitimate" child in the offing. In June, 1967, Huckleberry's for Runaways, financed by Glide, opened its doors in the Haight-Ashbury. It was designed primarily for girls, but during its first year in service over twice as many runaway boys as girls came to the house.[2] Its naming was probably unfortunate, since the hero of Mark Twain's novel had been too long a symbol of the freedom for boys that was denied to girls. The whole experience of running away would be rendered unsuccessful for many of these young girls if they were to seek help in an institutional setting, even one as emancipated as Huckleberry's. Like suffragettes, they sought their moment of emancipation from the old fears.

In brief, the girls were discovering that life could be fun even for girls, as the Beatles indicate in their song, and that home often created a permanent chastity belt for the girl's emotions and feelings, held in place formerly by parental fears

[2] In the first twelve months that Huckleberry's was in operation, 448 males and 216 females were given some help. See Rev. Larry Beggs, *Huckleberry's for Runaways* (New York: Ballantine Books, 1969).

for the physical safety of the girl child and the necessity for protecting her from stigma and disgrace as she matured. The boys, in turn, like Jude, were discovering that there were increasingly simpler and better ways to express sexual feelings, moving progressively from self-admiration, to admiration of the other in one's own image, to the expanding admiration of the biological stranger—the girl. In this interlocking process, both the boys and the girls were becoming people first, simple and human, with sexual difference a delightful variation but not a rank ordering.

The rank ordering was still the massive hang-up in my generation—and of course still persists all too generally. Women were the second sex, as Simone de Beauvoir has so aptly stated it. If a girl accepted this fact too calmly, like a lady, she was termed "masochistic" by the classical psychoanalysts, who formed a new chastity belt for the advantaged women of the 1940's and whose dicta extended far beyond their analysands. But if a girl tried to redefine her role so as to be a thinking and productive person, she was exhibiting "penis envy" and was man-like in her aggression. Psychoanalysis acted as a new and effective intellectual control over advantaged women; and it was difficult for a developing person who happened to be a woman to find a dignified place in the American society of the 1940's. However much Eleanor Roosevelt has come to be admired over the years, she was the butt of many sly jokes in the late thirties and early forties; even intelligent young women of my generation felt that she had placed her career first and in this way had damaged her own children, and no simple facts from her actual life history sufficed to refute this reasoning. If children turned out well, the father was given a good deal of credit; if they turned out poorly, the mother was obviously responsible.

For some weeks after the Human Be-In in January, 1967, I felt a curious glow from it, sensing the death of eligibility requirements for being a person and knowing that even a middle-aged woman like myself belonged to the future and had a thing. Yet, from time to time, the doubt would spread over me that the seekers were not really concerned about women, as such; and this had often been the plight of Utopias, beginning with Eden—to founder on this problem. Since the seekers in the Haight-Ashbury were openly allied in the struggle of the black man for his full humanity, it would seem logical for them to be also concerned about women. Alva Myrdal had long since pointed out that the plight of the Negro and of women and children had been intertwined in the history of America legally and morally;[3] my faith in the young seekers prompted my hope that they would know and understand the crucial connection between all groups of people who were denied full humanity, including women.

Near the end of February, 1967, a mimeographed handout appeared in the Psychedelic Shop announcing a "Haight Ashbury Girl Digger Meating [*sic*]" for the early part of March. "What can we get away with that males can't?" and "What's our thing?" were to be subjects for discussion. While this announcement echoed some of my own concern, it did not represent any full-fledged movement among the women, as far as I could ascertain. I had an uncomfortable feeling that women were once again taking up pioneer-women chores, glorifying weaving, the baking of bread, and so on, although some of them were becoming skilled artists, writing passably good poetry, organizing light shows with skill and originality, and so on. Still I felt uneasy and uncertain, as if the young women in the Haight-Ashbury were moving backward.

As with so many other puns of the seekers, the word "meating" was evocative for me, stirring up the dilemma of being a woman as I had experienced it in my own growing-up years—the endless preoccupation with what to eat, the preparation of meat and fowl for the table, the fear that a woman was loved for her build, her flesh, or for the luxury of the family's having a built-in servant; these fears I had dutifully recorded in my own journal for those crucial years. In the enormous schedule planned for a young woman—of being a competent cook, a gracious hostess, a forever-young lover, a significant and

[3] See Alva Myrdal's "A Parallel to the Negro Problem," Appendix 5 to Gunnar Myrdal, *An American Dilemma* (New York, Harper & Brothers, 1944) pp. 1073–1078.

quiet helper in her husband's career, a mother of handsome and successful children—where was there any time for finding one's own core of being? Being referred to as a "piece" was a part of the horror, as if one were a piece of meat on the scale of life; and there was the clear message from the young men that a young woman was somehow a better "piece" if she were not too smart. Somehow this feeling of being dehumanized was connected for me with the quite usual childhood trauma of learning that animals were killed for meat—even little lambs in the rolling meadows and fluffy baby chicks grew up to be killed and eaten. As a girl child, I had been taught to clean and cut up chickens for dinner that shortly before had been drowsing in the hen yard outside. Cutting the knuckles between the drumsticks and the second joints always seemed cruel and dehumanizing to me. Women were supposed to be gentle; yet somehow they participated in many ungentle tasks, and they in turn were themselves defined as flesh within the human family and were possessed, in some material sense, by paterfamilias, almost like new automobiles.

This question about the status and role of women was also an ongoing one at Fruitlands; and while the male members of that group tried desperately to solve some of the dilemmas involved in making women into equal human beings, the conflict remained unresolved, at least at one level, and effectively contributed to the final dissolution of that Utopian attempt. Both Charles Lane and Bronson Alcott felt that too much of a woman's time was spent in the indelicate task of preparing flesh and taking care of the dairy; and so the Fruitlands' diet precluded all meat, fish, and dairy products. "No hope is there for humanity," Lane and Alcott wrote in August, 1843, "while Woman is withdrawn from the tender assiduities which adorn her and her household, to the servitudes of the dairy and the flesh pots."[4] So strict was the taboo on eating any kind of flesh that one young woman who was a recruit to Fruitlands finally

[4] See letter on "The Consociate Family Life," as published in Sears, *Bronson Alcott's Fruitlands* (Boston and New York: Houghton Mifflin, 1915), p. 48.

fled from the haven in disgrace when the colony discovered that she had eaten "a little bit of the tail" of a fish at a neighbor's table.[5] This abstinence was partly based on the belief that animals, like children, women, and men, of whatever race or species, were entitled to "life, liberty, and the pursuit of happiness"; and Lane and Alcott made much of the fact that the presence of horses and cows at Brook Farm degraded that experiment, since it took advantage of dumb animals. This decision on the use of dumb animals led to some rather remarkable problems at times; Mrs. Alcott and her girls were once tied to a plow, substituting for work animals, according to Louisa May's account; and while the men were themselves work horses from time to time, they were often away on important missions of recruitment, and much of the heavy work fell on the women and girls.

Yet at the end of the Fruitlands experiment the more important anxiety about the status of women seemed to center around the fear on the part of Alcott and Lane that women were being taken advantage of by men who used them for their own purposes—unmentionable but obviously sexual and eventuating in the bearing of children. Since it was largely an unnamed anxiety, its resolution remained painful and incomplete. Lane himself advocated celibacy at the time he came to America; he had had an earlier unsuccessful marriage, and his only child by that marriage, William, came with him to Fruitlands. For a time, Alcott must have been tempted to this same solution. He already had four surviving children, all girls, and one son who died at birth, so in ten years of married life, they had had five children; Mrs. Alcott was then forty-three years old, so that it was possible that children could continue to be conceived. But surely by that time of life—Bronson being a year older than Mrs. Alcott—such unnecessary indulgences could be abandoned in the interest of the Utopian ideal, or so Lane must have argued, however delicately. There is no record, as far as I know, of such pressures from Lane on Alcott, but

[5] The description here is taken from Louisa May Alcott's fictionalized account of Fruitlands ("Transcendental Wild Oats," in Sears, *op. cit.*, p. 163), but the event is included in various firsthand reports on the experiment.

from the few recorded facts, some such crisis took place at Fruitlands. Both Lane and Alcott admired greatly a Shaker community near Fruitlands which had been actually established by the founder of that religion, Mother Ann Lee, and they often visited there. The Shaker religion, of course, precluded heterosexual congress. And Lane and Alcott felt that women had achieved equality with men under that regime. At the end of Fruitlands, Lane betook himself to the Shaker village with his son William; but Alcott refused to join the Shakers, apparently believing, under Mrs. Alcott's influence in part, that the sexual act was in itself a noble and ennobling occupation. Some years later, Lane left the Shaker colony and returned to England, where he married again and had in due course five more children, exceeding Alcott's record by one child. Thus both of the founders of Fruitlands decided, in the last analysis, that celibacy was not an integral part of Utopia; and the Alcott family seemed to have convinced Lane that happy marriage was indeed possible.

In the Haight-Ashbury there were some of the same concerns over the status and the role of women in the human scene; but there had been some profound changes over the years. One day when I was in the Print Mint, I saw a large poster photograph of D. H. Lawrence hung against the ceiling of the shop; the young man behind the counter seemed surprised when I recognized his picture. "Yes," he said, "we think a lot of D. H. Lawrence." It occurred to me abruptly that the young man before me looked a good deal like Lawrence, that indeed there were a population of D. H. Lawrences all around me, gentle harmless men who patted the heads of children, who sometimes baked bread (as Bronson Alcott had also done), who often manned brooms in the street outside for a sweep-in. It seemed not too long ago that I had talked with young women of my generation—who were, like me, English majors and would-be writers—about how terrific D. H. Lawrence was, because he thought that all men should know how to care for themselves, of how he made bread and swept up, darned his socks and washed his clothes. Now in the Haight-Ashbury, this change was beginning to take place for a whole generation of young men, and the young women were quietly adjusting to this change; like lost children, these young women were finding their way into new roles, not forsaking the old roles and skills, but exploring and fresh-faced with adventure, finding new space for themselves in sunlight. It would take time, but it was coming. One of the young women who talked to me intimately of her own experience with what was happening told me that in her own marriage there were no women-tasks and men-tasks per se, and that was true for most of their friends. "It may change when we have a child," she explained, "*but my husband wants me to have a mind.*" The words haunted me for days; in my generation, that would have been the ultimate compliment—for a man to openly cherish a woman's mind.

Some of the seekers were concerned about the eating of flesh, but this was not connected with the plight of women. From time to time, someone tried out one of the macrobiotic diets; and several young people may have died from undernourishment as the result of pursuing such a diet too conscientiously. But the ethical concern about the plight of animals used for food never reached the proportions that it did at Fruitlands or that it has in India; the experimentation in the Haight-Ashbury seemed more idiosyncratic and was not tied in with a basic commitment. The non-meat diet was often explained as a move toward awareness and insight; in this way it was related to the use of psychedelic drugs and often thought of as a substitution for them. Also a non-meat diet was far less expensive; and the ability to live on very little money was a great simplifier in the scheme of life that was courted in the new community. The cooking and preparing of food had been considerably simplified since World War II by various scientific discoveries for its processing and distribution, and none of the attendant tasks were arduous or thought of as belonging to women exclusively. Household chores, even in well-kept communes, were relatively simple by comparison with Fruitlands, so that there was a more natural melding of women and men tasks, without either sex being disadvantaged.

More importantly, the Haight-Ashbury seekers lived in the age of the pill, and women had begun to feel that indeed they could enjoy sex and admit to it without feeling unladylike. The concept of a woman being "used" by a man as a slave either at the table or in bed had begun to seem ridiculous, at least theoretically; and that was an important beginning. Thus the possibility for a viable Eden had improved considerably from the time of Fruitlands.

It had begun to occur to both the golden girls and the golden lads that they could each have the best of both possible worlds. The girls could leave home and survive; and they could "have fun" without collecting feelings of stigma that girls of my generation were convinced could be detected like geologic layers on the gynecologist's examining table. Young men could take care of babies as tenderly as girls and seemed to enjoy it; some of them seemed to have as much interest in observing a baby's development as Bronson Alcott had had. They could embroider, mend, cook, wash dishes, change babies, without losing their identities as male; and they could dress up in clothes as outrageous as those worn by women, as they had not been able to do with impunity since the War of 1812. The chores of daily living sometimes became joint ventures into who did what best, regardless of sex—even if the act of procreation implied certain specialized biological functions, both during and afterwards. In some households, this failure to have sex-designated chores led to silent struggles as to which person would give in first to the stench and the filth; but some of this casual housekeeping was a part of being young, had gone on for a long time, for example, in graduate students' living arrangements, and was an understandable rebellion against the strange elevation of soap to a symbol of culture and refinement second to no other chemical in a chemical world.

The shift in the role of women—her emancipation from childbearing as a burden, her sexual awakening, and her beginning emergence as a person in her own right—had some effect on the changing role of men, in an interactive pattern, as I have already noted. But the role of men was changing in and of itself, largely because of the Vietnam war. Most of the young men in the Haight-Ashbury were disturbed about either accepting the draft or evading it. The Haight-Ashbury experience was a kind of moratorium for many of them in the process of trying to decide what to do about it—go to Canada, go to jail, accept the draft and try to propagandize against war within the armed services, or whatever. In the beginning of the Haight-Ashbury experiment, there was some almost playful hiding-out from the draft, but this was at best only temporary and no solution. The names on the mailboxes in the main halls of some of the communes, apartments, rooming houses were often playful attempts to hide identities and to communicate the dilemma—Taka Shita, Wanta Brood, I. M. Peace, N. O. Fyte, and so on. The free-flowing hair on face and head and the wearing of beads—both in the wake of the style set by the Beatles and American rock bands—were also in the beginning a kind of playful making fun of the fact that these young men didn't want to be killed, that they were in fact "sissies" about it, much like one of their favorite heroes, Yossarian, in *Catch-22*.

In the Korean War, a relatively small number of young men had deliberately but circumspectly used pseudo homosexuality to evade the moral dilemma of war. But the Vietnam war had created a whole generation of advantaged young men who did not want to kill and be killed, so that not going to war and wanting to be harmless had suddenly been elevated into a state of being that had nothing to do with "choice of love object," as the psychoanalysts sedately term it.

This unrestrained growing of hair by the young men was reinforced early by the strong, irrational, and negative reaction of the establishment; and this reaction had a long pedigree in the history of America, for it expressed the genuine distrust—implicit in the strong conforming core of many Americans—for anything overtly "foreign," be it Jew, Bolshevik, Communist, or Wild Labor Leader. Thus, the reaction of the core society to *hair* reinforced what was originally only a relatively small "hair movement."[6] Many of the young men simply could not take seriously the original fuss made about sideburns, long locks,

[6] As I finish this book, over two years after the first Human Be-In, it is amazing to look at a photograph made that day of some of the people gathered together there; most of the men have hair styles that are conservative by today's standards, so rapidly have our standards for such things changed in two years.

flowing beards; but when they finally understood the depth of the establishment's feeling against hair, they began to use the hair itself as a deliberate symbol of a complex statement of their position: *Growing hair does not mean that I am or am not a homosexual. It does mean that I am willing to stand up for my rights as a human being and that includes my right to be harmless to all people. It also indicates my unwillingness to get on the treadmill of killing for a vast machine-like government. If I am scorned and called dirty because I allow hair to grow on my face and my head, then so much the better, for by this I indicate the seriousness of my belief. I scorn the society that has created this monstrous robot-like conformity that feeds the war machine as Hitler found robots to feed his war machine.*

Thus the scorn of the establishment for hair on young men became in and of itself a symbol of a young man's willingness to suffer for what was morally right—to be a harmless person. In the instant-theater technique of the Haight-Ashbury, young men began to let their hair grow longer and longer, to wear more and more beads, to carry flowers, and to demonstrate their tender feelings for all living things. In some such way, the miracle happened: Young men who had already made a heterosexual adjustment, or who were well on the road to that kind of an adjustment, suddenly discovered that there were many attractive aspects to the gentle arts traditionally reserved for women, for a few artists, or for the rather sad young men termed homosexuals who worked in decorator or hairdressing establishments. In short, they became people as the young women were becoming people. They had a common work goal for probably the first time since the nineteenth-century Utopias flourished in America: to be concerned about people, to care for people, to live in peace and tranquility, to do their thing, and to insist on the right of other people to do their thing.

From the beginning of my sojourn in the Haight-Ashbury, the faces of the young men had one remarkable characteristic for me—I recognized many of them when I saw them a second time. Their faces were made distinctive and memorable mainly by diversity of hair style on head and face. Everywhere I went in the neighborhood, I saw faces as distinctive as the pictures of my grandfather or my great-uncle as young men—pictures that I often examined as a child when I was allowed to look at an old family album. I can close my eyes even now and conjure up the picture of my maternal grandfather as a young man, his rather round face, his deep-set eyes accentuated by the rather wispy and inconsequential mustache, the gentle penciled sideburns, the whole picture being made completely unforgettable by a leaf of rose geranium in his buttonhole; the face of my great-uncle Frank from another side of the family was completely different, for the militancy of his mustache is offset by his large, luminous, and rather bulging eyes. In the same way I can summon up the faces of many young men that I saw in the Haight-Ashbury. Yet the faces of boys that I knew quite well in high school have faded over the years into a dull monotony of brushed, carefully trimmed hair and neat ties and shirts; interestingly enough, one face remains clear in my mind from that period—the face of a red-haired boy.

The clothes of the male seekers in the Haight-Ashbury added to the memorable effect, creating an array of characters that evoked smiles at times from the most uptight residents in the neighborhood. There was the gambler, gay and altogether charming, meticulously groomed with his mustache neat and trim as he swept along Haight Street at high noon, doffing his black broad-brimmed hat to the smiles and cheery greetings of all he met and swinging a handsome cane. On a later occasion, I saw the same person clad in mufti, wielding a broom at a sweep-in; but his greeting to passers-by was as cheery and gay as had been that of the gambler. There were innumerable Civil War spies, each with his own mission and each one distinctive in his drive for anonymity—a far cry from the nondescript civilian uniform of the F.B.I. man in our time. There was the young man, with a dark droopy mustache and a large black bowler hat, dressed in old Army fatigues, set off by a bow tie; with an old-fashioned portmanteau in hand, he looked like a reincarnation of Robert Louis Stevenson, as he is pictured arriving in Monterey some ninety years ago. But it is the faces of the Diggers that I remember best from the winter of my journey, as they ladled out soup in a clear sliver of afternoon sunlight on the Panhandle. Their faces and garb became the stained glass windows of the disciples throughout the churches of Christendom, feeding and comforting the multitudes. In the end, in the late summer of 1967, some of the Diggers wept, for there were not enough of them to comfort the new strangers, nor enough food to feed the hungry. Yet their despair was that of strong men who had tried gallantly, and that is the way I remember their faces.

There seems always to have been this two-sided part of America—the wish of some Americans to avoid falling into the vast and despairing conformity of the melting pot; and the wish of other Americans to push everyone into that same pot, making a firm exception for people with deviation in certain coloring of skin and slant of eye. Although both wishes were, from the beginning, part of America, there was a recurrent attempt by the conformists to deny the equally "native" tendency to be an eccentric, just as ancient on the American scene and just as stubborn. The cult of nativism—in itself, of course, a ridiculous pose, since everyone except the American Indian came here, often like cattle, from other lands—had firmly established itself in New England at the time of Fruitlands. One of the important members of that Utopia was Joseph Palmer, known throughout New England as "Old Jew Palmer," although the description was totally inaccurate. "Wearing a beard became a fixed idea with him," Sears writes, "and neither the law of the land nor the admonitions of the church could make him falter in his determination to claim freedom of action in this respect. He suffered ridicule, insolence, and persecution to a degree that was amazing, and which revealed the fact that in spite of a seemingly greater enlightenment on the part of the public, the same tendency, which drove the people to persecute so-called witches, and Shakers, and harmless persons with a little different viewpoint from their own, was still alive, and ready to flame forth as fiercely as ever."[7] The description fits well the kind of complaints that are and were

[7] The information on Joseph Palmer comes largely from Sears, *op. cit.*, pp. 53–67, *passim.*

made about the seekers, in the Haight-Ashbury and elsewhere, and the student activists who have adopted the same custom. Like many of the seekers and activists, Joseph Palmer went to jail for his belief. He resisted with a jackknife four men who set upon him to cut off his beard and thereupon was charged with committing an unprovoked assault. Refusing to pay a fine, he was kept in jail for over a year and repeatedly resisted attempts to have his beard shaved off. Many years later, when he died, his face with its flowing beard appeared on his tombstone, at his request, with the statement, "Persecuted for Wearing the Beard."

By the mores of his time, Joseph Palmer was an eccentric of the first order. His marriage was formalized, according to Sears, by his publishing "banns in his own handwriting on a large piece of paper which he had tacked to the trunk of a fine old pine tree which grew near his house," located on a tract of land known as "No Town." The formality of his marriage was challenged by the authorities, but he was well within his rights, since the land he lived on was not taxable and belonged to no township, having been given to his maternal grandfather by the Province of Massachusetts for valor in the wars against the Indians. Joseph Palmer was a religious man but he was intent, as many of the seekers were, on separating church and sex; many of the marriages that took place between Haight-Ashbury seekers were formalized by the two people standing together in the Park and stating intent to each other in front of friends, usually followed by suitable refreshments and music. Ruth Benedict has pointed out in *Patterns of Culture* that "in our own civilization the separateness of the church and of the marriage sanction is historically clear, yet the religious sacrament of wedlock for centuries dictated developments both in sex behaviour and in the church."[8] The religious sacrament is so persistent that even today it is difficult to find a justice of the peace who will perform the so-called civil ceremony without repeating the usual religious words. Both Joseph Palmer and the seekers in the Haight-Ashbury decided that the time had come to make some beginning toward separating the

[8] Ruth Benedict, *Patterns of Culture* (New York: Mentor Books, 1959), p. 50.

church from the institution of patterned sexual relations between two consenting adults, as church and state had been separated earlier.

All in all, Joseph Palmer, who became a hero to the new generation of the 1840's, would have been an admirable prophet for the young men and women in the Haight-Ashbury. And no one who had read about "Old Jew Palmer" or had known some of the young leaders on campus and in commune in the United States of the 1960's could believe that the race would die out because of a lack of courage.

There were some clear indications in the Haight-Ashbury society that an overt attempt at genuine sexual reform had been undertaken specifically by the young men, focusing on the redefinition of homosexuality. No stigma attached to it as a permanent adjustment; one of the major prophets of the group was an older man, a poet, who had established a permanent homosexual alliance. At the same time, homosexuality was adjudged by most of the young men as a way station in the journey of life; to stay at that particular station was tantamount to never learning another language or visiting another country. It was, in short, limiting. And since the expansion and deepening of experience was elevated into a meaningful way of life by the seekers, the denial of one particular kind of life experience was, at best, a denial of one's full rights.

In most of America, during at least the first half of the twentieth century, there was no open communication with the young on the ubiquitousness of homosexuality as a developmental phase particularly in the male, in spite of the first Kinsey report. In 1917, Edward Kempf, the eminent psychopathologist, had stated the facts of the case baldly, using his study of rhesus monkeys as an important comparison with human behavior:

In the infrahuman primates as well as in the genus *Homo*, homosexual interests predominate and normally precede heterosexual interests until the adult stage is well established. Homosexual interests occur in both sexes but are more common in the male. . . .

The transfer of the affective cravings from a homosexual type of object to a heterosexual object is a very delicate biological procedure and one that must not be inhibited by fear.[9]

Yet the society acted in such a way that the transfer from homosexuality to heterosexuality was increasingly more fearful, with no recognition at all of the "delicate biological procedure" involved, as Kempf describes it. There were a number of cultural attitudes that could operate either in tandem or separately to complicate the whole process of this transfer in the male. Foremost was the forbidden nature of sex and its alliance with the church in Western society, so that all of the Judeo-Christian culture was affected by the story of the Garden of Eden, the duality of human nature exemplified in the fruit of the tree of Good and Evil, as all of this was filtered through religious teachings.

But the democratic tradition had added its own handicap. The position of woman had been left up in the air within the democratic framework, in a way analogous to the position of the Negro in America but even more ubiquitous and difficult to deal with. The male child had strong affectional bonds with women in his growing-up years, at home and at school. And he often feared that the girl child—his sister or a schoolmate—was brighter than he was, whatever that means. Yet with the sound of the great founding ideals beating into his mind from the first years at school, he was also confronted with the accomplished fact that women were somehow considered inferior beings in the society. Thus the young male was forced to come to terms with the possibility that he was socially defined as "better than" the girl, but that in open scholastic competition, for instance, he might not be able to measure up to her.[10] This is a precarious position for negotiating a viable and

[9] Edward J. Kempf, "The Social and Sexual Behavior of Infrahuman Primates, with Some Comparable Facts in Human Behavior," *Psychoanalytic Review* 4 (1917): 127–154; *see* p. 153.

[10] I have been told reliably, for instance, that entrance and grading systems for men and women differ in two major university settings in this country, and I assume that it is widespread. The double standard is necessary in order to keep some kind of "balance" between men and women, since women almost consistently make better grades than men, particularly in tests for admission and in undergraduate classes. The adjustment is made

intimate sexual relationship with a young woman when the biological time comes.

English and American literature has many autobiographical references to this dilemna; but I shall cite here only one of the most famous of such references—D. H. Lawrence's description of Paul's conflict in *Sons and Lovers:*

> He looked round. A good many of the nicest men he knew were like himself, bound in by their own virginity, which they could not break out of. They were so sensitive to their women that they would go without them for ever rather than do them a hurt, an injustice. Being the sons of mothers whose husbands had blundered rather brutally through their feminine sanctities, they were themselves too diffident and shy. They could easier deny themselves than incur any reproach from a woman; for a woman was like their mother, and they were full of the sense of their mother. They preferred themselves to suffer the misery of celibacy, rather than risk the other person.

The dehumanizing of women in a democratic society, by failing to accord her equal status, made of her a possession. A young man was in this fashion placed in a buyer's market, in which a woman often became a status symbol in the same way that a car is; sometimes many young men would focus on the same girl in high school, for instance. The chance of rejection often held a shy boy in a frozen moment in which he continued to pursue whatever sexual satisfaction he had managed to achieve so far—by masturbation-with-fantasy, or by a prolongation of enchantment with the body of someone like himself, or by simple misery and an occasional nocturnal emission. This moment left frozen might effectively shut him off permanently from a transition that he wanted to at least try. In some such manner, homosexuality becomes for many young men simply a safer and less anxiety-provoking way of combating loneliness and achieving some measure of sexual relief.

In the Haight-Ashbury, there was a beginning realization that

---

by using less high standards for the men than for the women, so that there are two curves. Yet there has been widespread protest by college administrators against making some such adjustment for deprived Negro youth.

gentleness and encouragement could ease some of these cultural tensions on the way to heterosexuality. My first realization of this took place one evening in St. Martin's. I heard a group of young men welcome another young man who had apparently been out of the city for a while and congratulate him in a gently teasing fashion on the fact that he now wore two earrings instead of one—a signal in that society of a shift from homosexuality to heterosexuality. When I first heard the Beatles' song, "Hey, Jude," over a year after my encounter in St. Martin's, this scene at the coffee house flashed across my mind. It had the same flavor and tenderness: "Then you can start to make it better." The appeal of "Hey, Jude," seems definitely related to the delicate biological procedure by which the young man makes the shift to heterosexuality.[11] At the same time, "Hey, Jude" seems to recognize that the girl must be accorded equal status before the situation begins to get better: "Remember to let her into your heart/Then you start to make it better. . . . For well you know that it's a fool/Who plays it cool/By making his world a little colder." Much of the young man's dilemma in our society, as I have tried to outline it here, seems to be recognized and commented upon in the song.

The same idea of helping the young person "to make it better" is reported as a therapeutic device in dealing with young male schizophrenics on a famous mental hospital ward run by Sullivan in the 1920's. One of the therapeutic tools devised by Sullivan was often a predesigned discussion between two of his specially trained attendants on the wards, carried on in such a way that a patient could hear the discussion. Some of these discussions between the attendants in the presence of the patient

[11] In making this statement I am fully aware of the vulnerability of my interpretation; many people have tried to outguess the meaning of the Beatles' songs and have been occasionally slapped down by the Beatles for their attempt. If there is one thing I have learned from the hippies, however, it is that each person is entitled to his thing; in the culture of the young seekers, I had to go back to my own early thing, an intuitive understanding of what I observed through what Charles Cooley has called "sympathetic introspection." Thus, regardless of what the Beatles meant in "Hey, Jude," the song has this meaning in part to some very young men whom I have observed.

would focus on their fears about sex in their growing-up years. In one particular paper, Sullivan reports on a rapid recovery effected by such a discussion between two attendants in which they mentioned in the patient's presence "that it was too bad that so many people who had that sort of experience didn't seem able to think about anything else, and so never discovered that *there was a much better way of handling things.*"[12] In context, it is quite clear that the reference made by the attendants is to some form of homosexual encounter which the patient had also experienced and feared was infrahuman. This kind of handling of anxiety over sexual feelings avoids the moralizing position that any kind of sexual experience is per se bad. It simply implies that there are perhaps simpler ways for meeting a biological need that do not run the risk of so much anxiety. "I have come to recognize homosexuality as a developmental mistake," Sullivan has said, "dictated by the culture as substitutive behavior in those instances in which the person cannot do what is the simplest thing to do."[13]

Again, I would like to take note of the fact that young people in the Haight-Ashbury experimented with both forms of sexual activity, homosexual and heterosexual, with the girls openly engaging in some homosexual experimentation. And there was obviously a good deal of group sex experimentation going on, the assumption being that everything had to be tried, that the so-called rules established in the core society had been over many years little better than cheap window dressing for a variety of secret sexual arrangements, some of them consummated in cheap hotels, others on the floor of offices, and all too many in public toilets in the parks. The young people wanted to be open, to find out for themselves, and in general *to avoid harming the other person.*

Thus the editor of *The Oracle* was a stern advocate of fre-

[12] Harry Stack Sullivan, "Socio-Psychiatric Research" (1930) in *Schizophrenia as a Human Process* (New York: Norton, 1962), p. 265. [Italics mine.]

[13] Harry Stack Sullivan, *The Psychiatric Interview* (New York: Norton, 1954), p. 237.

quent visits to the VD clinic in this experimental period, so that the other person would not inadvertently contract a disease. A rather unusual ad appeared in *The Oracle* on this subject:

WHO HAS VD[14]

The graduate student from Cal
The fag from the Fillmore
The mechanic from the Marina
The hustler from the tenderloin
The blood donor at Irwin Memorial
The secretary from Montgomery Street
The stewardess of the Air Lines
The lover from Haight-Ashbury

WHO HAS VD?
Dear Mr. Cohen:

You may wonder why we have elected to submit this type of VD "article" to *THE ORACLE*. It has consistently been the policy of the San Francisco Health Department not to point the finger at any one segment of the population. Venereal Diseases are diseases of human beings. Therefore, the "Fillmore faggot" is not necessarily a Negro, since a number of gay Caucasians live in this loosely defined area. The Tenderloin hustler could be male or female working the bars or streets, as well as the call girl working out of the major hotels.

In case we have overlooked the dowager from Pacific Heights or the young divorcee living on Russian Hill, she may be a donor at the Irwin Memorial Blood Bank. So also could be the policeman, fireman, or young stud executive on his way up.

Very truly yours,
JAMES ASH
Disease Control
Investigator

The young people took this advice very seriously—a fact duly recognized by the city when the public health officials reported that the young seekers were a poor advertisement for a love generation, since they had such a high incidence of vene-

[14] *The Oracle*, No. 6 (February, 1967), p. 24.

real disease. The willingness of the seekers to be responsible for the health of the other person was equated in the establishment with immorality; and this was another instance in which the young could charge the adults with hypocrisy and lies.

The Biological Emancipation of Women

The casualness with which sex was discussed in the Haight-Ashbury, as reflected in *The Oracle*, for instance, had a particular effect on the young women, and over time had an impact on me, too; of necessity, it was of crucial importance to a change in the relationships between men and women. Young men have probably always been more aware than young women of their physical bodies and how to use them, partly because of the obviousness of an erection, for example. But young women, certainly of my generation, had little knowledge of their own bodies and all kinds of culturally built-in restraints on experimentation. If I were to try to summarize the admonition to young women of my generation, it would be "Control yourself." This necessity for control was symbolized by actual physical constraints placed on the body and by a pattern of secrecy about bodily functions, particularly menstruation. Chastity belts were not in vogue in my generation, but some of us, approaching puberty, were presented with curious contraptions called Ferris waists, complete with stays, which sometimes broke loose and emerged at the neckline, causing a sickening embarrassment in the eighth grade. Afterwards came brassieres and various awkward contraptions for holding up stockings.

But the *pièce de résistance* in the embarrassment of puberty was the sanitary belt and napkins, for these poorly engineered contrivances were regarded as shameful and unmentionable, even to peers. After the emphasis on sphincter control for urine and feces, the uncontrolled flow of menstrual blood from the girl's body once a month was a threat to her self-esteem. Since the flow came from the same general area of the body, it was regarded as a waste product, as distasteful and odoriferous as other waste products. The admonition for control became doubly important for menstruation: One must carefully time the periodicity of the menses, so as not to be caught without proper equipment. Sometimes a girl would carry—in anticipatory dread of the event—a brown paper sack to school for several days, containing a good deal of heavy armament for the enemy about to attack; there were no vending machines for sanitary napkins in the washrooms in grammar schools, so that heavy cloth napkins, sturdy sanitary belts, often made at home, and rubberized aprons, worn in reverse, were part of the standard operating equipment for the first few "heavy" days, as they were called. Two heavy cloth napkins, often made of diaper cloth and sometimes actually commandeered from baby diapers no longer needed in the family, were customary for the beginning days. At all costs, the girl would try to avoid changing the napkin during the day, because this meant carrying the soiled napkin around for the rest of the day; in an age of "waste not, want not," cloth napkins would be washed out secretly at home and used again for the next onslaught.

Paradoxically enough, there was only one thing worse than menstruating, and that was not menstruating, being "late." Mothers in my generation carefully checked as to whether the menstrual flow arrived on time, as some of them still do, of course, so both its advent and its tardiness were equally upsetting monthly events. If one were to lose control—to deviate from being a "nice girl," whatever that meant—then one lost even more control of the body, for one began to get terribly fat. When I was in the fifth grade, one of my classmates—a girl somewhat older than the rest of us—was expelled because she had done something terrible and her body had begun to "swell," as we spoke of it then.

These symbols of control—brassieres, garter belts and girdles, unmentionable and shameful sanitary belts and napkins, the menstrual flow that was both uncontrolled and controlling, and the nebulous fear of being discovered as "bad"—were all part of the internalized control operating in young women by the time they were of a "dating" age; and they continued to operate for the young woman, even if she left home to go away to college. The big argument against a woman's smoking was that it would lead to "other things." Once I used this argument myself when I was a freshman at college to counter a friend's charge that I was old-fashioned because I would not try a cigarette; I didn't do it, I told my friend, because it would lead to other things. Secretly I greatly admired this lovely soft feminine girl with lots of boy friends; but two years later she was a suicide on campus, shortly after her boy friend had died mysteriously; and campus legend had it that college authorities had opposed an autopsy, because they "knew *why*" she had killed herself. The grotesquely prophetic quality of my own fears made me begin to hate the whole pattern of restraint imposed on sex. And I sensed that this young woman had been caught in some monstrous and tragic *rite de passage* by which the innocent young were punished for being human.

The full import of these restraints from my own generation was borne in on me as a result of a conversation about the Haight-Ashbury that I had with a woman who was a senior staff member at the institute where I worked. She had agreed to talk with me about her impressions of the young seekers in the Haight-Ashbury. I had anticipated that she might make me feel defensive about the behavior of the young people, as many senior staff members in the institute did; but she often walked through the neighborhood on her way to work, and she had found them gentle, friendly, kind, and concerned, she told me. She was not annoyed that they "begged" from time to time; she felt that some of this casual attitude about money was in itself a movement toward reform.

In this connection, she began to tell me a story about a retired friend of hers, a very dignified, white-haired man, who had indicated to her that he had been quite displeased with the influx of hippies on Haight Street. He was a tennis enthusiast, and he occasionally went onto Haight Street because there was a sports shop there that had an excellent stock of tennis equipment. One day when he was in the shop, he was approached by a very beautiful young girl, dressed in hippie garb, who walked up to him and said, "Do you have any change?" And he was terribly shocked that this young beautiful girl should be begging. He was so shocked that he didn't know exactly what to do, so he reached in his pocket and pulled out a rather large handful of miscellaneous change and held it out to her. And she reached out her hand and extracted carefully two small coins.

And he said, shaken and curious, "Would you mind telling me what you want that change for?"

And she was very sweet and polite as she told him, "I need to buy some Tampax."

In reporting this story to me, the staff member stated that the man's whole attitude about hippies had changed from that point, that somehow he was not offended by the young girl's candor, although such a statement would have been completely unacceptable to him in the abstract; her directness, her expression of a human need, her answering his question directly and simply made him feel that he was young again and accepted by a beautiful young woman.

I was not surprised that the young woman had been casual in referring to her menstrual flow, for I had experienced the same matter-of-factness in the Haight-Ashbury, even in "mixed company," as we used to say. Nor did it matter to me whether or not the young girl had been really "putting on" the elderly gentleman, as some of my colleagues suggested. As instant life or instant theater, it had succeeded in breaking down some of the senseless restrictions on young women and some of the barriers between the generations.

After the staff member had told me this story about the kindly gentleman and the young girl, the two of us spent a few minutes in womanly communication, rare for my generation, over the embarrassment and horror of our own early encounters with the unexpected arrival of menses, of our social constraint in mentioning it, even to other girls of our own age, and of the wretched embarrassment we had experienced on various occasions. For several days after this conversation, scenes from my own girlhood kept flashing into my mind. I remembered going to the seashore with family friends when I was a young woman, and being quite unprepared for the appearance of the menses almost a week early. By then, I was familiar with the vastly superior institution of disposable sanitary napkins purchased in the drugstore, but I had never purchased them myself. I distinctly remember going into the drugstore in this seashore town four or five times before I found a woman at the appropriate counter so that I could ask for Kotex (which in those days was never openly displayed or discreetly wrapped and ready for merely picking up), being completely unwilling to ask the elderly male pharmacist behind the counter for a box of Kotex. And I began to sense how a girl's body in my generation was as carefully cut off from feeling and awareness through shame as if indeed a chastity belt complete with lock and key had been placed over the genitalia. No wonder that the middle-aged Mrs. Robinson in *The Graduate* is not able to talk companionably as a prelude to sexual relations and that this behavior seems inappropriate to the young hero, geared to a new generation and its pattern of life.

Early in my period of exploration of the Haight-Ashbury, I discovered that I could no longer tolerate tight undergarments; and after more than four decades of garment control of various parts of my anatomy, I rather permanently discarded certain constraints. Part of this stemmed from my realization that the young women in the Haight-Ashbury no longer wore brassieres, that as they walked along the street, with amulets swung between their breasts, they had a freedom and a pride in being women that my generation had missed. For the most part, the girls in the Haight-Ashbury had abandoned the wearing of lipstick, not even using the white lipstick then in vogue elsewhere; but the eyes were often deliberately made up in exotic fashion and became the important focus of attention in the girl's face, as if the girl were about to go before the footlights. If, as the legend had it, the eyes were the mirror of the soul, then it was the soul that the young women were focusing upon in facial make-up. But there was no denial of their sexual feelings and their longing for a suitable mate, in the soft contours of unbound bodies that so eloquently bespoke biological awareness and an almost innocent acceptance of that reality.

The conversation on menstruation with my colleague stirred some curiosity in me about a random bit of information that I had remembered from my visit to Fruitlands some years ago, and my unverified hunch about its meaning. Anyone who has visited there knows how relatively small was the house in which so many people lived and still more visited during that brief period in 1843. The original plan was that all four of the Alcott girls would occupy an attic room on the third floor, in order to save space. However, shortly after their arrival, Anna, the oldest girl, had been allowed a small room of her own, adjoining her mother's, on the second floor, even though this was a considerable allocation of space for one person in that household. The thought had stirred in me at the time I was first told this by the guide at Fruitlands that this change in plans was probably occasioned by Anna's reaching the menarche and the attendant problem of separating the younger Alcott girls from association with the fact of menstruation. In verifying this hunch recently, I have determined that Anna reached her twelfth birthday in the March preceding the Fruitlands venture. Whatever the stated rationale at the time (which is not recorded, as far as I know), it seems quite clear that Anna was accorded special privacy because of her symptom of young womanhood, for on June 15, she reports in her diary that she is "unwell," a word often used for menstruation even in my own growing-up years; and on June 26, 1843, Anna again reports: "I arranged a room for myself. It is to be my room and I to stay by myself in it."[15] So it seems that the new Eden took some account of Anna's new status, although obviously it was somehow shameful for Anna and something to be kept from the younger girls. It is also quite possible that the Alcotts wanted to afford her increased protection after she had reached womanhood. There were a number of "odd" characters at Fruitlands, including the male nudist mentioned before. While this kind of freedom was encouraged at Fruitlands, as it was in the Haight-Ashbury—often to the horror of the local inhabitants of both neighborhoods—it posed certain problems for the parents of a young girl who had reached womanhood.

This biological detail from the nineteenth century is of some interest here only because it highlights the obvious fact that attitudes toward women and the meaning of biological maturity had not basically changed in a hundred years. Yet the change going on in the mid 1960's in America was of sufficient

[15] Sears, *op. cit.*, pp. 92 and 102.

magnitude that I almost feel quaint and anachronistic as I report this attitude from my own generation and earlier.

The most important physical function of the female is, of course, to bear the young of each generation; and this was the function that underwent the most significant reform in the new generation, as I observed it in the Haight-Ashbury and elsewhere. Having a child was in its own right an exciting and wonderful event; and no legal or social sanctions could detract from the dignity with which a pregnant woman carried her child and later nurtured it. On the back of one of the paperback books on the Haight-Ashbury, there is an advertising quote in rather large letters, "'GOD IS THE FATHER OF MY CHILD,' the teen-age girl told police . . ."[16] This attitude was certainly the prevalent one for pregnant women in the Haight-Ashbury who were not living with the father of the child; and this was also the transcendental philosophy of Bronson Alcott and the Concord group. Indeed, it is quite possible that this is what Mary, the mother of Jesus, had in mind. The having of a child was a celebration of life. And since a child was not viewed as a piece of property but as a part of the divine process of life, the legal and social status of the mother was of no moment. The child was nurtured by many adults; some of the young children living in the communes in the Haight-Ashbury were unclear as to which adult in the environment was the "mother" or "father." Adults of both sexes were responsible for nurturing of the child; and while in practice some of the young parents were irresponsible at times, the philosophy was firm and moral; and I saw few uncared-for children in the Haight-Ashbury in this early period.

Because children were not possessions and were a cherished part of the world, they seemed to me to acquire a certain assurance and freedom early in life that was unusual. It was not uncommon to see a child of three or four walking around the concrete rim of the pond near the Haight Street entrance to the Park, while an adult stood or sat some distance away, calm, watching with pride and assurance as the child explored at his

[16] Burton H. Wolf, *The Hippies* (New York: Signet, 1968).

leisure and without admonition the rippling water, exulting in the freedom of the occasion. I suppose that an occasional child must have fallen in, although I never observed this happening. But if he did, there were, I am sure, ready hands to rescue him if he could not swim; and no one would have been excited or admonishing—of that I am certain. Children were a blessing; and they walked in this assurance. Only once did I hear a hippie-connected child scolded in the neighborhood, and that was by the owner of a so-called hippie shop. The event stunned me so much that I recorded it in my field notes, with the abrupt realization that the children in the Haight-Ashbury were less tense and generally happier than any group of children I have ever seen anywhere.

I knew of several young women in the Haight-Ashbury, not legally or socially involved with a man in a solid relationship, who became pregnant without planning it; in those instances, they discovered that indeed they did want to have the child; and this decision was made much simpler by the dignity and strength with which other young women of their acquaintance had established a one-parent household for themselves and their offspring. The idea of giving up a child for adoption was laughable to these young women.

Certainly there must be women who willingly give up a child, but I would think that it is much less prevalent than we have been led to believe by social agencies; the fear of hunger and want may persuade a young mother in a slum area to give up a child, but in such cases, it is usually the society that prescribes the solution. Adoption agencies in this country have been maintained by the social-work tradition of persuading the middle-class "unmarried mother," or more recently her counterpart from the slum, to *give up* her child as an unselfish act, "for the good of the child." Many of these young women have suffered monstrously after losing sight of their babies forever; and some of the adopted children, particularly girls, have grown up, within my knowledge, to face mental torture, sometimes eventuating in a mental break, finding it unbelievable as they themselves approach sexual maturity that their own biological mothers could have abandoned them to strangers, particularly in a society that idolizes the concept of "mother love."

Within another generation, women in America will for the most part refuse to put their children "up" for adoption; and this reform will be in no small part related to the reform begun by the seekers. The middle-class unmarried mother who is psychologically forced to give up her child is in much the same position as the poor black mother who leaves her young children in the city streets for long hours while she does day work to feed them, only to end up her life with sons and daughters in detention homes, jails, penitentiaries, or killed in street brawls. Young mothers in America, whether white or black, are beginning to find a common ground in their determination to end this kind of tyranny.

Since the seekers defined sexual love as in itself a celebration of life, young women were discovering that the joy of sexual feeling was not to be confused with the joy of having a child. They were two different delights that could be considered together, but they did not have to be. Young middle-class girls evinced an open curiosity about sex that would have been impossible only a few years before. In particular, sexual congress between animals, notably dogs, was openly watched and enjoyed, particularly by young girls in the neighborhood. My first realization of this phenomenon took place on the day after a police bust of two clerks in the Psychedelic Shop for the sale of so-called pornography. This was Lenore Kandel's *The Love Book*, which I have referred to earlier. There was a good deal of consternation on the faces of the young people in the shop, which was crowded. A member of the press was interviewing one of the clerks who had been arrested and was out on bail; the situation was understandably tense, and there was a good deal of muttering about the cops and their hang-ups. Near the door, two young girls stood gazing off into the corner of the shop with open delight, and I moved over so as to see what they were looking at. Two dogs in the back of the shop were sexually joined, and the girls watched this event with obvious joy. I found myself feeling sympathetic with their mood, for indeed it highlighted in a simple manner the travesty of what had gone on in the shop the day before. The poem that had been labeled pornographic by the police was a simple and direct expression in words of sexual human ecstasy. It was quite clear that in this particular instance, the dogs had considerably more freedom than human beings, and no one seemed to think that the sight of this was prurient. Again I had this feeling of instant theater, so that under the influence of these young people I began to observe the world around me with different eyes. Thereafter I learned to feel comfortable when I saw young girls standing in open-faced curiosity and delight, watching the sexual acts of animals on the street and in the park. By contrast, the curiosity of my generation and my sex seemed voyeuristic—the hiding of forbidden books, the surreptitious search in reference books for any kind of information on sexual congress, the surreptitious glance at dogs sniffing each other, the secret return to the monkey cage at the zoo so as to observe longer, but pretending not to notice, and so on.

The shift from rural to urban life in America had had a particular impact on girls as they made the transition to womanhood; on the farm, there was some awareness of the pattern of sex and life as it unfolded with the farm animals, although even there girls were actually protected from some of the more dramatic events which the boys participated in, such as the arrival of a stud animal from a neighbor's farm to be used for breeding purposes. But at least the young girl could see the young calf fed by its mother, and could understand the term "freshen" and what it meant. In urban America, there were few ways for a girl to find out about sex in a natural way; after women stopped nursing their babies publicly—the breast having been defined as not primarily for babies but for male adults—the girl had even less of a visual model for the mechanics of her own body. The opportunity for a boy to have sight of the sexual equipment of another boy was of course considerably greater than for a girl; in the prepuberty period, there was nothing for a girl to see of another girl that indicated what kind of sexual equipment was to gain importance; and in my generation, girls were not expected to see other girls in the nude before or after puberty. The boy had considerable knowledge of the sexual equipment of other human males from public urinals, if nowhere else. So that it is understandable that the young girls in the Haight-Ashbury had a new open curiosity about the act of sex in itself and expressed a good deal of interest in the whole visual experience of watching copulation of whatever species.

Out of this newly awakened curiosity, homosexuality between young girls was perhaps a more usual phenomenon than previously; it was certainly more open. In my generation, young women arrived at a homosexual adjustment mainly *after* they had abandoned any hope for marriage—usually in their late twenties. What I have referred to as the chastity-belt phenomenon usually served as a deterrent for sexual feelings in the earlier period, so that there was no early experimentation with homosexuality in girls as there was in boys. One indication for me of the rather widespread sexual reform that was taking place was the natural expression of physical warmth between girls and a clear indication that there might be a transitional homosexual phase in sexual development for girls as well as boys.

Sometime in the spring of 1967 the column known as HIPpocrates, written by Eugene Schoenfeld, M.D., M.P.H., began to appear in the *Berkeley Barb*;[17] readers sent Dr. Schoenfeld a good many questions on sex, drugs, and so on, and his answers were widely quoted in the Bay area; crucial questions and answers were often posted on the bulletin boards in the Haight-Ashbury. The questions, interestingly enough, often were questions that had troubled me in growing up. Some of them were obviously designed to shock Dr. Schoenfeld, but he answered them good-humoredly and matter-of-factly. HIPpocrates refused to preach or to be shocked, and this had considerable therapeutic value to the young seekers in the Haight-Ashbury. Thus the reader who inquired whether anal-lingus is to be avoided at all costs is told that the mouth has more bacteria than any other body orifice; the questioner is reminded that he or she should be certain that specific diseases are not present, presumably in either of the participants; otherwise, according

[17] My file of the *Barb* is somewhat incomplete for the early period, but the first column that I can find appears in the April 14, 1967, issue.

to Dr. Schoenfeld, "It just comes down to a matter of taste."[18] Although some of this straightforwardness may seem unnecessarily anatomical and distasteful to the denizens of another generation, this approach had much to commend it from a public health viewpoint. Good psychiatry, as it was practiced by a first-rate clinician like Sullivan, for instance, used this kind of approach, disposing matter-of-factly of the patient's fears that he had some aberrant longing, some infrahuman drive. Such preoccupations can usually be tackled realistically by focusing on medical facts and considerations and formulating the realistic choices the person may want to make interpersonally—that is, the matter of taste, literally or figuratively. Clear information often disposes of cravings that the inexperienced person feels are aberrant and is therefore hung up on.

In another column, appearing some time after the period of this book, a young woman writes to ask about the protrusion of the inner vaginal lips through the major lips and Dr. Schoenfeld assures the young woman that this is not abnormal. "Why some of my best friends . . ." he notes.[19] Such information, given with casual humor, could be obviously vitally reassuring to a good many young women. The whispered fears of my generation—the old wives' tales told and repeated almost in code—bore often the dread that one was physically deformed in some unknown way. This cloak of secrecy has begun to disappear under the persistent questioning of the young and the courage of some of the responsible adults in the society. I would think that part of the low suicide rate in the Haight-Ashbury for the period of this study can be credited to this kind of information dispensed in a variety of ways. Dr. Schoenfeld obviously deserves a lot of credit for some of his pioneering in this direction.[20]

In focusing on some of the positive aspects of the sexual reforms undertaken by the young, I do not mean to deny some

[18] See column in *Berkeley Barb*, June 23–29, 1967, p. 10.
[19] See column in *Berkeley Barb*, October 18–24, 1968, p. 21.
[20] Some of these columns are now available in a book: Eugene Schoenfeld, *Dear Doctor Hip Pocrates* (New York: Grove Press, 1968).

of the painful and obviously highly unsuccessful experimentation that went on. Sometimes the wish to free oneself from all rules was disorienting, however noble in intent it might be. Again, the wish to correct all injustice at one fell swoop, to make every human being feel that he was accepted, was simply a task too enormous for human frailty. Thus young white girls sometimes felt that the only way to correct the injustices meted out to black men was to accept them as sex-mates, as they termed it. In one such experiment, several young white girls, living in a kind of modified commune, were obviously quite unhappy with their sex-mates, who were black and considerably less well-educated than they were; and drugs were obviously used to dull the frustration of the situation. Part of the unhappiness stemmed from the fact that the girls were obviously trying to recompense the boys for society's massive put-down of black people for several centuries; thus they defined themselves as servants for the boys, waiting on them in a peasant-like way. The young men, bewildered but delighted, reinforced each other in requiring more and more of this special kind of service. When the girls were alone, they often literally wept on each other's shoulders, with no clear awareness of the futility of the task they had undertaken. Although I do not think that a group of middle-class white girls can undertake such a burden successfully as a general rule, I do not want to negate the positive aspects of the experiment; it is going on in a number of urban centers in the United States even now, and the old barriers of class and color are being broken down. Some of the pioneers are like all pioneers—they experience some hardship, and are at times relatively unhappy. The fact that such experiments are now out in the open increases the chance of some successful outcomes. And young girls are not stigmatized by their contemporaries for attempting this kind of significant social action; they are admired and respected, whether they succeed or not.

Like the Alcott girls, the girls in the Haight-Ashbury were moving in new and exciting directions. It is of some moment that two of the three Alcott girls who lived to maturity became artists of note. Bronson Alcott's desire to treat his daughters as people bore fruit in a remarkable way for that century. In much the same way, I would predict that many of the young women who lived in the Haight-Ashbury, or in other hippie communes now scattered throughout the hills and dales of the whole country, will in time emerge as artists of considerable note, doing away once and for all with the old wives' tale that women cannot generally achieve that level of creativity.

The put-down between the sexes had begun to decline. With tenderness, the golden girls and boys tried to reach each other, as people moving in unaccustomed ways, sometimes experimental to the point of danger, for they actually had no guidelines from the older generation, only the old chains of fear, lewd innuendo, advertised excitement. But, in general, they were moving and they were doing it without hurting each other, anxious to protect each other from disease, from disrespect, from hurt. Sex was not evil; it was only evil when it interfered with the happiness of someone else; and life and intimacy and sex began to move slowly together and in tandem, without being defined as sin.

CHAPTER 12

No More Silence

And in the naked light I saw
ten thousand people maybe more
People talking without speaking,
people hearing without listening
People writing songs
that voices never share
and no one dare
disturb the sound of silence.

—from "The Sound of Silence" by Paul Simon

When I spoke about incoherence I said I'd try to tell you what I meant by that word. It's a kind of incoherence that occurs, let us say, when I am frightened, I am absolutely frightened to death, and there's something which is happening or about to happen that I don't want to face, or, let us say, which is an even better example, that I have a friend who has just murdered his mother and put her in the closet and I know it, but we're not going to talk about it. Now this means very shortly since, after all, I know the corpse is in the closet, and he knows I know it, and we're sitting around having a few drinks and trying to be buddy-buddy together, that very shortly, we can't talk about anything because we can't talk about that. No matter what I say I may inadvertently stumble on this corpse. And this incoherence which seems to afflict this country is analogous to that. I mean that in order to have a conversation with someone you have to reveal yourself. In order to have a real relationship with somebody you have got to take the risk of being thought, God forbid, "an oddball."

—from James Baldwin, "Notes for a Hypothetical Novel" in Nobody Knows My Name *(New York: Dell Publishing Company, 1963) pp. 123–124*

Now, near the end of the decade, there is an answer to Paul Simon's song, "The Sound of Silence." Throughout America, on the campus and in the slums, on the Indian reservations and among the migrant workers in the great central valley of California, the word has gone out, *There will be no more silence.*

When I began this book almost two years ago now, I had just participated in the tragic and abortive October, 1967, March on the Pentagon; and my Prologue expresses my sense of mourning for the golden period of the Haight-Ashbury, which had been officially terminated a month before the Pentagon March. Yet the Prologue, which I have left essentially as I first wrote it, clearly expresses my feeling and hope that the influence of the seekers was widespread and would blossom again. During 1968, when I wrote the main part of this book, I was constantly torn between the task of re-creating the Haight-Ashbury experiment from my field notes and my intense sense of involvement in the great hopes and despairs of the events of that year as they impinged upon the whole American society: Eugene McCarthy's campaign, which so startled America by the way young people with flowers—some of them, within my knowledge, part of the original movement in the Haight-Ashbury—moved with him into snowy New Hampshire; the withdrawal of President Johnson from the presidential race, driven to that unexpected stance by these young people holding flowers for a mystic who was basically a non-hero; the murder of the disciple of nonviolence, Martin Luther King, Jr., following within a few days of President Johnson's announcement; the beginning realization throughout the Republic that war and violence must somehow be ended; the murder of Robert Kennedy in June, by a young man inflamed by his identification with an ethnic injustice, as half of the young in the world today are potentially capable of being inflamed; and the fear of youth and truth as it gripped the old and the hypocritical in Chicago at the Democratic Convention in August of that year.

During the first half of 1969, I have tried to write this end chapter, putting my experience into some perspective; but again, the events of the first half of that year kept moving me toward new evaluations and new perspectives, for the young move ever more swiftly as time goes on. Thus the first half of 1969 has been marked by increasingly strident demands from students that there be an end to the silent collaboration between the universities and the military-industrial complex, with a strong emphasis on the meaning of these big kingdoms to the small people crowded in slums around the gates of the castles, whether in Washington or in Berkeley, in Cambridge or elsewhere. And this demand of the students has carried new and horrible risks with it, for the young people are determined now as never before to set a new moral standard for university administrators who seem caught like flies on flypaper as they try to get loose from the need for maintaining their fiefdoms, largely dependent as of now on research money funneled through the Defense Department. Thus the People's Park episode at Berkeley in the spring of 1969 focused on the little people outside the castle walls, in the hope that the spirit of a Be-In would prevail somehow. But the University's concern over the meaning of its "private property"—a rather curious concern for a tax-supported state system of colleges and universities—triggered the gun which shot down, in terror, a young innocent bystander. Afterwards there was a reconciliation on Memorial Day, 1969, with the phoenix-like Mime Troupe from San Francisco performing in front of the fenced-off People's Park, and with young people twining flowers in the fence and fraternizing with the young National Guardsmen caught, like friendly animals at the zoo, behind the fence. For Spring finally came briefly to the fence put up by the University at Berkeley around the People's Park; but essentially the fence remains, and the end is not yet in sight.

Across the continent from Berkeley, in the spring of 1969, stridency came to the Harvard Yard; and I saw in *The New York Times* the name of one of the more militant student leaders in that event, a boy whom I had known in California in the earlier days when he was just finishing high school and seemed destined to be a philosopher or a poet—certainly a scholar. Yes, the young and the unliberated will be heard; indeed they must be heard. And they will risk everything for the right to expose the secret and essentially evil conspiracy between the university administrations and the moneyed interests in this country.

There *is* a corpse in the closet, as James Baldwin suggested;

but now there are an army of "oddballs" who insist on talking about that corpse and about all the other corpses in the American closet of secrets. Some of these people who insist on bringing up these unpleasant subjects are indeed odd in their dress, in their hair styles, in their language—that is, odd by affluent, middle-aged standards. But they are not odd in their values. The Republic's history—indeed the history of the world—is filled with men and women of all ages who have spoken of the same values, who could sit down in comfort with these oddballs —the hippies, the yippies, the activists, or whatever—and speak the language of humanity, as they might have spoken to "the three consecrated cranks" of Concord—Emerson, Alcott, and Thoreau.[1]

There seems to be a kind of social rhythm in America, a periodic renewal of some vitality that stems from the history of the country. After the initial founding of the country, this rhythm first manifested itself in the new generation of the 1840's in New England. That generation, struggling against the immorality of slavery and the Mexican War, and out of sympathy with the emergent affluence of their parents and their stress on material comfort, took as their prophets Emerson and his followers. The movement was small in relative numbers, yet in twenty years this redefinition of American values had pushed the Republic toward a final tragic clarification of at least one of those issues—slavery. As Van Wyck Brooks points out,

> the more sensitive minds of the younger generation [of the 1840's], the imaginative, the impressionable, the perceptive, those who characterize a generation,—for the practical people never change, except in the cut of their clothes,—were thoroughly disaffected. The shape of the outward world had ceased to please them. The Fourth of July orations had ceased to convince them that "freedom" had any connection with freedom of mind or that "liberality" in religion had any connection with religious feeling. . . . The young people were radicals and mystics. They had no interest in

[1] This phrase is found in Father Isaac T. Hecker's reminiscences on Alcott, as reported in Sears, *Bronson Alcott's Fruitlands* (Boston and New York: Houghton Mifflin, 1915), p. 48.

size, numbers and dollars. They had begun to explore the inner life, the depths of thought and sentiment. They had returned, on another level, to the mental habits of their Pilgrim forbears.[2]

They were imbued, like the young in the 1960's, with the desire to make a contribution to society. In order to achieve that end, it was necessary to examine all the assumptions of the world as it existed, as it had been bequeathed to them. The parallels are so striking that indeed Brooks' description of the younger generation of the 1840's might well have been written about the young people in the Haight-Ashbury in the spring of 1967:

For, whether their minds were social or poetic, they all agreed regarding the state of the world. It was a cold, unfeeling civilization, bred by commercial interests and isolation, a negative moderation, an excess of prudence, compromise, provincial good taste. It cast a censorious eye on human nature, on all the free flights of the picturesque, the goodly growths of fancy. It offered employment to no one but the decorous and the complacent. It was timid, imitative, tame; worse, it was mean and cruel. It taught the mind of the young to aim at low objects,—and never had the young been so unsubmissive. They did not care a button for common sense. They were bored by the ideal of the marble statue as a pattern of social behaviour. They did not wish to "get," they wished to "have." They did not wish to "do," they wished to "be." As one of them said, in a burst that amused their elders,

Greatly to Be
Is enough for me,
Is enough for thee.

To reaffirm the senses and the soul. To exist, expand, feel, to possess their own uniqueness. . . . To have, when it came to "having," a flute, perhaps, a little telescope with which to study the tree-tops from Wachusett, a book of Tennyson's poems to sing and recite on long walks over the Andover hills. . . . If one parted one's hair in the middle and let the locks flow down over one's shoulders, if one wore a blouse or a frock on fitting occasions, one could forget, at least for a day or two, the brutal, monkish regimen of the college.[3]

[2] Van Wyck Brooks, *The Flowering of New England* (New York: E. P. Dutton, 1952), p. 187.
[3] *Ibid.*, pp. 188–189.

In many ways, this challenging of old ideas and old values was the fertile soil in which the Anti-Slavery movement was nourished, which in turn, for instance, was crucial in the writing of *Uncle Tom's Cabin,* probably the most important book in the history of the Republic. In many of the same ways, the young people of the 1960's, on a much swifter time schedule, moved from the gentle demand for political and social reforms of the early 1960's to the transcendental position of internal reform as advocated by the seekers in the Haight-Ashbury, to the more strident demand for radical reform in the society as a whole as the decade closed.

For the young of today are speaking about the same kind of fundamental human issues as the young of the 1840's, and they will be heard. If they speak softly or sing softly the words that outline their great human values, and we do not hear them, then they will shout. And if their shouts are not heard, then they will act. In the end, unless we listen, they will all act, the political activitists and the seekers melded into one. So far, throughout the 1960's, they have moved between political stridency and the peaceful demonstration of the need for change or the power of love, changing costume rapidly, never completely committed to the show of force. But they cannot afford to wait for twenty years, as the generation of 1840 did, for they have grasped the lesson of Hiroshima.

In a thousand ways, from a thousand lips, including those of the President of the United States, we are told that these young oddballs of the 1960's are a minority, that they are not representative of most of the young in America. "We live in a deeply troubled and profoundly unsettled time," President Nixon said at Madison, South Dakota, on June 3, 1969. "Drugs, crime, campus revolts, racial discord, draft resistance—on every hand we find old standards violated, old values discarded, old precepts ignored. A vocal minority of the young are opting out of the process by which a civilization maintains its continuity: the passing on of values from one generation to the next. Old and young shout across a chasm of misunderstanding—and the more loudly they shout, the wider the chasm grows." President

Nixon is obviously suggesting that conformity and the "sounds of silence" represent traditional good American behavior and that there is a discrete body of American values, neat and tied in red, white, and blue tape, that can be passed on to each new generation. But what are these values?

Some of the assumptions in the President's statement obviously prescribe a continuation of certain aspects of the American character, for Tocqueville wrote in 1835 of the stultifying conformity of many Americans and of the omnipotence of the majority as representing the greatest danger to the new Republic:

> If ever the free institutions of America are destroyed, that event may be attributed to the omnipotence of the majority, which may at some future time urge the minorities to desperation, and oblige them to have recourse to physical force. Anarchy will then be the result, but it will have been brought about by despotism.[4]

Indeed the President's own daughter, Patricia, might be seen as illustrating some of what Tocqueville had observed. In 1964, when Miss Nixon was eighteen years old and presumably living in New York City with her family, the Negroes in the South began to test the new Civil Rights Act signed into law by President Johnson in July, 1964. On July 3, 1964, according to *The New York Times,* three Negroes drove into the parking lot of Mr. Lester Maddox's restaurant. Waving a pistol, Mr. Maddox ordered them off his property. He kicked the side of their car, took an ax handle and struck the top of the car, shouted to his white customers to "get some ax handles," which he had in a box in the restaurant; and about two dozen customers, including some women, armed themselves from this box.[5] It was during this period that Mr. Maddox first received national attention in the press and on television, so that it seems safe to assume that it was during this same period that Miss Nixon wrote a letter to Mr. Maddox suggesting that he make his

[4] Alexis de Tocqueville, *Democracy in America,* edited by Richard D. Heffner (New York: Mentor Books, 1956), p. 121.

[5] Story by Peter Millones, *The New York Times,* July 4, 1964, p. 1.

restaurant a private club.[6] Obviously Miss Nixon's suggestion took account of the omnipotence of the white majority in the South and advocated a solution less violent than Mr. Maddox's, so it fit into the pattern of an omnipotent majority having its own way in a conformingly polite manner; but she was advocating the evasion of a federal law and disregarding a moral stance that had been firmly established by the whole trauma of the Civil War. It seems rather doubtful from what we know of the Nixon family that Miss Nixon was in rebellion against her parents when she wrote this letter. Were these values then a part of the attitude of the Nixon family at that time? And are these the values that President Nixon would like to see passed on from one generation to another, or have his values and those of his family changed since 1964? And if so, how?

It is true that Miss Nixon was very young when she wrote this letter—only eighteen. But it is well to remember that eighteen-year-olds are facing the possibility of going to jail for resisting the draft in an immoral war never legally declared by the Congress of the United States. Does the President think that draft resistance in our time, as he implies in his speech, is immoral and un-American, and that it is in a worthy American tradition for his daughter to write a letter to an avowed racist, violent and criminal in his actions and intent, and counsel him on resistance to a federal law? Just what is this tradition of America that President Nixon wants the young to transmit to new generations?

It seems to me that throughout the history of the Republic, its founding dream has been kept fresh and alive by only a handful of people, many of them young. Sometimes that dream has been almost completely lost, but some call to conscience has always been sounded at the crucial moment; and when that call has sounded, most Americans have heard it finally and been stirred to dedicate themselves anew to the dream. Yet all too often the call for a new dedication has been accompanied by a fierce reaction to the new generation, as if it

[6] From an unsigned special story to *The New York Times* (dateline, Washington, May 9), May 10, 1969, p. 18: "A Shy Tricia Nixon Emerges from Her White House Cocoon."

had indeed expressed an idea at complete variance with the American spirit, or the human spirit, at its best. In our time, the cry against the younger generation has been more rabid than ever, bordering on the hysterical; and we talk long and earnestly about the "generation gap." There *is* a dangerous gap in our time; but the gap exists between our consciences and our actions. And those who see that gap, whether young or old, are trying to close it, as mankind has always tried to close it throughout the history of the civilized world; the effort of the young to close that gap between conscience and action must renew the hope of those of us who also once hoped, tried, and mainly failed.

For there is potentially a new flowering in our time, just as there was a flowering in New England in the 1840's. Then, as now, the society succeeded, in a moment of affluence, in producing a crop of young people who had the time to think, the knowledge to question, the daring to dream. Most of their elders were speechless and dismayed, although the new generation had been encouraged by their parents and their teachers in the intellectual pursuits that had made the flowering possible. Brooks has referred to the parents of the 1840's as a "buffer generation that lay between the hard old Puritan ways and the minds of the younger people." My generation was in many ways also a buffer generation that opened the doors for its children. Yet by a series of historical accidents, my own generation were often silent, did not develop our own young idealism, only passing on to our children the hope, liberally sprinkled with the cynicism engendered by our own failure to further the dream. My generation made the flowering of the advantaged young possible; we moved them toward compassion for all men, taught them reverence for life and justice, for racial equality, for ethical values, for freedom; and *the advantaged young took us seriously*, forgetting our cynicism and our fears which had become, out of historic necessity, our companions-in-despair. In a sense, my generation transmitted the hopes with one hand; but with the other hand, we gave to the young as recommended reading books like *Brave New World*, or *Nineteen Eighty-Four*. It is this cynicism that most upsets the young, for it cancels out the hope.

If the seekers and the activists in America today merely represent a minority viewpoint, if they do not encapsulate the basic ideals of most Americans of all ages in these years of decision, then indeed the American dream has failed, we stand before the world as people controlled by hundreds of Hitlers, dressed in the garb of multimillionaires growing corpulent like leeches on the rich stores of oil hidden under the tidelands; or in the costume of patriotic industrialists purveying fire and poison in endless supply to be used against mankind by kill and overkill experts in the Pentagon; or in the sanctimonious raiment of the "concerned" officials in the federal government who continue year after year to try to find some way to make sure that starving people's morals will not be endangered by allowing them to eat; or even in the robes of trusted men in high public office who, having gained power, become irresponsible with it.

I cannot accept the fact that we, in my generation, were somehow basically different when we were young, that we cannot learn to close this "gap." Through an historically tragic series of events—depression, wars, the political repression of the fifties, the bogeyman equating of the great ideals of socialistic communism with the political repression of Stalinism, so that we were cut off from knowledge of over half the world's search for a better way of life—we were slowly eroded into a conspiracy of silence. When we were not silent, we were punished; and through this process going on about us, we learned to be cynical, in fact to make a virtue out of being cynical. We must understand that process in order to forgive ourselves. *Until we learn to forgive ourselves, there will continue to be a generation gap, for the young speak to our consciences; and it is this which we cannot forgive them.*

The cynicism of my generation reverberates in my mind these days, sometimes waking me at night with words never spoken, memories of earlier feelings that frighten me with their messages of lost opportunities. For my cynicism is gone now at last, and I feel at times naked and alone in my own generation. I find myself engaged in a dialogue that too long ago I abandoned, because no one dared to listen, until I was afraid of my own voice.

When Bruno Bettelheim's book on his work with disturbed children in Chicago first appeared, I was working as a junior researcher on a ward for disturbed children in another hospital; the title of the book, *Love Is Not Enough*, upset me greatly, particularly as it was translated by professionals in the setting where I worked, for the phrase was often used to rationalize decisions made not for the benefit of patients but for staff: "We have to use our heads," someone would say. But I buried the feeling, as did other junior staff members; we did not want to "rock the boat," as the ward chief reiterated when any tensions arose. And gradually this philosophical position became so fixed on a ward staffed by many experts that any display of affection for patients by lower echelon staff, particularly attendants, might be labeled as anti-therapeutic—a ruling of the intellect by the heart that actually might set the patient's progress back. Now sometimes I feel like screaming out in the middle of the night, torn awake by some almost forgotten dream about one of those patients: "Love may not be enough, but it's almost all we've got. Maybe it's all we've got. Maybe the Beatles are right, 'All you need is love.' "

Or again, I think of my experience at Southside Hospital. In the research group with which I was associated there was a phrase used to describe new staff members, particularly psychiatric residents and student nurses, many of whom were coming into a mental hospital for the first time. If they worried about what was happening to a patient or patients on the ward to which they were assigned, they were experiencing what the research staff called "the rescue fantasy." The rescue fantasy, like love itself, could supposedly actually interfere with the giving of expert help. Yet most of the researchers, themselves human and sensitive, avoided any research that took them on the wards for extensive periods and primarily engaged in studies of staff attitudes, for instance, so that they could maintain some distance from the unnecessary tragedies taking place on the wards, conducting interviews whenever possible, even with patients, in the safe confines of the research offices, where the researchers would not be tempted to be "troublemakers." One researcher who spent considerable time on the ward reported to research staff on some of the unnecessary risks to patients' well-being and life involved in ill-considered administrative decisions made without adequate information on ward life; and this researcher was accused by a senior researcher of focusing on Southside's "id rather than its superego," although he did not challenge the reliability of the information. In some such way, a good hospital developed a new and fatal public relations attitude that Southside could do no wrong; and in the end, the hospital became more and more famous while the rate of patient suicides reached its highest point since the hospital had opened its doors several decades earlier. Now too late, I have the courage of my convictions; and the words beat a refrain in my head: "Yes, I *am* concerned about the hospital's id. And I *do* want to rescue patients. What else is a hospital for?" And in my dreams I am running through the wards opening windows, shouting over the loud-speaker system to the senior consultants, "Come to the wards and see what is happening. Come and see. And do something."

Yet the people in charge at any and all of the hospitals at which I worked were usually dedicated and gifted; often their only flaw was that they felt it necessary to placate the bureaucracy—the state government, a granting agency, or even the United States Congress—in order to obtain adequate funds to staff the hospital, and/or to train students, to do research, and so on. Although this kind of cynicism and its effect can be more microscopically examined in a small institution, like the mental hospital, it existed throughout American society during my generation, reaching its peak, perhaps, in 1953, when the Rosenbergs were put to death by the state without proper legal safeguards and with no adequate definition of their crime, while powerful and informed men stood by silently, many of them quite clear on what was happening. Thus three days after the execution of the Rosenbergs, Justice Felix Frankfurter stated, "To be writing an opinion in a case affecting two lives after the curtain has been rung down upon them has the appearance of pathetic futility. But history also has its claims."[7] In much the same way, hospital staff often discussed *afterwards* what had been going on on the ward *before* the patient committed suicide. In both instances, the silence was broken too late, too incompletely, so that guilt over silence still haunts my generation. Thus my generation often finds it difficult to explain to the young—whether deprived and poor or advantaged and seeking—that we recognize the conspiracy of silence in which we were engaged and that in a thousand ways we tried to do something about it, always too little and too late, but that we tried.

Yet I do not mean to imply that a *mea culpa* attitude is adequate for explaining what happened to my relatively silent generation; nor does it take into account the countless unknown and often relatively powerless people within the system who maintained courage in the face of overwhelming odds, who found significant ways to be concerned and thus kept the cancerous silence from spreading fatally throughout the society. In every generation, in every setting, and at every level, there have always been *the people who care;* my generation was no exception. Not all the actions of my generation could be classed as cynical—there was often a consensus of concern and despair between people who cared, a signal of recognition that something must be done to curb the spread of human disaster, a refusal to run away from shared despair, which somehow often bore some small—even sweet—fruit. Within the circumference of my own small world of the mental hospital, the cry for something to be done and the response to that cry were often literally silent, conveyed by a glance, swift and certain, between two people; when all else failed, the communication established in this conspiracy of silence contained some small modicum of hope. One's eyes were caught and held by another's in moments of deepest despair. I was not able to formulate in words this eye communication and its importance until I had become absorbed in the life of the seekers and discovered that even in the most troubled human situations, this silent communication of despair no longer appeared on the faces of the

[7] As cited in the prefatory pages to Walter and Miriam Schneir, *Invitation to an Inquest* (New York: Doubleday, 1965).

young people in the golden days of the Haight-Ashbury; even the disturbed young novitiates sought help openly and optimistically.

Near the end of my formal encounter with the seekers in the Haight-Ashbury, I tried to formulate in a field note the difference between the silent cry for help, so prevalent in my generation, and the determined pursuit of change and the emergence of hope in the faces of the young:

When I was working as a ward observer at Southside, I discovered an eye gesture, so peculiar, so pronounced, and so desperate that I had to begin to search my experience for where I had seen that gesture before, what it meant, and exactly what was communicated. Once I had isolated this gesture, this signal, a whole series of events before and since gained a new meaning. I saw this signal sometimes in the eyes of a public official in the television coverage of some public event; and I can now think back over my entire life and see its shape in our whole society.

At the particular time of which I speak, Southside was in a state of collective upset and suicide risk, so severe that for a while there was some talk among senior staff of closing the hospital down temporarily—a state that was never reached. At the height of this situation, I met the head nurse of one of the wards as I came into the hospital one morning. She was a very sensitive person, and her ward was the only one in the hospital that had escaped having at least one suicide on it. Her lips were drawn in a tight line, and she barely nodded to me, although she and I had had a pleasant and rather close relationship centered around our concern for patients. But her eyes were sharp and incisive; they searched my face in a swift and penetrating way, desperate and defensive at the same time. They were trapped eyes, and they shouted for something to be done. I sensed what she was saying:

Things are worse than ever in the hospital this morning. The senior staff continues to make moves from fear which aggravate the situation. You have been on the ward; you know how hard I have tried and that I speak for patients who are helpless. You are a link between the ward and the administration. None of the senior staff spend any time on the ward. What can you do?

There was not much I could do, but I went up on the ward and read the nurses' notes on what had happened in the night; the situation was indeed acute. Whether or not this made any difference on that occasion, I do not know. I presume that it had made a difference at some time, for she and I had evolved this method for consensing on our despair over what was happening; and both of us had some indication from patients and ward staff that this kind of collaboration had been crucial in many crises. Yet essentially, as I look back, it was such a feeble effort compared to what either or both of us could have done by speaking out.

It has finally dawned on me that while I still see this signal of despair particularly in the faces of lower echelon people at the University Medical Center—secretaries, nurses, and so on—I do not see that despair on those same faces if I happen to run into them in a coffee house in the Haight-Ashbury. Most of the lower echelon people at the Medical Center have some after-hour life in the Haight-Ashbury; and while they, like the students, have given up on the morals of the higher echelon professionals at the Medical Center, they speak to me with animation of the Haight-Ashbury and what I am studying there. This is not an idle observation, for I have noted that on a ratio of about 10 to 1, non-professionals at the Center (or people low on the totem pole) express interest in my work in the Haight-Ashbury, as compared to the professionals.

The look of despair is missing in the eyes of the young in the Haight-Ashbury. Sometimes I see the glazed look of drugs in their eyes, but I do not sense the kind of hopelessness of which I speak. It is rather a kind of sickness, at times, that represents a crisis, but there is the hope that when the crisis is over the person will be made whole. I think that in a remarkable number of instances, this is true, that the person emerges from the Haight-Ashbury experience, including the drug experience, with a new determination to avoid the pitfalls of an older society—the role of the person caught in the establishment's system, unable to help the victims, the bodies that keep the establishment going so well.

Whatever else has happened, the young are no longer silent. One hundred and twenty-five years ago, the young and their prophets in New England put an end to silence in much the same way. They objected at first by non-violent means and by civil disobedience to slavery, to the immoral Mexican War, to the materialistic values emergent from the new affluence of little men bent on making bigger and bigger money. They did not believe that the teachers at Harvard University were teaching the things that mattered, and they had as one of their chief mentors a man who had never spent a day in a college or a university—Bronson Alcott. That small movement of transcendental conscience, begun by men and women who were termed fanatics by the establishment of that period, finally moved a Republic to a great Civil War and made it for the first time a government of free men—although not yet of free men *and* women. And what had begun on the high road of non-violent reform in Concord, at Brook Farm, and, more specifically, at Fruitlands, had to change radically in order to be heard. So it was that Ralph Waldo Emerson, who had disapproved of Thoreau's and Alcott's decision to go to jail rather than pay taxes to an immoral society, was finally forced to say of the Fugitive Slave Act, "I will not obey it, by God." So it was that Bronson Alcott with the vision of a Utopia in 1843, ruled by introspection and good living, finally had to give his full support in 1859—as did Thoreau and Emerson—to an armed man, Captain John Brown. In much the same way, Alcott's daughter, Louisa May Alcott, who was a girl of eleven at Fruitlands, went as a woman of thirty with her father's blessing to nurse the wounded in a Civil War hospital in Washington—a remarkably activist position for a woman of that period, even though her tour of duty was short, curtailed by an illness from which she never fully recovered.

Yet throughout the period from 1840 to the outbreak of the Civil War, politicians, then as now, kept reiterating the refrain that this protest represented only a vocal minority. Thus on January 6, 1860, only a little more than sixteen months before the firing on Fort Sumter, Emerson was still trying to convince the Republic that John Brown's stand at Harper's Ferry was significant:

> I am not a little surprised at the easy effrontery with which political gentlemen, in and out of Congress, take it upon them to say that there are not a thousand men in the North who sympathize with John Brown. It would be far safer and nearer the truth to say that all people, in proportion to their sensibility and self-respect, sympathize with him. For it is impossible to see courage, and disinterestedness, and the love that casts out fear, without sympathy.[8]

[8] From a speech on John Brown given at Salem, January 6, 1860; in Ralph Waldo Emerson, *Miscellanies* (Boston: Houghton, Mifflin, 1892), p. 262.

Nor can I believe that the gap is so wide between the institutions of the society and the militant students, between the hippies and their conforming elders, between the affluent and the dispossessed in city slum, in hill country, on reservation, or in the great central valley of California. It is the call to conscience that frightens us all so much, the fear that one has somehow lost one's way on the gleaming strip of life, so brief, so beautiful; that one has strayed onto sordid byways and can hear no longer the cry of a child. Yet a sensitivity to life, to every other person, still lingers on in all of us, waiting to be miraculously brought back, to be resurrected. It is not too late for any of us, no matter how we have wasted our precious golden days in needless striving, in careless indifference. In a mystical sense, this is the time for resurrection.

Tolstoy's last great novel, *Resurrection*, explores the same phenomenon in his society. He ponders over the fact that prisoners on their way to Siberia were moved from the prison to the railroad carriage in terrible heat so that three of them perished on the way, basing this part of his novel on an actual happening in the early part of the 1880's, when five convicts died of sunstroke in one day on their way from a prison in Moscow to the railway station. "Nobody is to blame, and yet the men are dead," Tolstoy's hero muses, "murdered by these very men who are not to blame for their deaths."

"All this happened," Nekhlyudov said to himself, "because all these people . . . consider that there are circumstances in this world when man owes no humanity to man. Every one of them . . . if he had not been a governor, an inspector, an officer, would have thought twenty times before sending people off in such heat and such a crowd; they would have stopped twenty times on the way if they had noticed a man getting faint and gasping for breath—they would have got him out of the crowd and into the shade, given him water and allowed him to rest, and then if anything had happened they would have shown some pity. They did nothing of the sort: they even prevented others from helping; because they were thinking not of human beings and their obligations towards them but of the duties and responsibilities of their office, which they placed above the demands of human relations. That is the whole truth of the matter," thought Nekhlyudov. "If once we admit, be it for a single hour or in a single instance, that there can be anything more important than compassion for a fellow human being, then there is no crime against man that we cannot commit with an easy conscience."[9]

Sometimes in these days of new stresses, I grieve especially for the young girls in the Haight-Ashbury, searching and eager with their flowers in hand and their belief that they could eventually move a Republic toward peace and a fullness of life and love for every soul; and finding in their hope, as Louisa May Alcott did, the courage to be people, to be fully human. For if—and I say if—we shall again have a great civil war on our hands, these young women will not be nurses; they have moved past that sheltered position for women. They will pin up their long locks and join hands with young black women with African haircuts, and they will fight alongside the young bearded John Browns black and white of this generation. For they are determined that mankind will survive even if they do not.

However else my generation failed, we have produced a generation comparable to that of the 1840's, strong and courageous, many of them advantaged enough to seek a new way to solve the old problems, moving in the sunlight of clear vision, trying to learn the wisdom of the disadvantaged, struggling mightily to end the silence.

From every college campus, from every slum, from every commune, they shout at us: *There is yet time. Spring does not have to be silent any more. 1984 does not have to come. Life can be celebrated. There can be a Human Be-In.*

[9] L. N. Tolstoy, *Resurrection*, translated by Rosemary Edmonds (Balitmore, Md.: Penguin Books, 1966), pp. 447–448.

Epilogue

October 15, 1969
Cambridge, Massachusetts

In Cambridge, the day is golden with October, filled with the thin brilliant sunlight from the south that in this northern clime cuts its warmth onto the old brick in Harvard Yard with a special rosy glow. As we walk on the outside edge of the Yard toward Cambridge Common where the Moratorium march to Boston Common is to begin, the bell tolls from the oldest church in Cambridge, lamenting the dead in Vietnam and echoing for me the poem on Hiroshima's children in *The Oracle* that I read first almost a million years ago, it seems: "Send them back, send them back," the bell beats the words through my whole being. And whether it is the bell in the oldest church in Cambridge mourning with the young gathering in Cambridge Common that produces the effect, or some other unknown cue, I know that I am again at a Human Be-In with people who are color-blind and age-blind and celebrating life —this time by mourning together all their dead who at Hiroshima and Hanoi, Belsen and Hue, Saigon and Leningrad, and in a thousand nameless villages, were caught in meaningless destruction before Spring had ever come.

On Cambridge Common, there is an air of calm activity as people move almost deliberately toward the speakers' platform —some alone, some in small clusters, some in more deliberate groupings with banners flying, a new gathering of the tribes. On the speakers' platform, the white-thatched gentleman who had already said the important words some months ago is trying to say them again; but the sound equipment is poor and the words are as familiar as the words of an old Beatles record. We stand respectfully but the ritual is unimportant, and when a small band comes out of one of the side streets playing a tune, we move into the street with one accord, like children following the Pied Piper for a new and distant meadow.

The bell still tolls, and our feet are restless as the march moves briefly and then pauses, moves again, again stops, as marches always seem to do, with some unknown obstacle up front, out of sight. We shift our feet on the pavement like horses at the barrier, knowing that if we hurry there is yet time to save some of the children, but sensing suddenly that not all the children can be brought back, that some like Hiroshima's children are gone forever, unfulfilled, unknown, sometimes even unmourned. There is a tremulousness in the air as we are finally stopped quite definitely and for a long time, it seems, almost in front of the tolling church bell, and we wait tensely for this human march to begin. As we wait, faint and then pungent through the autumn air drifts the smell of pot, not much different, I note for the first time, from the smell of burning leaves, which is indeed a happy smell for me too—for in the yard of my childhood the event of leaf-burning took place at the same time as the setting of new bulbs for the spring blooming, while visions of fields of white narcissus and rows upon rows of stiff hyacinths, far beyond the confines of the allotted space, raced through my mind.

We continue to wait, more relaxed now, and the bell continues its beat. How many times over the years have I waited in such marches? I begin to count them over, sometimes having to search my memory for the specific issue, but remembering the city and the season of the year, the despair and the hope, the search for meaning. Only a few times over the years have the marchers in my particular journey felt a surge of triumph, the feeling that the old injustices would yet be righted in our lifetime. Once after Marian Anderson sang in front of the Lincoln Memorial in Washington, we walked home along the streets of Washington afterwards in an unexpected march of triumph, tears of joy streaming down the faces of black and white people, our hands linked in a spontaneous movement together that seems forever gone on the streets of Washington as I know them now.

More usually, the waiting has been a presentiment of frustration. On the march to the Pentagon in Washington, the waiting had been filled with horror and shame and fright, for it was clear that the delays stemmed from the panic of official

Washington, which lay like a dangerously charged electrified fence between the little people and their government, so that both the White House and the Capitol grounds were off-limits for the first time in my memory. At the end of that march, there were steel-helmeted men on the roof of the great five-sided fortress, with machine guns trained on the little people gathered beneath, so that I felt like an ant in a disturbed ant hill.

This waiting today is different, because it seems a necessary preliminary for such a vast swell of people, who are all about me, coming in from all sides. This is a huge cortège, not for the Moses-like heroes of our adolescent hopes—John Kennedy, Martin Luther King, Robert Kennedy—but for the non-heroes, the little people who can no longer be dignified by war, so that the little people will no longer waste their fragrance on polluted air. I can close my eyes and hear distinctly the gentle English professor in Contemporary Lit, now himself long dead and gone, read aloud and beautifully W. W. Gibson's poem, "Peter Proudfoot," while many of us in the classroom wept quietly, trusting that never again would we send the lost, the forgotten, into the false nobility of war:

He cleaned out middens for his daily bread:
War took him overseas and in a bed
Of lilies-of-the-valley dropt him dead.[1]

The Peter Proudfoots in Vietnam, many of them at least, came from hill and slum without even the dignity of having a job cleaning up refuse, Uncle Sam being their first and only employer; and where are the beds of flowers in which to sleep in such a war as this one?

Yet this is not simply a funeral cortège, it is a wake, celebrated in true Irish fashion in this city so formed by the Irish-American spirit, it is a celebration of the life left all around us; and the people on the march are filled with good humor for life, the will to live and to grieve and to laugh again. As we finally begin to move down Mt. Auburn Street toward Massa-

[1] "Peter Proudfoot," in Wilfred Gibson, *Collected Poems* (1905–1925) (London: Macmillan, 1929), p. 489.

chusetts Avenue, young faces lean out of crowded quarters on the top floors of old shabby buildings and call out cheery greetings: "We're coming, too," they say in a sudden surge of companionship, raising their hands in the V-sign.

But in one newer office building the windows are crowded with the staid and quiet ones—the ones President Nixon claims are his constituency, silent and disapproving of any projected change in their living—and they do not return the V-sign; some of them turn down their thumbs while those who march are stunned and unbelieving, asking each other, "How can this be?" One very young girl asks me wistfully, "How can *anyone* be against peace?" For a moment I am that young girl myself, recalling the sharp sting when I first reached voting age and realized that the words taught to me as a child as good had suddenly turned into a joke, a taunt; when I announced that I had read the Socialist Party platform, and yes, it was the closest to my ideals and I would vote that way, I was reminded by an array of adults whom I had treasured and admired that I was being a starry-eyed idealist and that this kind of talk acted upon produced the "most dangerous" kind of behavior.

The march has gained momentum now and we are falling behind slowly. Somewhere between Harvard Square and the Mass Avenue bridge, I find myself walking in front of a huge square formation of young people, carrying, in almost military precision, a large American flag, parallel to the street, with young hair flying in all directions around the edge of the flag, like an uneven and unmatched fringe. And being still gun-shy in the old way, I have a moment of sheer dread, thinking I have been caught up in this march with some Birchites who have sneaked in. I mention my fear to my companion nervously, as I had two years ago wondered out loud on the bridge over the Potomac, on our way to the Pentagon, whether we were being delayed interminably and intimidated by FBI agents posing as hippie monitors of the march—which indeed later turned out to have been a reasonable fear. But, "no," my companion tells me firmly about the flag; today we are all redefining the flag—it is our flag, too. And I feel a kind of Walt Whitman patriotism run through me, a sense of the continual search for "companionship thick as trees along all the rivers of America, and along the shores of the great lakes, and all over the prairies. . . ." I still have this kind of patriotism, I suppose, much as I have come to abhor the word as it has been mouthed by the nativists. But the young people who carry the flag today are reviving a new kind of country, and insisting that this new kind of country is American, too, and that therefore they have the right to bear the flag. If the flag is a symbol of that kind of country, then it is my symbol, too, although I have never been much in favor of any flags.

There is a pause in the march to allow for traffic to cross on the street ahead of us; and in the lull, as we pause, a young woman with a baby in a carriage begins to cross the street just in front of us, and she is only halfway across the wide street before the march begins again. The flag people have been given the signal to resume their precision movement, and the great flag moves with a single rippling impulse once again, when suddenly the advance scouts who control the people around the flag's edge see the baby carriage and the young mother, who like a gentle rip tide moves swiftly against the main flow of the march. There is a moment of indecision, and we all turn around, almost mischievously, to watch what will happen to the flag. But one of the monitors is equal to the occasion: he says, "Lift the flag," and all the arms go up and bear the flag aloft over the head of the woman and the carriage, and there is a triumphant cry of sheer relief and joy from all of us, while the flag rides over the woman and her baby like a religious canopy shielding and protecting them from all harm. And I find myself hoping to the point of prayer, although this was never my wont, that never will that configuration of color and design be folded and presented to that woman at some crowded grave site, twenty years from now, using that flag in a vain attempt to make of killing a noble profession, as long as the killing is done in the name of orderly or disorderly government, with or without the consent of the governed.

In front of me there is a young man wearing a blazer with a sign on it saying, "Tonkin Gulf Yacht Club," in yellow and black, reminding me abruptly of the yellow submarine, in reverse, and I smile at the juxtaposition of the tragic and irreverent as they bombard my senses this day. No such Yacht Club could ever fool these young people again into a false legitimization of killing to support the rich and the powerful; and even though my assurance is still shaky at times, I am glad to have even briefly this feeling of faith in the young and their clear-eyed sophistication about clichés. Again, I hear a young man saying, "Today makes me feel like the Fourth of July used to make me feel," but this goes too far in my temporary exultation of the national role, for I have always felt a curious shame about the Fourth of July, as if it intoned "We are the greatest, none like us. . . ."

As we near the Charles River, some of the marchers shout at the M.I.T. buildings in a sudden surge of realization that here is the Pentagon posing in the guise of academia, and I do not catch their particular words, but I know their meaning. How short a time ago, I think sadly, these Cambridge institutions—Harvard and M.I.T.—stood proudly in the splendor of a New England tradition of scholarship; and now they seem almost corrupted by fear and timidity and the omnipresent need for the everlasting-dollar-for-good-research (What can we do?), until now the buildings themselves look shoddy at times.

Shortly we move on to the Mass Avenue bridge across the Charles River. Even the river seems worth saving today; in fact both the sky and the water are joined here in a sudden burst of heavenly housekeeping, so that they seem safe and pure, the water pure enough to drink, the air clear enough to breathe, until I catch a whiff of something that denies that promise. Yet I still feel that it can yet be saved, this land and water now knee deep in our own pollution—not by any more laws but by this kind of salt march, this will of the Human Be-In.

Overhead a sky-writing plane begins to inscribe a white edging of frosting on a huge blue birthday cake, and we watch breathlessly, turning backward as we near the Boston side of the Mass Avenue bridge, while the peace symbol is funneled into the circle—a birthday cake for mankind. And one single cry of exultation goes up from the marchers on the bridge, as if we had all been holding our breath in unison, waiting to see whether we could cheer our own survival, and yes, we could; the peace symbol in the sky is a sign. On the Pentagon march there had been a group of young mystics who had believed that chanting would bring down the walls at the Pentagon, that they would come tumbling down by the forces of good. But the walls had been quite firm while the young wept against the walls with their own urine, unwilling to give up their vigil and bereft of any public chemical toilets that were the usual courtesy on a public march in Washington. Now there is a sign in the sky, as surely as if the Pentagon walls are tumbling.

Our monitors are a man and a girl, she in long, street-length, rather dramatic-looking greatcoat, with a military knapsack flung over it, he barefoot at one end, well covered at the other by a growth of thick hair. The police confer with them politely and naturally from time to time; since my early encounters with the police in San Francisco, the denizens of law and order have become more sophisticated about long hair and different clothing—with some slight recognition, additionally, that odd attire sometimes covers a distinguished and powerful name, I think cynically. But then I take on the more determined attitude of seeking out good where it exists and discover that, indeed, some of the policemen look happy and relaxed, and the policeman in San Francisco who finally smoked pot on the City Hall steps runs idly through my mind, although I don't suppose . . . not in Boston, surely, where the Irish-American pubs are still in good working order. Or are they?

After we cross the bridge and swing onto Commonwealth Avenue, our ranks are split into two parts, one on each side of the middle parkway down Commonwealth, with our merry monitors assuring us that there is no sinister meaning attached to those marchers who are shunted off to the right. Shortly the end is in sight—the Public Gardens and beyond, the Common itself where one of the public speakers, a U.S. Senator, is already speaking. Overhead there is a new peace symbol in the sky, but, like the speechmaking, it seems somehow redundant at this stage. For now we can rest briefly on the grass, sinking down in peace, with some part of a long mission completed. The mission is a Human Be-In, and a small part of the huge confusing mosaic that has been scattered through my mind for so long seems to slip into place. Another plane goes overhead with a streamer behind, "We support Nixon," but no one bothers to boo or notice. We are supporting mankind and no magic name can ever rouse us again to a false hope or even an unnecessary fear. Only the long march of human feet matters, summoning us to live together in the brief period before we sink into the earth and other feet, hopefully, march over the same ground, supported by our gentled dust. The peace settles over the great five-sided Common. The feet have done it, cheered on even by truck drivers, many of whom had made the V-sign as we walked along Mass Avenue. We are a motley crew—we are people, bizarre and varied, not conforming in dress or speech, coming from the steppes of Russia, the vineyards of southern Italy, the coastal plains of Africa, the magic slopes of China, the garden hillsides of Japan, the communes of every bizarre tribe on the face of the earth, moving together in slow and painful stages, now holding tenderly and proudly each our own peculiarities of soul and physique, woven together for a moment into a paisley of hope.

The ground begins to grow damp beneath us, and knots of people mostly on the far side of thirty begin wearily to gather themselves up from the ground where they have been resting. There is a new speaker on the platform now, but no one is listening particularly, although the crowd is quiet and respectful. It is as if our feet have traced out a new elegy in a country churchyard, and we no longer need words. And while we stand for a brief moment, stiff and damp from the earth that stirs up the memory of the wind-grieved ghosts that haunt our American life, we catch the afternoon sun full in our faces; so we move contentedly toward the subway station and home.

Afterwards the Boston *Globe* in a lead editorial marvels at the fact that at the end of the October 15 meeting on Boston Common, young people picked up the trash, leaving the Common neater than it had been before; and "across from the Common on Beacon Street, even the ancient bricks were washed down nice and clean." Having attended the first Human Be-In in San Francisco, I begin to fathom the mystery of what these young people do, so I am not surprised. October 15 was filled with Spring; and when Spring is in the offing, the spirit of man is equal to any occasion.

Index